AAT

Synoptic Assessment
Level 3
Advanced Diploma in
Accounting
Question Bank

Fourth edition 2019

ISBN 9781 5097 8172 0

British Library Cataloguing-in-Publication Data

A catalogue record for this book is available
from the British Library

Published by

BPP Learning Media Ltd
BPP House, Aldine Place
142-144 Uxbridge Road
London W12 8AA

www.bpp.com/learningmedia

Printed in the United Kingdom

BPP
LEARNING MEDIA

Contents

Introduction

This is BPP Learning Media's AAT Question Bank for the *Advanced Diploma in Accounting Level 3 Synoptic Assessment*. It is part of a suite of ground-breaking resources produced by BPP Learning Media for AAT assessments.

This Question Bank contains these key features:

- Tasks corresponding to each assessment objective in the qualification specification and related task in the synoptic assessment. Some tasks in the Question Bank are designed for learning purposes, others are of assessment standard.

- AAT's AQ2016 practice assessment 2 and answers for the *Advanced Diploma in Accounting Level 3 Synoptic Assessment* and further BPP practice assessments

- In the main Question Bank there are occasionally links to online information (such as AAT ethics). These are there to assist you in the practice of these questions. In the real assessment, you will be supplied with a number of appendices which may include extracts of the AAT *Code of Professional Ethics* and/or VAT information. In the practice assessments in this book, you will have an appendix (at the back of this book) which is similar to that found in the real exam.

- AAT practice assessment 1 should be completed online to enable you to gain familiarity of the 'look' of the exam and how the additional information will be presented to you.

The emphasis in all tasks and assessments is on the practical application of the skills acquired.

Test specification for the Level 3 synoptic assessment – Ethics for Accountants, Advanced Bookkeeping, Final Accounts Preparation, Management Accounting: Costing and Spreadsheets for Accounting

Assessment method	Marking type	Duration of assessment
Computer based assessment	Partially computer/partial human marked	2 hours + 45 minutes plus an additional 15 minutes to upload your work

Guidance from the AAT regarding completion of the Level 3 synoptic assessment

	Assessment objectives for the Level 3 synoptic assessment	Weighting
1	Demonstrate an understanding of the relevance of the ethical code for accountants, the need to act ethically in a given situation, and the appropriate action to take in reporting questionable behaviour	15%
2	Prepare accounting records and respond to errors, omissions and other concerns, in accordance with accounting and ethical principles and relevant regulations	15%
3	Apply ethical and accounting principles when preparing final accounts for different types of organisation, develop ethical courses of action and communicate relevant information effectively	15%
4*	Use relevant spreadsheet skills to analyse, interpret and report management accounting data	25%
5*	Prepare financial accounting information, comprising extended trial balances and final accounts for sole traders and partnerships, using spreadsheets	30%
Total		**100%**

*Sections 4 and 5 will be in the form of downloadable spreadsheet files which must be completed and uploaded when completing the actual assessment.

When using the practical materials in this question bank, the relevant downloadable files can be found at https://learningmedia.bpp.com/catalog?pagename=AAT_Spreadsheets.

Approaching the assessment

When you sit the assessment it is very important that you follow the on screen instructions. This means you need to carefully read the instructions, both on the introduction screens and during specific tasks.

When you access the assessment you should be presented with an introductory screen with information similar to that shown below (taken from the introductory screen from one of the AAT's AQ2016 practice assessments for the *Advanced Diploma in Accounting Level 3 Synoptic Assessment*).

BPP
LEARNING MEDIA

- Read the scenario carefully before attempting the questions; you can return to it at any time by clicking on the 'Introduction' button at the bottom of the screen.

- Complete all 5 tasks.

- Answer the questions in the spaces provided. For answers requiring free text entry, the box will expand to fit your answer.

- You must use a full stop to indicate a decimal point. For example, write 100.57 **not** 100,57 or 100 57

- Both minus signs and brackets can be used to indicate negative numbers **unless** task instructions say otherwise.

- You may use a comma to indicate a number in the thousands, but you don't have to.
  For example, 10000 and 10,000 are both acceptable.

- Where the date is relevant, it is given in the task data.

- **Tasks 1.1 to 1.3** in Part 1 require you to enter your answer in the assessment environment.
  Tasks 2.1 to 2.2 in Part 2 require you to download files and work outside the assessment environment in a spreadsheet software program.

  You should ensure that you have uploaded all files required before you finish and submit the assessment.

Information

- This assessment has a total of **5 tasks** which are divided into subtasks across two parts.

- The total mark for this paper is 100.

- The marks for each sub-task are shown alongside the task.

- The data you need to complete a task is contained within that task or through the pop-up that appears on the task page; you will not need to refer to your answers for previous tasks.

The actual instructions will vary depending on the subject you are studying for. It is very important you read the instructions on the introductory screen and apply them in the assessment. You don't want to lose marks when you know the correct answer just because you have not entered it in the right format.

In general, the rules set out in the AAT assessments for the subject you are studying for will apply in the real assessment, but you should carefully read the information on this screen again in the real assessment, just to make sure. This screen may also confirm the VAT rate used if applicable.

A full stop is needed to indicate a decimal point. We would recommend using minus signs to indicate negative numbers and leaving out the comma signs to indicate thousands, as this results in a lower number of key strokes and less margin for error when working under time pressure. Having said that, you can use whatever is easiest for you as long as you operate within the rules set out for your particular assessment.

You have to show competence throughout the assessment and you should therefore complete all of the tasks. Don't leave questions unanswered.

In some assessments, written or complex tasks may be human marked. In this case you are given a blank space or table to enter your answer into. You are told in the assessments which tasks these are (note. there may be none if all answers are marked by the computer).

If these involve calculations, it is a good idea to decide in advance how you are going to lay out your answers to such tasks by practising answering them on a word document, and certainly you should try all such tasks in this Question Bank and in the AAT's environment using the assessment.

When asked to fill in tables, or gaps, never leave any blank even if you are unsure of the answer. Fill in your best estimate.

Note that for some assessments where there is a lot of scenario information or tables of data provided (eg tax tables), you may need to access these via 'pop-ups'. Instructions will be provided on how you can bring up the necessary data during the assessment.

Finally, take note of any task specific instructions once you are in the assessment. For example you may be asked to enter a date in a certain format or to enter a number to a certain number of decimal places.

The synoptic assessment for the Advanced Diploma in Accounting will be made up of **two** component parts. Students will complete component one in the 'locked down' environment of SecureClient in the same way as all other assessments. Component two requires the assessment system to be 'unlocked' to enable students to access spreadsheet software.

Each component has a time allocation. Part 1 has 75 minutes and Part 2 has 105 minutes (90 minutes plus 15 minutes upload time for your working papers). Any time remaining following the completion of component one cannot be transferred to component two. It will not be possible for students to return to component one once they have completed it and moved onto component two.

It is strongly recommended that students visit the AAT Study Support Area and familiarise themselves with the software. There is a useful video 'How to sit an Advanced Diploma synoptic assessment' which explains how to navigate using the software. Do review this prior to sitting your assessment.

Grading

To achieve the qualification and to be awarded a grade, you must pass all the mandatory unit assessments, all optional unit assessments (where applicable) and the synoptic assessment.

The AAT Level 3 Advanced Diploma in Accounting will be awarded a grade. This grade will be based on performance across the qualification. Unit assessments and synoptic assessments are not individually graded. These assessments are given a mark that is used in calculating the overall grade.

How overall grade is determined

You will be awarded an overall qualification grade (Distinction, Merit, and Pass). If you do not achieve the qualification you will not receive a qualification certificate, and the grade will be shown as unclassified.

The marks of each assessment will be converted into a percentage mark and rounded up or down to the nearest whole number. This percentage mark is then weighted according to the weighting of the unit assessment or synoptic assessment within the qualification. The resulting weighted assessment percentages are combined to arrive at a percentage mark for the whole qualification.

Grade definition	Percentage threshold
Distinction	90–100%
Merit	80–89%
Pass	70–79%
Unclassified	0–69% Or failure to pass one or more assessment/s

Re-sits

Some AAT qualifications such as the AAT Advanced Diploma in Accounting have restrictions in place for how many times you are able to re-sit assessments. Please refer to the AAT website for further details.

You should only be entered for an assessment when you are well prepared and you expect to pass the assessment.

AAT qualifications

The material in this book may support the following AAT qualifications:

AAT Advanced Diploma in Accounting Level 3, AAT Advanced Diploma in Accounting at SCQF Level 6 and Further Education and Training Certificate: Accounting Technician (Level 4 AATSA).

Supplements

From time to time we may need to publish supplementary materials to one of our titles. This can be for a variety of reasons. From a small change in the AAT unit guidance to new legislation coming into effect between editions.

You should check our supplements page regularly for anything that may affect your learning materials. All supplements are available free of charge on our supplements page on our website at:

www.bpp.com/learning-media/about/students

Improving material and removing errors

There is a constant need to update and enhance our study materials in line with both regulatory changes and new insights into the assessments.

From our team of authors BPP appoints a subject expert to update and improve these materials for each new edition.

Their updated draft is subsequently technically checked by another author and from time to time non-technically checked by a proof reader.

We are very keen to remove as many numerical errors and narrative typos as we can but given the volume of detailed information being changed in a short space of time we know that a few errors will sometimes get through our net.

We apologise in advance for any inconvenience that an error might cause. We continue to look for new ways to improve these study materials and would welcome your suggestions. If you have any comments about this book, please email nisarahmed@bpp.com or write to Nisar Ahmed, AAT Head of Programme, BPP Learning Media Ltd, BPP House, Aldine Place, London W12 8AA.

Question Bank

Assessment objective 1 – Ethics for Accountants

Task 1.1

Rajesh is a part qualified accounting technician who has recently become employed by RMS Accountancy, a medium sized firm which provides a variety of bookkeeping and accounting services for local businesses.

Rajesh and Jennifer, another accountant at RMS, have been discussing professional ethics and the ways in which the AAT *Code of Professional Ethics* applies to them. During this discussion Rajesh made the following comments.

(a) Are these statements true or false?

Statement	True	False
'I know I act ethically as I have never broken the law and always comply with regulations.'		
'The AAT *Code of Professional Ethics* is legally binding if you are a member of the AAT.'		

One of RMS's clients, Carmichael Ltd, has been allocated to Rajesh. Carmichael Ltd is owned by Rajesh's sister, Manju.

(b) This situation represents which one of the following threats to Rajesh's compliance with the fundamental principles?

	✓
Familiarity	
Self-interest	
Advocacy	

(c) If Rajesh carries out this work, which fundamental principle would he be most at risk of breaching?

	✓
Integrity	
Objectivity	
Confidentiality	

(d) **Which is the most appropriate action for Rajesh to take?**

Action	✓
Resign from RMS Accountancy	
Inform RMS Accountancy of his link with Carmichael Ltd	
Inform the AAT of his link with Carmichael Ltd	

RMS Accountancy prides itself on its strong ethical culture which can, in part, be attributed to the 'tone-at-the-top'.

(e) **Which of the below statements best describes what is meant by the tone-at-the-top?**

	✓
Leaders of the firm have issued clear policies on the ethical behaviour expected at RMS Accountancy.	
Leaders of the firm demonstrate the importance of compliance with the fundamental principles.	
Leaders of the firm require that any potential threat to the fundamental principles is communicated to them in order for the most appropriate action to be taken.	

The Institute of Business Ethics (IBE) has set out simple ethical tests for business decisions. It claims that an understanding of the transparency, effect and fairness of the decision can help to assess whether or not it is ethical.

(f) **Complete the following statement**

[▼] can be assessed by considering whether or not the decision maker would mind other people knowing the decision that they have taken.

Picklist:

Effect
Fairness
Transparency

The AAT *Code of Professional Ethics* identifies safeguards for members in practice which can be used in the work environment to protect against threats to the fundamental principles.

(g)   Are these statements about safeguards true or false?

Statement	True	False
Disciplinary procedures are an example of a safeguard.		
Safeguards always eliminate threats of unethical behaviour from the organisation.		
Undertaking continuing professional development is considered to be one safeguarding measure.		
The AAT *Code of Professional Ethics* makes the recommendation for breaches of ethical requirements to be reported.		
AAT only accept complaints of unethical behaviour from employers or members of the public.		

(h)   Charlotte Brown is an accountant in practice, working in a small firm of accountants. She has discovered that a client has been fraudulently selling counterfeit goods and money laundering the proceeds of these sales.

Complete the following statement.

Charlotte should disclose confidential information on this matter directly to

▼

Picklist:

the firm's nominated officer.
the National Crime Agency.
HM Revenue & Customs.
the Conduct Committee.

....

Task 1.2

(a) **Are the below statements regarding professional ethics and the ethical responsibilities of accountants true or false?**

Statement	True	False
The AAT *Code of Professional Ethics* provides a set of rules to help accountants determine ethical behaviour.		
The accountancy profession has a responsibility to act in the public interest.		

Tony is an AAT member working in practice who provides accounting services to a number of clients. While Tony is on annual leave his colleague, Janis, is carrying out work for one of his clients on his behalf. Janis has found a significant number of errors in the work Tony has carried out for this client. The client has told Janis that he has lost a large contract due to the overstatement of the loan in his financial statements. Upon his return, Tony is surprised by the number of errors found and states they were due to a lack of skill.

(b) **If Tony is found to have failed to exercise reasonable care and skill, could he be liable to the client for the following?**

Action	Yes/No
Breach of contract	▼
Negligence	▼
Fraud	▼

Picklist:

Yes
No

Betsy is an accountant working in a small business. One of the company's directors, Marie, has reviewed the financial statements compiled by Betsy and has made a number of changes, including removing information on the names of the directors. Betsy does not agree with this action, however, Marie is insistent that these accounts are filed.

(c) **What is the most appropriate course of action for Betsy to take?**

Action	✓
Betsy should file the financial statements as the director has signed them.	
Betsy should report the company director to the National Crime Agency.	
Betsy should raise her concerns internally stating her concerns in an email to the Board of Directors.	

(d) **'The risk of loss resulting from inadequate or failed processes, people and systems or from external events' is a definition of which of the following?**

Operational risk	
Business risk	
Control risk	

Behaving in an ethical manner involves acting appropriately.

(e) **Complete the following statement**

Behaving ethically means acting with transparency, honesty, fairness and ▢▼ in dealings with clients, suppliers, colleagues and others.

Picklist:

confidentiality
respect
discretion

Janis has a number of documents she needs to pass to a partner to sign off. When she takes the documents to his office she finds there is file regarding the troubled financial state of a client's company. Janis is very familiar with the company as it is her husband's employer.

(f) Complete the following statement.

This is a potential [▼] threat on behalf of the junior and looking at the partner's file would be a breach of the [▼] principle.

Picklist 1:

advocacy
familiarity
intimidation
self-interest
self-review

Picklist 2:

confidentiality
integrity
objectivity
professional behaviour
professional competence and due care

(g) Are the below statements true or false?

Statement	True	False
The principle of confidentiality must always be carefully abided by in all situations.		
In some situations it is entirely plausible that the principle of integrity could be over-ridden as a result of the circumstances.		

Task 1.3

(a) Which of the following statements best describes why accountants should comply with a professional code of ethics?

	✓
It is required by law that they do so.	
To maintain public confidence in the profession.	
To prevent dishonest individuals from entering the profession.	

Denys and Maria are student accounting technicians who are employed by a large accounting firm. During a conversation about the relevance of the AAT *Code of Professional Ethics*, Maria makes the following comments.

(b)   Are these statements true or false?

Statement	True	False
'The AAT *Code of Professional Ethics* does not apply to me yet as I am only a student accounting technician.'		
'Ethical codes provide advice as to how to comply with the law.'		

(c)   If you have an ethical concern at work, usually the most appropriate first course of action would be to raise this with

[▼] or [▼] .

Picklist:

employee helpline
the AAT
trusted colleague
your immediate supervisor

The firm is about to take on a new client and Denys is assisting Jane, a more senior accountant, to carry out due diligence producers.

Denys asks Jane the following questions.

(d)   Select using the picklist whether Jane would be more likely to answer yes or no to each of Denys' questions.

Action	
Are customer due diligence procedures only required for new clients?	▼
Is it always acceptable for accountants to pay a referral fee to obtain a new client?	▼
Is it acceptable to offer a commission to employees for bringing in a new client?	▼

Picklist:

Yes
No

In order to help prevent and identify money laundering and terrorist financing, financial institutions and non-financial businesses and professions are required to adopt specific measures. One of these measures is to implement customer due diligence.

(e) **How long such customer due diligence information be retained?**

	✓
5 years	
7 years	
Indefinitely	

Whistleblowing is the disclosure by an employee of illegal or unethical practices by his or her employer.

(f) **Are these statements relating to whistleblowing true or false?**

Statement	True	False
Whistleblowing should occur as soon as illegal activity is suspected.		
Employees are protected under the Public Information Disclosure Act to ensure they cannot be dismissed for whistleblowing.		
If the disclosure is in the public interest, then the fundamental principle of confidentiality is not breached.		
If the employee is bound by a confidentiality clause in their contract, or has signed a non-disclosure agreement, then the employee could still face dismissal.		

Task 1.4

(a) **Complete the following statement.**

The UK accountancy profession as a whole is regulated by the

[▾] and global ethical standards are set by the

[▾] .

Picklist:

AAT
CCAB
FRC
IESBA

All professional accountants have a duty to comply with the five fundamental principles.

(b) **Are these statements true or false?**

Statement	True	False
The duty to comply with the fundamental principles is more relevant to accountants working in practice than accountants working in business.		
Compliance with the law, as well as the policies and procedures of the organisation for which you work will ensure that you never break the five fundamental principles.		

Sharon, an AAT member, is preparing the accounts for a client who has employed her services for a number of years. The client has had a difficult year and will struggle to survive if it cannot secure new finance from a potential investor. The client has asked Sharon to omit details of a number of loans they have taken out during the year. Sharon knows that if she does not do as the client asks, it is likely that they will lose the investor and risk going out of business completely.

(c) **This situation is most likely to represent which of the following threats to Sharon's compliance with the fundamental principles?**

	✓
Familiarity	
Self-interest	
Intimidation	

(d)   **Which of the fundamental principles is threatened?**

	✓
Integrity	
Professional competence and due care	
Confidentiality	

Sharon does not agree to the clients request as she feels this would be a breach of her ethical duty as an accountant.

However, when she presents the accounts to her line manager, Andrew, for review he also suggests that she changes the accounts. Andrew is aware that the firm as a whole is reliant on the client for its own survival and, were this client to go out of business, it is likely that their accountancy business would do. He quietly suggests to Sharon that, if the accounts remain as they are, it is likely that it would not be long before they were both out of a job.

(e)   **Select which additional threats to fundamental principles may now also arise.**

Action	✓
Familiarity	
Self-interest	
Intimidation	
Self-review	

(f)   **Which of the following actions would be the most appropriate for Sharon to take next?**

	✓
Change the accounts as requested	
Refuse and explain her reasons for doing so with Andrew	
Refuse and inform the media as it is in the public interest to disclose the matter	

Task 1.5

(a) Are these statements true or false?

Statement	True	False
Under the AAT *Code of Professional Ethics*, as a minimum you are expected to comply with the laws and regulations of the country in which you live and work.		
The ethical code exists primarily to enhance the public image of accountancy and increase public confidence in the profession.		

(b) Which of the following best describes what is meant by 'independence'?

	✓
Ensuring all work is carried out in the public interest	
Having no previous or current links, financial or otherwise, with a client	
Carrying out work objectively and with integrity	

(c) Rotating senior assurance team personnel helps ensure compliance with the five fundamental principles by safeguarding against which of the following threats?

	✓
Self-review	
Self-interest	
Familiarity	

Marcia is an AAT member who is carrying out an audit of BigBreak Ltd (BB), a holiday company specialising in weekend breaks. During the engagement, Marcia celebrates her 30th birthday and is given an all-inclusive luxury spa break as a birthday gift from the client.

(d) **Which of the below statements best describe the action that Marcia should take.**

	✓
She should accept the gift as it is insignificant and will not influence her audit.	
She should reject the gift as it may appear to others to compromise her objectivity.	
She should reject the gift as it may appear to others to compromise her integrity.	

(e) **Complete the following statement.**

Accountants [　　　▼　　　] accept significant gifts or preferential treatment from a client. This is because it represents [　　　▼　　　] to the fundamental principles.

Picklist:

a familiarity threat
a self-interest threat
no threat
should
should not

The fees paid to accountants by a client for undertaking an assurance engagement could be based on a number of factors.

(f) **Show which of the below could be taken into account when determining fees.**

Action		
The skills required to carry out the engagement		▼
The outcome of the engagement		▼
The value of the service to the client		▼

Picklist:

Could be taken into account
Must not be taken into account

(g) Are these statements true or false?

Statement	True	False
Tipping off is an offence which may be carried out by accountants.		
Accountants can go to jail if they are found guilty of having been involved in money laundering.		

Task 1.6

(a) Show whether the below statements are true or false?

Statement	True	False
There are no disadvantages to professional accountants of complying with the AAT *Code of Professional Ethics*.		
Accountants are required under the AAT *Code of Professional Ethics* to comply with all relevant laws and regulations		
Accountants are required to uphold the reputation of the accounting profession in both their professional and private lives.		

The Institute of Business Ethics (IBE) encourages high standards of ethical behaviour in businesses and it sets out simple ethical tests for a business decision.

(b) Putting yourself in the place of the people on the receiving end of the decision you are about to make helps you to assess which one of the following?

	✓
Transparency	
Effect	
Fairness	

(c) In which of the following situations would an accountant be required to breach the fundamental principle of objectivity?

	✓
When it is in the public interest to do so	
When it is required by law to do so	
An accountant should never breach the objectivity principle	

Johnson is a trainee accountant who is applying for a job in a new company that will represent a significant step up in his career. He really wants the job and to help his case he exaggerates the extent of his experience to better suit the expectations set out in the job specification.

(d) **Which ONE of the below statements best describes this situation?**

	✓
Johnson has not compromised his professional ethics; everyone embellishes a little to get a job.	
Johnson has acted irresponsibly and has therefore breached the professional ethic of self-interest.	
Johnson has misled a potential employer and has therefore breached the professional ethic of integrity.	
Johnson has misled a potential employer and has therefore breached the professional ethic of confidentiality.	

Johnson's new employer is a direct competitor of his former employer. When Johnson starts his new job he uses the skills, knowledge and experience that he gained from working for the competitor.

(e) **Show whether the below statements are true or false?**

Statement	True	False
It is fine for Johnson to use these skills, knowledge and experience as the new firm would expect a degree of insider knowledge to be obtained as a perk of employing a former employee of the competition.		
It is fine for Johnson to use these skills, knowledge and experience provided he does not disclose any confidential information.		
It is fine for Johnson to use these skills, knowledge and experience, but only after a reasonable amount of time has elapsed to prevent conflicts of interest arising.		

Professional accountants must maintain the confidentiality of information and not to disclose anything without proper authority.

(f)   Show whether the below statements are true or false in relation to the above?

Statement	True	False
This is an ethical principle.		
This is a legal obligation.		

Task 1.7

(a)   Business ethics suggest that businesses have a duty to act in the best interests of which of the following?

	✓
The shareholders or other key investors	
The employees of the organisation	
Society as a whole (including shareholders and employees)	

(b)   In which of the following situations would an accountant be required to breach confidentiality?

	✓
Providing working papers to a new firm who is taking on a former client	
As a result of an enquiry by AAT	
To a financial institution who has requested the information directly to your firm of accountants	
To protect a member's professional interest in a court of law	

(c)   Which of the following statements best describe what is meant by 'tone-at-the-top'?

	✓
Senior management set clear policies and procedures that are cascaded down through the organisation.	
Senior management lead by example.	
Senior management establish a clear disciplinary procedure to ensure ethical breaches are escalated to be dealt with at the top of the organisation.	

Rita has discovered that she may have been involved in a money laundering operation without her knowledge. She is worried that she may be incriminated if she reports the issue and is fearful of losing her job and damaging her reputation. The money laundering scheme was very small scale and so Rita makes the decision not to disclose the matter. She confronts the perpetrator and informs them that she will have no further dealings with them.

(d) Could Rita be guilty of money laundering?

	✓
No, she was unaware of being involved in money laundering and withdrew from the engagement as soon as she suspected wrong doing.	
No, the money laundering scheme was very small scale and would therefore be below the threshold for criminal conviction.	
Yes, if she has been part of the scheme, even unknowingly, she could still be guilty of money laundering.	

(e) Show whether the below statements are true or false?

Statement	True	False
Rita has tipped off the client.		
If Rita does fail to disclose her suspicions of money laundering she may face additional charges.		
If Rita was to make a protected disclosure she may have a defence against any money laundering charges brought against her.		
If Rita was make an authorised disclosure she may have a defence against any money laundering charges brought against her.		

(f) Complete the following sentence.

When unethical or illegal behaviour is uncovered, whistleblowing should be carried out [▼]. External whistleblowing should take place [▼] internal discussion with management.

Picklist:

as a last resort
following
immediately
prior to
rather than

Task 1.8

(a) **Complete the following sentence.**

The AAT requires its members to behave in a way that maintains its reputation, maintains [▼] and protects the [▼].

Picklist:

best interests of the industry
future of the industry
public confidence
public interest
superior quality of output
users of accounting information

Raffaella is being investigated by the AAT for misconduct as a result of failing to complete the CPD requirements expected of her. She has also failed to reply to an item of correspondence from the AAT.

(b) **Do Raffaella's actions represent conclusive proof of misconduct?**

Action	Yes/No
Failing to comply with the AAT's CPD requirements	▼
Failing to reply to an item of correspondence from the AAT	▼

Economic, social and environmental responsibilities of finance professionals are interlinked and is sometimes referred to as a 'triple bottom line' approach.

(c) **Using the picklist below show whether the following suggestions help to address the economic, social or environmental responsibilities of finance professionals**

Action	Economic/Social/Environmental
Carrying out a conference call between various members of regional staff	▼
Holding an away day for members of the finance department	▼
Reducing the future cost of electricity by investing in solar panels	▼

Picklist:

Economic
Environmental
Social

Christie is a professional accountant in practice who has had Alpha Ltd as a client for many years. In her professional capacity, Christie has been asked by Alpha Ltd's new landlord to give a written reference confirming that the company is likely to be able to pay rent over the next five years. Alpha Ltd is paying a large fee for supplying the reference.

(d) **Show whether the below statements are true or false?**

Statement	True	False
Christie should not accept this engagement as the large fee compromises her integrity.		
It would be acceptable practice for Christie to include a disclaimer or liability in the written reference.		
Christie should not accept this engagement as the length of the relationship with the client compromises her objectivity.		
Christie should not accept this engagement as a safeguard against the threat of intimidation presented by this situation		

(e) **Complete the following sentence**

If Christie gives the reference, even though she knows that Alpha limited has no means of paying the rent, she would be committing [▼] .

Picklist:

fraud by breach of position
fraud by failing to disclose information
fraud by false representation

(f) **Are the following statements relating to taxation services true or false?**

Statement	True	False
When a member in practice submits a tax return on behalf of a client the responsibilities of the member should be made clear in a letter of engagement.		
When a member in practice submits a tax return on behalf of the client, the member assumes all responsibility for the return and computations.		

Task 1.9

(a) Threats to professional competence and due care may be safeguarded by continuing professional development (CPD).

Can CPD also help to safeguard against threats to the following fundamental principles?

Fundamental principle	Yes	No
Confidentiality		
Integrity		

There are certain services that an accountant cannot legally offer unless they are authorised to do so by the relevant regulatory body in the UK. These services are known as 'reserved areas'.

(b) **Which of the following services are considered to be reserved areas**

Action	✓
Internal auditing	
Insolvency practice	
Taxation services	

(c) **'Meeting the needs of the present without compromising the ability of future generations to meet their own needs' is the definition of which of the following?**

	✓
Corporate Social Reporting (CSR)	
Ethical business practices	
Sustainability	

You are an accountant working in practice and have, for several years, carried out work for two competing hairdressing businesses, Hair By Me and Hair to Infinity. A lease has just become available on the high street in the town in which the two businesses operate. It is in a highly desirable location and both businesses are keen to take on the lease. They have both asked you to act for them in relation to the bid for the lease. On discovery that they were both bidding for the same lease both hairdressing businesses have, independently, offered you an additional £4,000 to act for them exclusively. Neither business is willing for you to act for both parties with respect to the lease.

(d) **Select which of the following fundamental principles are threatened by the above situation**

Action	✓
Integrity	
Objectivity	
Confidentiality	
Professional competence and due care	
Professional behaviour	

The AAT *Code of Professional Ethics* provides general principles for ethical issues relating to taxation.

(e) Complete the following statement

The AAT *Code of Professional Ethics* says that 'a member providing professional tax services has a duty to put forward the best position in favour of [▼] .'

Picklist:

a client or employer
the public
the tax authorities

Rakhee, an AAT member working in the charity sector, has taken on a new member of staff, Mo. Mo is frequently on the phone during normal working hours and sometimes disappears from his desk for long periods of time to make extended personal calls.

(f) What is the most appropriate action for Rakhee to take?

	✓
Escalate the matter to her line manager	
Report Mo to the AAT	
Discuss the situation with Mo and encourage him to make his phone calls outside normal working hours	

Task 1.10

(a) Overall responsibility for ethics in the accountancy profession rests with which of the following organisations?

	✓
IFAC	
IESBA	
CCAB	

A report by the Nolan Committee established *The Seven Principles of Public Life*. These are the principles we would expect holders of public office to take into consideration in their actions in public life.

(b) **Which TWO of the following are set out by the Nolan Committee in the *Seven Principles of Public Life*?**

	✓
Honesty	
Confidentiality	
Accountability	
Discretion	

The fundamental principle of professional competence and due care requires accountants to only undertake work in which they have suitable skills and experience in order to be able to complete.

(c) **Which of the following types of legal action could be faced by an accountant who fails to act with sufficient expertise. Select the most appropriate option(s).**

Action	✓
Breach of contract	
Breach of trust	
Professional negligence	
Fraud accusations	

Lana is a self-employed accountant who specialises in carrying out bookkeeping and accountancy work for other small businesses. She has become aware that one of her clients, a self-employed electrician has been offering clients a lower rate for cash payment. The electrician is not VAT registered, but you suspect that he may be working for cash in order to avoid declaring this income on his tax return.

(d) **Which of the following actions would be most appropriate for Lana to take?**

	✓
Report the electrician to his trade regulatory body	
Cease to work on behalf of the electrician	
Disclose the matter publically as the matter is one of public interest	

Alfred is a professional accountant working in practice. He has begun to suspect one of his clients, François, of money laundering.

(e) **Select which of the following statements are true or false?**

Statement	True	False
If Alfred does not disclose his suspicions of money laundering, then he himself will have committed a criminal offense.		
Failure to disclose money laundering suspicions can result in a fine up to £10,000.		
Alfred must ensure that he makes François aware that the relevant disclosures have been made.		

(f) **Which ONE of the following disclosures should Alfred make in this scenario?**

	✓
Protected disclosure	
Authorised disclosure	
Anonymous disclosure	

Task 1.11

(a) **Which of the following statements relating to the threat of advocacy are true or false?**

Statement	True	False
An accountant who is employed by an organisation is more likely to face an advocacy threat than an accountant working in practice.		
A dominant individual attempting to influence your decisions is an example of a threat of advocacy.		
The fundamental principle most likely to be compromised as the result of an advocacy threat is objectivity.		

Hannah is working on an audit engagement for a client. She is struggling to complete the work in the amount of time available and is finding that she is having to work very long days in an attempt to finish the engagement on time.

(b) **Which of Hannah's fundamental principles listed below could this compromise?**

	✓
Professional behaviour	
Professional competence and due care	
Integrity	

(c) **Using the picklist below, show whether the following offences would be prosecuted in a criminal court or heard in a civil court.**

Action		
Misappropriation of assets		▼
Money laundering		▼
Negligence		▼
Fraud		▼

Picklist:

Civil
Criminal

After the loss of several client records, ABC company brought in an IT consultant who proved that ABS company has recently had their computer system hacked.

(d) **Which of the following types of operational risk is presented by the above situation?**

	✓
Internal fraud	
External fraud	
Systems failure	

Lucy has just finished an audit engagement for an events management company and has issued an unqualified report. She enjoyed the time spent with the client, in particular discussing her shared love of music festivals with some of the key staff.

At the end of the engagement, Lucy finds the following message in her inbox.

Hi Lucy,

Hope that you are well.

Thank you for your hard work in auditing our accounts and issuing an unqualified report. The whole team is really happy with the result and we would like to offer you two tickets to the sold out Magic Fields festival along with backstage passes so you can meet your favourite band.

(e) **Which of the following actions should Lucy now take?**

	✓
Go to the festival, it is a once in a lifetime opportunity and she knows that she carried out her work in accordance with the AAT *Code of Professional Ethics*	
Inform her manager that the offer has been made to her	
Refuse the tickets and report the matter to AAT	

Peter is an accountant working in practice. He has just realised that he is caught up in a client's money laundering activities. He panics and shreds the evidence in his client's files.

(f) **Select whether the following statements are true or false in this scenario?**

Action	True	False
Peter could be found guilty of money laundering.		
Peter could be found guilty of the offense of tipping off.		
Peter could be found guilty of prejudicing the investigation.		

Assessment objective 2 – Ethics for accountants/Advanced Bookkeeping/Final Accounts Preparation

Task 2.1

Liz Turner has been trading for just over 12 months as a dressmaker. She has kept no accounting records at all, and she is worried that she may need professional help to sort out her financial position, and she has approached you.

You meet with Liz and discuss the information that you require her to give you. Sometime later, you receive a letter from Liz providing you with the information that you requested, as follows:

(i)   She started her business on 1 October 20X7. She opened a business bank account and paid in £8,000 of her savings.

(ii)   During October she bought the equipment and the inventory of materials that she needed. The equipment cost £3,800. All of this was paid for out of the business bank account.

(iii)   A summary of the business bank account for the twelve months ended 30 September 20X8 showed the following.

Bank statement extract

	£		£
Capital	8,000	Equipment	3,800
Cash banked from sales	32,000	Purchases of materials	20,750
		General expenses	400
		Drawings	14,370
		Balance c/d	680
	40,000		40,000

(iv)   All of the sales are on a cash basis. Some of the cash is paid into the bank account while the rest is used for cash expenses. She has no idea what the total value of her sales is for the year, but she knows that she has spent an additional £3,200 in cash on materials and an additional £490 in cash on general expenses. She took the rest of the cash not banked for her private drawings. She also keeps a cash float of £100.

(v) The gross profit margin on all sales is 50%.

(vi) Total purchases for the year are £25,550 and total cost of sales for the year is £24,350

You are required to:

(a) **Calculate the sales for the year ended 30 September 20X8.**

£

(b) **Show the entries that would appear in Liz Turner's cash account. Use the picklist provided to select the correct account name.**

Cash account

Account	£	Account	£
▼		▼	
▼		▼	
▼		▼	
▼		▼	
▼		▼	
Total		Total	

Picklist:

Balance c/d (float)
Bank account
Capital
Drawings
General expenses
Purchases of materials
Sales

(c) **Calculate the total drawings made by Liz Turner throughout the year.**

£

(d) **Select the TWO principles from the list below which are outlined in the AAT *Code of Professional Ethics*.**

	✓
Integrity	
Selflessness	
Honesty	
Objectivity	

(e) **Which of the following statements reflects THREE purposes behind the AAT *Code of Professional Ethics***

	✓
Maintain the reputation of the accountancy profession	
Increase opportunities for AAT members	
Act in the public interest	
Ensure protection from negligence claims	
Ensure professional knowledge and skill of AAT members and students	

Task 2.2

Green Bean Limited is a business which makes ready meals for sale to supermarkets. It has several large non-current assets in its factory, and needs some assistance in accounting for some adjustments during the financial year ending 31 December 20X8.

Company policy is to charge a full year's depreciation charge in the year of acquisition and none in the year of disposal.

The following details have been extracted from the non-current asset ledger as at 1 January 20X8.

	Cost	Accumulated depreciation	Carrying amount
Aygosh 100	120,000	20,000	100,000
Masher A	85,000	70,000	15,000
Scrawler B	45,000	20,000	25,000

The following additional information is available

- The Masher A was disposed of on the 1 December 20X8. It was sold for £20,000.

- Depreciation has not yet been calculated for the year ended 31 December 20X8, These assets are depreciated on a diminishing balance basis at 25%.

(a) Calculate the depreciation expense for the year ended 31 December 20X8

£

(b) Complete the following journal to account for the disposal of the Masher A asset.

	Debit £	Credit £
Bank and cash		
Non-current assets – cost		
Non-current asset – accumulated depreciation		
Profit and loss account		

At the year end, Green Bean invests in a new piece of machinery, the Boggler 25 which cost £45,480.

It is planned to be depreciated at a rate of 25% on a diminishing balance basis.

(c) **Calculate the depreciation charge for the first THREE years based on a reducing balance basis (round to two decimal places)**

(d) **Indicate whether the following statements are true or false.**

Statement	True	False
An error of commission does not cause an imbalance in the trial balance.		
The suspense account can appear in the financial statements.		
An error of principle causes an imbalance in the trial balance.		
A trial balance is prepared before the financial statements.		

You are updating the extended trial balance for bank and cash details when you discover that the petty cash records do not reconcile with the petty cash receipts that have been filed. It appears that over a course of time one person has been over claiming travel expenses.

(e) **Which fundamental principle (as stated in the AAT *Code of Professional Ethics*) has been breached here? Select the MOST appropriate answer.**

	✓
Integrity	
Honesty	
Selflessness	
Professional competence and due care	

33

(f) What action is required in these circumstances?

```



```

Task 2.3

You are preparing the year end accounting records for Thomas Brand, who is a sole trader and has a plumbing business.

Thomas' friend, Bill Bailey, did a few months of an accountancy course and decided he would be able to do Thomas' accounts for him. However, Bill has decided that the business is too complex, so Thomas has brought the accounts to Blithe & Co Accountants.

Bill has drafted a trial balance as at 31 December 20X9. However, you discover a number of items which need to be recorded in the accounts.

Account	Debit £	Credit £
Bank	22,450	
Capital		13,200
Purchase ledger control account		4,095
Sales ledger control account	6,725	
Sales		45,200
Purchases	32,570	
Administration costs	750	
	62,495	62,495

A number of items require your attention

- A new vehicle has been acquired for £16,200. It is expected to be sold after five years for £3,800. Vehicles will be depreciated on a straight line basis, with a full year's depreciation in the year of acquisition.

- Sales for December of £1,700 have not yet been recorded. The customer had not paid his invoice at year end.

- A customer paid his outstanding invoice of £800 on 31 December, and this has not yet been recorded.

- Drawings of £1,600 have not yet been recorded in the accounts.

(a) **Calculate the depreciation charge for the year on the new vehicle.**

£ [   ]

(b) **Complete the journal entries using the picklist below, for the acquisition of the new vehicle.**

Details		£	Debit ✓	Credit ✓
	▾			
	▾			

Picklist:

Accumulated depreciation
Bank
Depreciation expense
Purchase ledger control account
Sales ledger control account
Vehicle cost

(c) **Complete the journal entry, using the picklist below, for the depreciation charge on the new vehicle.**

Details		£	Debit ✓	Credit ✓
	▾			
	▾			

Picklist:

Accumulated depreciation
Bank
Depreciation expense
Purchase ledger control account
Sales ledger control account
Vehicle cost

(d) **Complete the extended trial balance below, including your information calculated in parts (b) and (c) and the missing information in the narrative in respect of sales, drawings and trade receivables. Calculate the totals at the bottom of the debit and credit columns in your final trial balance.**

Account	Ledger balance Debit £	Ledger balance Credit £	Adjustments £	Trial balance Debit £	Trial balance Credit £
Bank	22,450				
Capital		13,200			
Purchase ledger control account		4,095			
Sales ledger control account	6,725				
Sales		45,200			
Purchases	32,570				
Administration costs	750				
Drawings					
Vehicles – Cost					
Vehicles Accumulated depreciation					
Depreciation expense					
Totals	62,495	62,495			

Task 2.4

Wahleed Mansoor is a sole trader who manufacturers skateboards. The following information has been provided about events on the last day of the year:

- Minor Limited, a customer with a receivable outstanding of £950 has gone into liquidation. It is not expected that this debt will be recoverable.

- A new machine is purchased for £5,000. It will have a useful life of 5 years, and a full year of depreciation is charged in the first year of acquisition. The purchase of the machine has been entered into the trial balance, however, the depreciation has not yet been calculated.

(a) **Prepare the journal using the picklist provided for the allowance for irrecoverable debts adjustment against the debt of Minor Limited.**

Details		Debit £	Credit £
	▼		
	▼		

Picklist:

Bank
Irrecoverable debt expense
Sales ledger control account

(b) **Calculate the depreciation charge for the year ended 31 December 20X8.**

£ [   ]

(c) **Prepare the journal for the depreciation charge as calculated in part (b). Use the picklist provided.**

Details		Debit £	Credit £
	▼		
	▼		

Picklist:

Accumulated depreciation
Depreciation expense

(d) **List the FOUR enhancing qualitative characteristics as laid out in the *Conceptual Framework.***

Wahleed has been trying to clear an unknown balance on his trial balance. He knows he needs to look at the following transactions, but is at a loss as how to clear the balance. The following information is provided:

- A stationery invoice of £1,450 was correctly posted to the bank account, however, it was posted to the office expenses account as £1,540.

- Drawings of £750 had been reflected in the bank and cash account only.

- Rent payment of £900 was posted as a credit to the rent account and a debit to the bank.

(e) **Using the information provided, complete the suspense account and clear the outstanding balance for Wahleed.**

Suspense account

Details	£	Details	£
Balance b/d	660	▼	
▼		▼	
Total		Total	

Picklist:

Balance c/d
Bank
Drawings
Office expenses
Rent accrual
Rent expense

Task 2.5

Bella Parker is a sole trader who sells wooden toys. She has drawn up her trial balance at the end of the year 31 December 20X7.

	Debit £	Credit £
Revenue		265,500
Purchases	143,250	
Opening inventory	10,000	
Closing inventory	13,500	13,500
Office expenses	750	
Insurance	1,400	
Drawings	24,000	
Trade receivable	1,200	
Trade payable		1,350
Accruals		3,200
Prepayments	900	
Capital	70,000	
Cash at bank	16,050	
Suspense	2,500	
	283,550	283,550

The following items were noted:

- Drawings of £2,000 were correctly credited to the bank account, however, no entry was made on the drawings account.

- Cash sales of £500 were banked, however, Bella forgot to include them in the sales account.

- An insurance invoice was posted correctly to the trade payables account, however, the entry was then credited to the insurance account. The invoice was for £500.

- A van was purchased for £8,000 on the last day of the year. It is expected to last 5 years after which it will be sold for scrap for £500. A full year's depreciation will be charged in the year of acquisition.

(a) **Using the information in the narrative above, show the correcting entries in the suspense account below which clear the account.**

Suspense account

Details		£	Details		£
	▼			▼	
	▼			▼	
				▼	

Picklist:

Balance b/d
Balance c/d
Drawings
Insurance
Sales

(b) **Calculate the depreciation charge for the van.**

£ [   ]

(c) **Enter the adjustments into the extended trial balance below, showing the revised figures for the draft financial statements.**

	Initial trial balance			Revised trial balance	
	Debit £	Credit £	Adjustments £	Debit £	Credit £
Sales		265,500			
Purchases	143,250				
Opening inventory	10,000				
Closing inventory	13,500	13,500			
Office expenses	750				
Insurance	1,400				
Drawings	24,000				
Trade receivable	1,200				

	Initial trial balance		Adjustments £	Revised trial balance	
	Debit £	Credit £		Debit £	Credit £
Trade payable		1,350			
Accruals		3,200			
Prepayments	900				
Capital	70,000				
Cash at bank	16,050				
Suspense	2,500				
Motor vehicle					
Depreciation expense					
Accumulated depreciation					
	283,550	283,550			

(d) **Calculate the gross profit of Bella's business for the year ended 31 December 20X7.**

£ [   ]

Assessment objective 3 – Ethics for Accountants/Final Accounts Preparation

Task 3.1

Andrew, Brown and Carter are a partnership ("ABC") who design and install kitchens.

You are an Accounting Technician at MSP Accountants ("MSP"), and have been asked to prepare the partnership accounts for the ABC partnership.

You have the following information about the partnership's business:

- The financial year ends on 31 March.
- Brown and Carter each introduced a further £10,000 capital into the bank account on 1 October 20X6.
- Goodwill was valued at £80,000 on 31 March 20X7.
- There was no interest on drawings.

	Andrew	Brown	Carter
Profit share, for the period	40%	30%	30%
Capital account balances at 1 April 20X6	£40,000	£30,000	£30,000
Current account balances at 1 April 20X6	£1,160 credit	£420 credit	£5,570 credit
Drawings for the year ended 31 March 20X7	£2,500 each month	£38,000	£45,000

The appropriation account for the year ended 31 March 20X7 has already been prepared by the accountant.

Partnership appropriation account for the year ended 31 March 20X7

	Total £
Profit for appropriation	156,000
Salaries:	
Andrew	15,000
Brown	18,000
Carter	24,000

	Total £
Interest on capital:	
Andrew	2,860
Brown	1,980
Carter	1,980
Profit available for distribution	92,180
Profit shares:	
Andrew	36,872
Brown	27,654
Carter	27,654
Total profit distributed	92,180

(a) Prepare the current accounts for the partners for the year ended 31 March 20X7. Show clearly the balance carried down. You MUST enter zeros where appropriate in order to obtain full marks. Do NOT use brackets, minus signs or dashes.

Use the picklist provided to select the appropriate account name.

Current accounts

	Andrew £	Brown £	Carter £		Andrew £	Brown £	Carter £
▼				▼			
▼				▼			
▼				▼			
▼				▼			
▼				▼			
Total							

Picklist:

Balance b/d
Balance c/d
Capital – Andrew
Capital – Brown
Capital – Carter
Current – Andrew
Current – Brown
Current – Carter
Drawings
Goodwill
Interest on capital
Salaries
Share of profit or loss

During your work, you discover an anomaly in the underlying records of ABC. You have reason to suspect that one of the partners is incorrectly recording his expenses.

(b) **Who would usually be the most appropriate first person to raise this with** [▼] **or** [▼] .

Picklist:

employee helpline
the AAT
HMRC
your immediate supervisor

A fellow junior colleague asks what the term 'whistleblowing' means.

(c) **Are these statements relating to whistleblowing true or false?**

Statement	True	False
Employees are protected under the Public Information Disclosure Act provided that they have acted in good faith and the belief is that the environment is being damaged.		
You should start the whistleblowing process as soon as illegal activity is suspected.		
The fundamental principle of confidentiality is not breached, if the disclosure is in the public interest.		
If the organisation has an ethics committee, this should be approached before getting to the whistleblowing stage.		

Task 3.2

James Doolittle is a sole trader who has prepared the following trial balance for his business.

	Debit £	Credit £
Bank	11,950	
Capital		74,300
Payables		40,800
Receivables	35,450	
Allowance for doubtful debts		3,200
Drawings	19,000	
Fixtures and Fittings	24,500	
Electricity	2,050	
Insurance	2,800	
Miscellaneous expenses	1,500	
Motor expenses	3,100	
Motor vehicles at cost	48,000	
Purchases	245,000	

	Debit £	Credit £
Accumulated depreciation – Fixtures and fittings		8,550
– Motor vehicles		29,800
Rent	3,400	
Sales		344,450
Opening inventory	40,200	
Telephone costs	1,950	
VAT		3,050
Wages	54,750	
Closing inventory	43,500	43,500
Depreciation expense – fixtures and fittings	2,450	
Depreciation expense – motor vehicles	7,800	
Accruals		1,000
Prepayments	1,250	
	548,650	548,650

(a) Prepare the statement of financial position as at 31 March 20X7 based on the information in the trial balance. Use the picklist provided to select the account names as required.

	Cost £	Accumulated depreciation £	Carrying amount £
Non-current assets			
▼			
▼			
Current assets			
▼			
▼			
▼			
▼			

	Cost £	Accumulated depreciation £	Carrying amount £
Current liabilities			
▼			
▼			
▼			
Net current assets			
Net assets			
Financed by:			
▼			
▼			
Less			
▼			

Picklist:

Accruals
Capital
Cash and cash equivalents
Closing inventory
Depreciation charges
Drawings
Electricity
Fixtures & Fittings
Insurance
Miscellaneous expenses
Motor expenses
Motor vehicles
Opening inventory
Prepayments

BPP
LEARNING MEDIA

Profit for the year
Purchases
Rent
Sales
Telephone
Trade payables
Trade receivables
VAT
Wages

(b) **The two fundamental qualitative characteristics of financial information, according to the IASB's *Conceptual Framework* are:**

> [   ] and [   ]

(c) **Select which ONE of the following statements which best explains the term 'going concern'.**

	✓
The effect of transactions being recognised when they occur	
That the business will continue in operation for the foreseeable future	
To ensure similar businesses can be compared to allow for investors to assess them	
To ensure the financial statements have been prepared on time	

Task 3.3

Beth Green is a sole trader who has prepared the following trial balance for her business.

	Debit £	Credit £
Drawings	8,050	
Repairs and maintenance	1,250	
Electricity	1,025	
Insurance	900	
Miscellaneous expenses	750	
Motor expenses	1,550	
Motor vehicles at cost	24,000	
Purchases	122,500	
Rent	1,700	
Revenue		171,800
Opening inventory	20,100	
Telephone costs	975	
Bank		3,964
Capital		10,772
Accruals		1,389
Closing inventory	21,750	21,750
Depreciation expense – machinery	1,225	
Depreciation expense – motor vehicles	3,900	
	209,675	209,675

The following information is also available

- A customer with an outstanding invoice of £475 has gone into liquidation. This has not yet been reflected in the TB.

(a) **Prepare the statement of profit or loss for the year ended 31 December 20X8.**

	£	£
Sales revenue		
Less:		
▼		
▼		
▼		
Cost of goods sold		
Gross profit		
Less:		
▼		
▼		
▼		
▼		
▼		
▼		
▼		
▼		
▼		
Total expenses		
Profit/loss for the year		

Picklist:

Accruals
Bank and cash
Capital
Closing inventory
Depreciation charges
Disposal of non-current asset
Drawings
Electricity
Insurance
Irrecoverable debt expense
Miscellaneous expenses
Motor expenses

Opening inventory
Prepayments
Purchases
Rent
Repairs and maintenance
Sales revenue
Telephone
Trade payables
Trade receivables
VAT

Beth is planning on going into business with her new investor, they are going to become a Limited Liability Partnership.

(b) **List THREE differences which Beth must be aware of if her business becomes a LLP, compared to her current status as a sole trader.**

BPP
LEARNING MEDIA

Task 3.4

When a partner joins or leaves a partnership there will be a number of procedures to be made to the partnership accounts. These can include adjustments to amounts in the capital accounts and also a new agreements on the profit share ratio. One adjustment that may be needed is to goodwill.

(a) **Explain what is meant by 'goodwill'.**

(b) **What ethical principle is most at risk with goodwill valuations and suggest a safeguard that could help reduce your chosen risk.**

Maria Lemieux has a business selling sportswear and she currently operates as a sole trader. Maria has asked for your advice outlining the advantages and disadvantages of bringing her best friend, Wendy Gretsky into the business. Wendy has experience of designing sportswear for a large national business.

(c) **Write an email to Maria, explaining the advantages and disadvantages of operating as a partnership. Also comment on any actions to take if she chooses to bring Wendy into the business as a partner.**

| To |
| From |
| Date |
| Subject |
| |

Task 3.5

Jemima works as an accounts assistant in a mid-sized accountancy firm and her work has so far involved the preparation of financial statements for sole traders. Her supervisor has now requested for Jemima to prepare a set of financial statements for limited company without any additional training.

(a) **According to the AAT *Code of Professional Ethics*, identify the ethical principle that Jemima is most at risk if she undertakes this work.**

(b) **Outline suggested safeguards that Jemima can follow to reduce the risk of breaching this principle**

(c) **Explain FIVE differences between financial statements preparation for companies and those of sole traders that Jemima should be aware of.**

(d) **Which ONE of the following statements is correct?**

	✓
If a company goes into liquidation, the maximum amount that the shareholder lose is the amount of capital they have agreed to invest in the company	
The information provided in the financial statements is strictly limited.	
All directors are shareholders in a company limited by liability.	
The amount of time each shareholder can work in a company is restricted.	

Jemima has received some financial information from one of the clients, Peter Lapin, a sole trader.

- All of Peter's sales are on a cash basis with no customers receiving any credit terms. He receives credit terms from his suppliers.

- Sales are calculated at a 25% gross mark up

- Here is an incomplete cash at bank extract which Peter has pulled together for Jemima.

Cash at bank

Account	£	Account	£
Balance b/d	10,000	Motor expenses	650
Receipts from customers	36,000		
		Payments to suppliers	25,000
		Balance c/d	14,850
Total		Total	

(e) **Calculate the drawings (assuming all transactions go through the bank account) for Peter Lapin**

£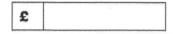

(f) **Calculate the cost of sales figure for Peter's business using the information provided.**

£

Task 3.6

While producing a set of accounts for a partnership, Tomaz identifies that entertainment expenses have increased by 500% from previous years. On further investigation Tomaz discovers the partnership previously had two people required for expense authorisation; one to raise an expense claim and another to check and authorise the claim. However, now only one individual raises the claim and authorises payment.

(a) **Identify the threats and ethical principles that are most at risk here.**

(b) **What safeguards can be put in place to reduce the risks that Tomaz faces?**

(c) **What are the typical contents of a partnership agreement?**

Task 3.7

A large business has set its materiality level at £5,000 and it has been discovered that two purchase invoices have been fraudulently raised and paid to a member of staff. Each invoice was worth £1,000. A colleague has stated as these amounts are well below the materiality threshold level set there is no need to follow this issue up or investigate further.

(a) **What is meant by the term materiality?**

(b) **How should you respond to your colleague regarding whether it should be followed up and if so, what steps should be taken?**

Amy is an accounting technician and is in the process of preparing a set of accounts for a sole trader, ABC Supplies. While collecting sales revenue information a customer telephones and asks for Amy to email across other customer details of ABC Supplies. He says he wants this information to be more competitive and without it he may have to take his custom elsewhere.

(c) **What ethical principle and threat is most relevant here?**

(d) **What should Amy do in these circumstances and identify when Amy may disclose customer information.**

Task 3.8

When preparing a set of final accounts it is important for the preparer to be aware for any potential conflict of interests.

(a)   Explain what is meant by a conflict of interest.

(b)   What is the appropriate procedure for dealing with potential conflicts of interest?

Jaz is an accountant in a large accountancy practice and is the process of preparing the final accounts for two separate clients, A and B. After reviewing a member of her staff's working papers Jaz discovers that client A has made a substantial loan (£1m) to B. Jaz is fully aware that B is facing serious financial difficulties and there are doubts whether B will continue to be a going concern in the foreseeable future.

(c)   What is the threat that Jaz is facing here and suggest safeguards that Jaz can put in place?

Task 3.9

(a)   When preparing financial statements for a sole trader explain what is meant by the term 'Capital'.

A sole trader has a capital balance of £56,730 on 1 January 20X6. During the year ended 31 December 20X6 the business made a profit of £38,920 and the owner withdrew cash totalling £24,650 along with inventories taken for personal use amounting to £3,000.

(b)   Calculate the capital balance at 31 December 20X6.

£	

X and Y are partners in a business selling laptop computers. Both partners have signed a partnership agreement that permits drawings to be made in cash at the end of the financial year. During th;e most recent reporting period Y has taken a laptop computer for his own personal use and this has not been recorded anywhere in the partnership accounts. Y has not informed X that he has taken this laptop.

(c)   Explain the consequences of Y's actions on the partnership.

Task 3.10

A business trading as a sole trader or a partnership will be financed by capital invested into the business by its owners and money taken out of the business for the benefit of the owners will be in the form of drawings.

(a) **Looking at capital and drawings explain how this differs from an organisation trading as a limited company?**

An accountant has prepared a limited company set of accounts that has an inflated equity figure effectively overvaluing the company by a considerable amount. This value was used to secure a substantial bank loan. The company has since ceased to trade with the loss of many jobs. After financial press interest in the matter it was found the accountant did not perform the necessary checks to see if his reported equity figure was correct even though equity had increased to £2m from just £25,000 reported in the previous year.

(b) **Identify the two ethical principles that are most at risk here.**

(c) **Explain what is meant by the term professional scepticism.**

....

Task 3.11

Buildings, machinery, IT equipment and goods purchased for resale are assets which typically have a substantial value in a business. To help reduce the risk of any material misstatement in the final accounts there are two accounting standards that provide guidance on valuation of these types of assets.

Required

(a) **Identify the two accounting standards that provide guidance on the accounting treatment of non-current assets such as buildings and current assets of goods purchases for resale.**

(b) **If an accountant did not keep up to date with changes in accounting standards what ethical principle would be most at risk?**

(c) **How can an accountant keep up to date with changes in the accountancy profession and identity the consequences when skills are not up to date.**

....

Assessment objective 4 – Spreadsheets for Accounting/Management Accounting: Costing

Task 4.1

BetterYou is a company which provides short training courses in mindfulness.

The training courses are delivered in person to small groups of individuals. There are four trainers, Alex, Janine, Simone and Karesh. They are responsible for recruiting individuals to attend their courses.

BetterYou offers four training packages. Level 1, Level 2 and Level 3 are progressive one day courses. Level 2 can only be attended on completion of Level 1, and Level 3 can only be attended on completion of Level 2.

The fourth package 'Complete Mindfulness' incorporates Levels 1–3 and is provided at a reduced cost compared to booking the courses individually. The learner pays for the whole course up front then books on the individual courses as they progress through the levels.

You have been given a spreadsheet **Question Task 4.1 BetterYou.xlsx** which shows sales figures achieved by each trainer for the April–June quarter in 20X6. It contains two worksheets: 'Sales' and 'Price structure'.

Download this spreadsheet file from www.bpp.com/aatspreadsheets and save in the appropriate location. Rename it using the following format: **'your initial-surname-AAT no –dd.mm.yy-Task4.1'**.

For example: J-Donnovan-123456-12.03xx-Task4.1

A **high degree of accuracy** is required. You **must save your work as a .XLSX file** at regular intervals to avoid losing your work.

(a) **Open the renamed spreadsheet and on the 'sales' worksheet insert a column between the columns 'course' and 'units'.**

- **Give the column the title 'unit price'.**
- **Use a lookup function to insert the unit price on the sales tab.**

(b) **Add a column in Column F called 'Total value' and apply a formula to all cells in that column to show the total value of the units sold in each row.**

- **Split the screen so that the headings remain visible.**
- **Use the SUM function in cell F50 to determine the total values of sales for the quarter.**
- **Format the numbers in this column to contain a thousand separator and make the contents of cell F50 bold.**

(c) **Create a pivot table and pivot chart showing the total value of sales, broken down by course, made by each of Alex, Janine, Simone and Karesh.**

- **Place the pivot table and pivot chart on a new sheet, and rename this sheet 'Total Values'.**

- **Add a chart title 'Total sales Values Apr–Jun'.**

If any of the trainers manage to recruit 20 or more individuals on to any of the courses in a month, that trainer will receive a bonus of £5 per individual booked on that course.

(d) **Give Column G the heading 'Bonus' and use an IF function to show the amount of bonus payments due.**

- **Total all bonuses to be paid.**

- **Create a pivot table in a new worksheet which shows the total bonus to be paid to each trainer.**

- **Sort the data in this pivot table to arrange the trainers in ascending order in terms of the bonus payment due to them for the quarter.**

- **Rename the tab 'Bonuses'.**

(e) **Password protect the entire workbook and using the password Better123.**

Task 4.2

You have been given a spreadsheet **Question Task 4.2 FinanceTeam.xls** which shows qualification details of members of the finance team at ABC co. It contains two worksheets: 'Finance Team' and 'Subs'.

Download this spreadsheet file from www.bpp.com/aatspreadsheets and save in the appropriate location. Rename it using the following format: **'your initial-surname-AAT no –dd.mm.yy-Task4.2'**.

For example: J-Donnovan-123456-12.03xx-Task4.2

A **high degree of accuracy** is required. You **must save your work as a .XLSX file** at regular intervals to avoid losing your work.

(a) **Open the renamed spreadsheet and open the subs worksheet.**

- **Format the data on this page as a table, include the headings.**

- **On the finance team worksheet, use a LOOKUP function to complete the subs column.**

- **Format the subs figures in a red font colour.**

ABC company offers free health check-ups to all employees aged 40 or older.

(b) **Use conditional formatting to highlight all employees aged 40 and over.**

- **Sort the data based on employee number, from lowest to highest.**

ABC company employees are given 24 days of holiday per year. When they have served at the company for 5 or more years, they receive an additional 5 days leave per year.

(c) **Rename column J as 'holiday'.**

- **Use an IF statement to complete the data in this column to show how many days holiday per year to which each individual is entitled.**

(d) **Format the data as a table with light blue shading.**

- **Use the filter function to display only individuals who are members or students of the AAT who have not yet paid their subs.**

....

Task 4.3

You have been given a spreadsheet **Question Task 4.3 Orders.xls** which shows an extract of a spreadsheet of purchases made by various departments in the organisation. It contains one worksheet: sheet 1.

Download this spreadsheet file from www.bpp.com/aatspreadsheets and save in the appropriate location. Rename it using the following format: **'your initial-surname-AAT no –dd.mm.yy-Task4.3'**.

For example: J-Donnovan-123456-12.03xx-Task4.3

A **high degree of accuracy** is required. You **must save your work as a .XLSX** file at regular intervals to avoid losing your work.

Since this spreadsheet was prepared, the company 'Cater Co' has been rebranded and the name of the company has changed to 'Corporate Catering Company'.

(a) **Open the renamed spreadsheet.**

- **Use find and replace to update any cells which refer to 'Cater co' to show the new name of the company.**

- **Rename the worksheet 'order list'.**

(b) **Create a pivot table and also a pivot chart in a new worksheet to represented the amount spent with each supplier. Put the pivot chart to the right of the pivot table.**

- **The pivot chart should show the supplier details on the horizontal axis and the total spend by supplier on the vertical axis.**

- **Rename the chart as 'Spend per supplier'.**

- **Rename the worksheet 'Supplier spend' and ensure the order of the worksheets is such that the order list worksheet is on the left and the supplier spend worksheet is on the right.**

- **Using conditional formatting in the pivot table, select all suppliers who have a total spend above £350. The cell colour and the font should change for these suppliers.**

- **Filter the pivot chart to show only the suppliers with a spend above £350**

- **In cell B8, insert an Average function to show the average supplier spend for these largest suppliers.**

- **Ensure the Average function formula is visible.**

(c) **Copy the Order List worksheet and rename this duplicate tab "Department spend".**

- **Insert a new pivot table for this data, this needs to be positioned on the existing worksheet to the right of the data**

- **Sort the pivot table to show the spend per department**

- **Insert a 3D pie chart, label it 'Total spend by department'**

Task 4.4

You have been given a spreadsheet **Question Task 4.4 Inventory.xls** which shows inventory held at a distribution centre. It contains four worksheets: 'Inventory list', 'Locations', 'Price List' and 'Order June 20X6'.

Download this spreadsheet file from www.bpp.com/aatspreadsheets and save in the appropriate location. Rename it using the following format: **'your initial-surname-AAT no –dd.mm.yy-Task4.4'**.

For example: J-Donnovan-123456-12.03xx-Task4.4

A **high degree of accuracy** is required. You **must save your work as a .XLSX file** at regular intervals to avoid losing your work.

(a) **Open the renamed spreadsheet and go into the location tab.**

- **Rename column E as location code and format the cell to be the same as the others in this row.**

- **Create a location code in cell E2 comprising of the aisle, location and bin number, eg 1A3.**

- **Apply this formula to all relevant cells in Column E.**

(b) **Open the inventory list worksheet and use lookup functions to complete:**

- **The location information in Column B**

- **The unit price information in Column C**

- **Insert a formula to calculate the value of each item of inventory in Column E**

(c) **Insert an IF function to determine whether or not items are due to be re-ordered in Column G.**

- **If the item is above the re-order level, this should return the value 0. If the item is on or under the re-order level, this should return the value 1.**

(d) **Format the data contained in cells B1:H22 as a table, using Table style medium 14**

- **Format cells A1:I1 using font Arial 12, in bold. Merge and centre the title across the top of the table. Select a suitable purple shade of background.**

- **Hide the gridlines to improve the look of the worksheet.**

- **Sort the data by using the filter on column H to remove all items that have been discontinued.**

- **Hide Column H.**

(e) **Use the filter function to show only those items that need to be reordered.**

- **Copy and paste the relevant items on to the Order June 20X6 worksheet to create an order list.**

- **Ensure you do not copy over the table format to the new order list.**

Task 4.5

You have been given a spreadsheet **Question Task 4.5 Timesheet.xls** which is used by employees of ABC Co. to record the hours they have worked and where they have spent their time. Your spreadsheet currently contains one worksheet: Week 1. This contains details of the time spent by one employee, Harrison, during that week.

Download this spreadsheet file from www.bpp.com/aatspreadsheets and save in the appropriate location. Rename it using the following format: **'your initial-surname-AAT no –dd.mm.yy-Task4.5'**.

For example: J-Donnovan-123456-12.03xx-Task4.5

A **high degree of accuracy** is required. You **must save your work as a .XLSX file** at regular intervals to avoid losing your work.

ABC company operates a flexitime system. It counts one working day to be 7.5 hours long. However, employees can work more or fewer hours in any given day, so long as the time is made up elsewhere. If employees accumulate 7.5 hours of flexitime, they can choose to take a 'flexi-day'. A flexi-day is a day off in lieu of the time that has been worked to accumulate these hours and, from the employees point of view, works like an additional day of annual leave.

(a) **Open the renamed spreadsheet.**

- **Add a formula to cell C31 to calculate the amount of flexi-time earned or used on Monday. Apply this formula to the rest of the days of the week.**

- **Add a formula to cell C32 to calculate the current balance of flexitime on Monday. Apply this formula to the rest of the days of the week.**

- **Replace the formulas in cells I25 and I28 with more robust formulas to check for errors in the summing of data.**

As part of the flexi-time system, employees are not allowed to work for less than six hours in any given day.

(b) **Use a data validation function in cells C29:G29 to identify any days where less than six hours are worked.**

- **Set the data validation to circle in red any days where fewer than six hours have been worked.**

Employees are also not allowed to charge more than two hours to the admin account in any given day.

(c)   **Use a data validation function to prevent more than two hours of admin being charged on any given day.**

-       **Give a suitable warning title and a brief message on the limit of administration time allowed per day.**

-       **Attempt to change the admin charge on Monday to three hours.**

You are given the following information about Harrison's working patterns for the following two weeks:

In week two, Harrison was on annual leave all five days.

In week three, Harrison attended a training course for 8 hours on both Monday and Tuesday. On Wednesday he charged 3 hours to each of projects 1 and 2 and 2 hours to admin. On Thursday he charged 4 hours to project 1, 3 hours to supervision and 2 hours to admin. On Friday he charged 7 hours to project 3 and one hour to admin.

(d)   **Insert two new worksheets.**

-       **Change the name of the new worksheets to 'Week 2' and 'Week 3'.**

-       **Copy the format and formulas used on Week 1 to Week 2 and Week 3 and populate the spreadsheets with the information given above.**

-       **Link the formula related to flexi-time to ensure the balance from Week 1 is carried over to week 2 and so on.**

(e)   **Insert a new worksheet and rename it 'Summary'.**

-       **Use the data from Weeks 1–3 to produce a summary sheet which collates the total number of hours charged to each activity per week.**

-       **Format the summary sheet in the same style as the weekly worksheets.**

-       **Use the split function to keep the header rows in place.**

....

Task 4.6

You have been given a spreadsheet **Question Task 4.6 Sickness.xls** which shows an extract from a record of employee sick leave taken. It contains two worksheets: 'Record' and 'Employee names'.

Download this spreadsheet file from www.bpp.com/aatspreadsheets and save in the appropriate location. Rename it using the following format: **'your initial-surname-AAT no –dd.mm.yy-Task5.5'**.

For example: J-Donnovan-123456-12.03xx-Task5.5

A **high degree of accuracy** is required. You **must save your work as a .XLSX file** at regular intervals to avoid losing your work.

(a) **Open the renamed spreadsheet and go into the Record tab.**

- **Use a lookup function to complete the employee name column.**

Sickness certificates from a medical professional are required in order to verify any sickness period in excess of 5 days.

(b) **Use an IF statement in Column I along with a lookup function in Column E to determine whether or not a certificate is required.**

- **The IF statement should return the values 0 for no and 1 for yes and the lookup should refer to the table in Columns J and K.**

- **Hide Columns I, J and K.**

Employees should not take more than 15 sickness days in total per year.

(c) **Insert a pivot table on a new worksheet (area A1:F31) which summarises the total number of sickness days taken by each employee.**

- **Rename this worksheet 'Summary'.**

Employees are a cause for concern for the organisation if they take frequent short periods of sickness.

(d) **Return to the 'Record' worksheet and sort the data by employee number.**

- **Use a subtotal function to count the instances of sickness taken by each individual.**

- **Highlight the entire worksheet and apply conditional formatting to highlight the employee number of any individuals who are at risk of falling into the frequent sickness category. Highlight any employees who have taken more than one episode of sickness in the period.**

Task 4.7

Note. Preparation of histograms is no longer assessed at Level 3, however, this question is retained as knowledge of how a histogram works is required. You have been given a spreadsheet **Question Task 4.7 TestResults.xls** which shows scores achieved by students in four tests and an overall score. It contains one worksheet: 'Test Results'.

Download this spreadsheet file from www.bpp.com/aatspreadsheets and save in the appropriate location. Rename it using the following format: **'your initial-surname-AAT no –dd.mm.yy-Task4.7'**.

For example: J-Donnovan-123456-12.03xx-Task4.7

A **high degree of accuracy** is required. You **must save your work as a XLSX file** at regular intervals to avoid losing your work.

(a)   Open the renamed spreadsheet.

- **Run a data validation test to remove any duplicate entries.**

- **In Column G, calculate the average score for each candidate using formula across tests 1-4.**

- **Name the worksheet "Test results"**

- **Create a copy of the worksheet and call it "referrals". Perform the remaining tasks in part (a) in the "Referrals" worksheet.**

- **For this data range C2:F46 only, format the cells using conditional formatting whereby scores of less than the pass mark are highlighted in red cells. The maximum a candidate can score in the test is 150, and the pass mark is 70%.**

- **Insert a new column H called 'Comments' and using an IF statement where any average scores of less than 120 are achieved, the comment should read 'Refer'. No comment is required for students achieving above that score.**

- **Format the table to Medium 3, filter the results so that only referred candidates are shown.**

Students who have scored over 130 are considered suitable candidates for a scholarship. The five highest scoring students will automatically gain a place in the scholarship program. There are ten places available. The remaining students who fall into this category will be offered an interview for this program.

(b) **Return to worksheet 'test results' and format the data as a table using table style medium 2.**

- **Use the filters within the table to identify only those students who will be offered an interview for the scholarship program.**

- **Reorder the data using the filter to rank the potential scholarship candidates from highest scoring to lowest scoring.**

(c) **Add a column called 'outcome' in Column H.**

- **Insert the text 'Scholarship' in this column next to the top 5 students, and 'Interview' against the remaining students.**

- **Remove the filters, and rename this worksheet "scholarship"**

(d) **Password protect the entire workbook and using the password Test123.**

Task 4.8

You are Ian Chesterton, a part-qualified accounting technician. You work for Hammond Co, which manufactures luxury office furniture.

You cover all aspects of bookkeeping and accounting for the business. You report to Tom Howard, Chief Accountant.

Today's date is 3 January 20X0.

The board of Hammond Co is currently considering an investment in new plant and machinery, which will enable the company to sell a more comfortable make of its office chair. The board will make a decision about this next week. The investment will take place immediately afterwards if the board decides to go ahead.

You have been asked to produce an analysis for the board meeting of this investment, using the net present value (NPV) and payback methods of investment appraisal. In order to fulfil Hammond Co's criteria, the investment must have both a positive NPV and a payback period of less than three years.

You have been given the following details about the investment:

- The investment appraisal should cover a time horizon of four years.

- Hammond Co will need to make an immediate investment in plant and machinery of £240,000.

- Expected sales revenue of the new chair in Year 1 will be £200,000 and expected variable costs will be £100,000.

- Sales revenue and costs are expected to rise by the following percentages in Years 2–4 compared with the previous year.

Year	2	3	4
	10%	5%	3%

- Expected fixed costs will be £20,000 per year and will not change over the four year period.

Download the spreadsheet file **Question Task 4.8 Hammond.**xlsx from www.bpp.com/aatspreadsheets. Save the spreadsheet file in the appropriate location and rename it in the following format: 'your initial-surname-AAT no-dd.mm.yy-Task4.8'. For example: H-Darch-123456-12.03.xx-Task4.8

A **high degree of accuracy** is required. You must **save your work as an .XLSX file** at regular intervals to avoid losing your work.

(a) **Open the renamed file. Calculate the revenues and variable costs for Years 1–4 using the information provided, showing variable costs as a negative figure.**

(b) **Enter the fixed costs for Years 1–4, showing them as a negative figure.**

(c) **In cell A6 enter the narrative Capital expenditure. Enter the amount of capital expenditure in the correct cell and show it as a negative figure.**

(d) **In cell A7 enter the narrative Cash flows and calculate the net cash flows for Years 0–4.**

(e) **In cell A9 enter the narrative Discounted cash flows and calculate the discounted cash flows for Years 0–4, using the cash flows you have calculated and the discount factors given in cells B8–F8.**

(f) **Calculate the NPV and insert it in cell B10. Put an IF statement in cell C10 that will show ACCEPT if the NPV is positive and REJECT if the NPV is negative.**

(g) **Tidy up the NPV calculation by showing all negative figures in brackets and all figures rounded to the nearest £, with commas for 000s.**

(h) **For the payback calculation, copy and paste cells A7–F7 into A12–F12.**

(i) **Show the cumulative cash flows for each year as a running total in cells B13–F13.**

(j)   For the last negative cumulative cash flow, in the cell immediately beneath it in row 14, insert this figure as a positive number. Highlight this figure, the first positive cumulative cash flow and the year number in which the last negative cumulative cash flow occurs by placing a black border around the cells.

(k)   Use the highlighted figures to carry out a payback calculation in cell B15, expressing your answer as a decimal rounded to two decimal places.

(l)   Put an IF statement in cell C15 that will show **ACCEPT** if the payback period is less than three years and **REJECT** if the payback period is more than three years.

(m)   Perform a spell check and ensure that the contents of all cells can be seen.

(n)   Use the proforma email to do the following:

- Comment on the results of your calculations.
- Give two advantages of using the payback method of investment appraisal.

To:	Tom Howard
From:	Ian Chesterton
Date:	3 January 20X0
Subject:	Investment in plant and machinery

Task 4.9

You are Barbara Wright, a part-qualified accounting technician. You work for Riley Co, which manufactures cups.

You cover all aspects of bookkeeping and accounting for the business. You report to Lynne Dupont, Finance Director.

Today's date is 25 January 20X1.

Lynne Dupont has asked for your assistance in appraising an investment in new machinery, which should enable it to produce cups that are harder-wearing and less likely to break. Lynne Dupont thinks that Riley Co will be able to charge a higher price each year for its new cups, although the variable cost per cup will also increase. Lynne has asked you to use the net present value (NPV) and payback methods of investment appraisal. In order to fulfil Riley Co's criteria, the investment must have a positive NPV or a payback period of less than four years.

You have been given the following details about the investment:

- The investment appraisal should cover a time horizon of four years.

- Riley Co will need to make an immediate investment in machinery of £300,000.

- Riley Co expects to sell 50,000 new cups a year. The selling price of each cup in Year 1 will be £5 and the expected variable cost per cup will be £3.

- Sales price and variable cost per cup are expected to rise by the following percentages in Years 2–4 compared with the previous year.

Year	2	3	4
Sales price	10%	8%	5%
Variable cost	6%	4%	3%

- Expected fixed costs will be £40,000 per year and will not change over the four year period.

Download the spreadsheet file **Question Task 4.9 Riley Co.xlsx** from www.bpp.com/aatspreadsheets. Save the spreadsheet file in the appropriate location and rename it in the following format: 'your initial-surname-AAT no-dd.mm.yy-Task4.9'. For example: H-Darch-123456-12.03.xx-Task4.9

A **high degree of accuracy** is required. You must **save your work as a .XLSX file** at regular intervals to avoid losing your work.

(a) **Open the renamed file. Calculate the revenues and variable costs for Years 1–4 using the information provided, showing variable costs as a negative figure.**

(b) **Enter the fixed costs for Years 1–4, showing them as a negative figure.**

(c) **In cell A6 enter the narrative Capital expenditure. Enter the amount of capital expenditure in the correct cell and show it as a negative figure.**

(d) **In cell A7 enter the narrative Cash flows and calculate the net cash flows for Years 0–4.**

(e) **In cell A9 enter the narrative Discounted cash flows and calculate the discounted cash flows for Years 0–4, using the cash flows you have calculated and the discount factors given in cells B8–F8.**

(f) **Calculate the NPV and insert it in cell B10. Put an IF statement in cell C10 that will show ACCEPT if the NPV is positive and REJECT if the NPV is negative.**

(g) Tidy up the NPV calculation by showing all negative figures in brackets and all figures rounded to the nearest £, with commas for 000s.

(h) For the payback calculation, copy and paste cells A7–F7 into A12–F12.

(i) Show the cumulative cash flows for each year as a running total in cells B13–F13.

(j) For the last negative cumulative cash flow, in the cell immediately beneath it in row 14, insert this figure as a positive number. Highlight this figure, the first positive cumulative cash flow and the year number in which the last negative cumulative cash flow occurs by placing a black border around the cells.

(k) Use the highlighted figures to carry out a payback calculation in cell B15, expressing your answer as a decimal rounded to two decimal places.

(l) Put an IF statement in cell C15 that will show **ACCEPT** if the payback period is less than four years and **REJECT** if the payback period is more than four years.

(m) Perform a spell check and ensure that the contents of all cells can be seen.

(n) Set the print area for cells A1:G16, ensure the page orientation is set to landscape when printed.

(o) Give the printed area a header of "Riley NPV Calculation" and a footer showing the date and time.

(p) Change the title of "NPV" in cell A1 to "NPV Riley Calculation", change the font to Calibri 16 and merge and centre the titles across cells A1:D1.

(q) Use the proforma email to do the following:

  • Comment on the results of your calculations.

  • Give two reasons why the NPV method is a better method of investment appraisal than the payback method.

To:	Lynne Dupont
From:	Barbara Wright
Date:	25 January 20X1
Subject:	Investment in machinery

Task 4.10

You are Susan Foreman, a part-qualified accounting technician. You work for Kingsley Co, a company that manufactures economy DVD players.

You cover all aspects of bookkeeping and accounting for the business. You report to Charles Frere, Managing Director.

Today's date is 29 February 20X2.

Charles Frere is considering investment in new technology costing £675,000, that will make the production of DVD players more efficient. He has prepared estimates of increases in DVD player sales, based on being able to cut the price as a result of using the new technology. The new technology will lead to increased fixed costs and Charles Frere acknowledges that total variable costs will also increase as a result of increased sales.

Expected total variable costs for Year 1 are £180,000. They are expected to rise by the following percentages in Years 2–4 compared with the previous year.

Year	2	3	4
Variable costs	15%	12%	10%

Fixed costs are expected to be £40,000 in Year 1, and to rise by 5% in each of the following three years.

Charles Frere has asked you to carry out an appraisal of the investment in the new technology, using the net present value (NPV) and internal rate of return (IRR) methods of investment appraisal. In order to fulfil Kingsley Co's criteria, the investment must have a positive NPV or an IRR of more than 11%. Charles Frere has provided you with the results of NPV calculations using discount rates of 10% and 15%, to help in your IRR calculation. For 10% the result is +£27,756, for 15% the result is –£47,539.

Download the spreadsheet **Question Task 4.10 Susan Foreman.xlsx** file from www.bpp.com/aatspreadsheets. Save the spreadsheet file in the appropriate location and rename it in the following format: 'your initial-surname-AAT no-dd.mm.yy-Task4.10'. For example: H-Darch-123456-12.03.xx-Task4.10

A **high degree of accuracy** is required. You must **save your work as a .XLSX file** at regular intervals to avoid losing your work.

(a)   **Open the renamed file. Enter the narrative for Variable costs and Fixed costs in cells A4 and A5. Calculate the variable costs and fixed costs for Years 1–4 using the information provided, showing them as negative figures.**

(b)   **In cell A6 enter the narrative Capital expenditure. Enter the amount of capital expenditure in the correct cell and show it as a negative figure.**

(c)   **In cell A7 enter the narrative Cash flows and calculate the net cash flows for Years 0–4.**

(d)   **In cell A9 enter the narrative Discounted cash flows and calculate the discounted cash flows for Years 0–4, using the cash flows you have calculated and the discount factors given in cells B8–F8.**

(e)   **Calculate the NPV and insert it in cell B10. Put an IF statement in cell C10 that will show ACCEPT if the NPV is positive and REJECT if the NPV is negative.**

(f)   **Tidy up the NPV calculation by showing all negative figures in brackets and all figures rounded to the nearest £, with commas for 000s.**

(g)   **Carry out the IRR calculation in cell B11, using the information supplied by Charles Frere. Express your answer to two decimal places. Use conditional format to show an IRR that meets Kingsley Co's criteria in green and an IRR that does not meet Kingsley Co's criteria in red.**

(h)   **Insert a comment for cell B11 stating that "For the IRR >11 the criteria set by Kingsley Co is valid". Ensure that the comment is visible at all times on the spreadsheet.**

(i)   **Perform a spell check and ensure that the contents of all cells can be seen.**

(j)   **Use the proforma email to do the following:**

- **Comment on the results of your calculations.**
- **Give two reasons why the NPV method is a better method of investment appraisal than the IRR method.**

To:	Charles Frere
From:	Susan Foreman
Date:	29 February 20X2
Subject:	Investment in new technology

Task 4.11

You are Steven Taylor, a part-qualified accounting technician. You work for Merroney Co, a manufacturer of socks.

You cover all aspects of bookkeeping and accounting for the business. You report to Avril Rolfe, the Chief Finance Officer.

Today's date is 14 March 20X3.

Avril Rolfe is currently contemplating a proposal for Merroney Co to invest in machinery to produce a new range of novelty socks. The machinery will cost £320,000. Fixed costs associated with the machinery are expected to be £60,000 in Year 1 and are not expected to change in subsequent years.

Avril Rolfe has prepared estimates for sales price per unit, variable cost per unit and expected sales for the next four years. Avril however has had to move on to other work and has asked you to complete the investment appraisal.

Avril wants you to use the net present value (NPV) and internal rate of return (IRR) methods of investment appraisal. In order to fulfil Merroney Co's criteria, the investment must have a positive NPV and an IRR of more than 9%. Avril has provided you with the results of NPV calculations using discount rates of 5% and 10%, to help in your NPV calculations. For 5% the result is +£37,191, for 10% the result is -£6,005.

Download the spreadsheet file **Question Task 4.11 Merroney.xlsx** from www.bpp.com/aatspreadsheets. Save the spreadsheet file in the appropriate location and rename it in the following format: 'your initial-surname-AAT no-dd.mm.yy-Task4.11'. For example: H-Darch-123456-12.03.xx-Task4.11

A **high degree of accuracy** is required. You must **save your work as a .XLSX file** at regular intervals to avoid losing your work.

(a) **Open the renamed file. Enter the narrative for Revenues and Variable costs in cells A6 and A7. Calculate the revenues and variable costs for Years 1–4 using the information given in Rows 3–5.**

(b) **Enter the fixed costs for Years 1–4, showing them as a negative figure.**

(c) **In cell A9 enter the narrative Capital expenditure. Enter the amount of capital expenditure in the correct cell and show it as a negative figure.**

(d) **In cell A10 enter the narrative Cash flows and calculate the net cash flows for Years 0–4.**

(e) **In cell A12 enter the narrative Discounted cash flows and calculate the discounted cash flows for Years 0–4, using the cash flows you have calculated and the discount factors given in cells B11–F11.**

(f) **Calculate the NPV and insert it in cell B13. Put an IF statement in cell C13 that will show ACCEPT if the NPV is positive and REJECT if the NPV is negative.**

(g) **Tidy up the NPV calculation, by showing all negative figures in brackets and all figures rounded to the nearest £, with comma for 000s.**

(h) **Carry out the IRR calculation in cell B14, using the information supplied by Avril Rolfe. Express your answer to two decimal places. Use conditional format to show an IRR that meets Merroney Co's criteria in green and an IRR that does not meet Merroney Co's criteria in red.**

(i) **Perform a spell check and ensure that the contents of all cells can be seen.**

(j) **Use the proforma email to do the following:**

   • **Comment on the results of your calculations.**

   • **Give two advantages of using the IRR method of investment appraisal.**

To:	Avril Rolfe
From:	Steven Taylor
Date:	14 March 20X3
Subject:	Investment in machinery

···

Task 4.12

You are Dodo Chaplet, a part-qualified accounting technician. You work for Maxwell Co, a company that manufactures high quality cosmetic creams.

You cover all aspects of bookkeeping and accounting for the business. You report to Kate Harvey, the Head of Accounts.

Today's date is 11 April 20X4.

Maxwell Co had originally budgeted to make and sell 40,000 units of cosmetic cream in the quarter to 31 March 20X4. However it actually made and sold 45,000 units in the quarter.

Information about the original budget and the actual results are provided.

Download the spreadsheet file **Question Task 4.12 Maxwell.xlsx** from www.bpp.com/aatspreadsheets. Save the spreadsheet file in the appropriate location and rename it in the following format: 'your initial-surname-AAT no-dd.mm.yy-Task4.12. For example: H-Darch-123456-12.03.xx-Task4.12

A **high degree of accuracy** is required. You must **save your work as a .XLSX file** at regular intervals to avoid losing your work.

(a) Open this renamed file. Calculate the percentage to flex this budget in line with the information about sales and insert this percentage figure into cell D1.

(b) In cell D3 enter the title Flexed budget. Calculate the flexed budget for the relevant entries using absolute referencing where appropriate.

(c) In cell E3 enter the title Actual results. Use copy and paste to take the actual results from the information you've been given into the correct positions in Column E.

(d) In cell F3 insert the title Variances. Calculate the variances for each revenue and each cost. Show these in Column F.

(e) In cell A15 insert the title Operating profit. Calculate the operating profit for the original budget, flexed budget and actual results.

(f) Calculate the overall variance in cell F15.

(g) Use conditional formatting in Column F to show all favourable variances in green and adverse variances in red.

(h) Put an IF statement in cell F17 that will show 'Balanced' if the column totals balance and 'Check' if they do not.

(i) Colour cell F17 with a yellow background and black border.

(j) Make sure all column headings are in bold.

(k) Copy the range A2 to F15 and paste into the new area of the worksheet called Maxwell Co Original budget for the quarter ended 31 March 20X4 (cost summary).

(l) Delete the row that contains the Revenue amounts.

(m) Produce subtotals for each of: materials, labour, variable overheads and fixed overheads.

(n) Show subtotals in original budget, flexed budget, actual results and variances columns.

(o) Hide the detail to only show the subtotals and grand total, not the individual components.

(p) Return to the original budget, perform a spell check and ensure that all the contents of the cells can be seen.

(q) From the variances in cells F5 to F14 identify the most significant favourable variance and the most significant adverse variance. Insert appropriate text in Column G adjacent to each variance, for example 'Most significant favourable variance' and 'Most significant adverse variance'.

(r) Use the proforma email to do the following:

- Report the flexed budget, actual operating profit and total variance.

- Explain one possible cause for each of the two variances identified as most favourable and most adverse.

To:	Kate Harvey
From:	Dodo Chaplet
Date:	11 April 20X4
Subject:	Variances in quarter to 31 March 20X4

Task 4.13

You are Ben Jackson, a part-qualified accounting technician. You work for Williams restaurant, a large city centre restaurant.

You cover all aspects of bookkeeping and accounting for the business. You report to Abby Hudson, the Accountant.

Today's date is 1 May 20X5.

In the quarter to 31 March 20X5, the restaurant budgeted to serve 4,500 meals (each budgeted meal consists of an average food and drink cost based on previous customer behaviour). However the restaurant only served 3,825 meals in the quarter to 31 March 20X5.

Download the spreadsheet file **Question Task 4.13 Williams Rest.xlsx**from www.bpp.com/aatspreadsheets. Save the spreadsheet file in the appropriate location and rename it in the following format: 'your initial-surname-AAT no-dd.mm.yy-Task4.13'. For example: H-Darch-123456-12.03.xx-Task4.13

A **high degree of accuracy** is required. You must **save your work as a .XLSX file** at regular intervals to avoid losing your work.

(a)   Open this renamed file. Calculate the percentage to flex this budget in line with the information about meals sold and insert this percentage figure into cell D1.

(b)   In cell D3 enter the title Flexed budget. Calculate the flexed budget for the relevant entries using absolute referencing where appropriate.

(c)   In cell E3 enter the title Actual results. Use copy and paste to take the actual results from the information you've been given into the correct positions in Column E.

(d)   In cell F3 insert the title Variances. Calculate the variances for each revenue and each cost. Show these in Column F.

(e)   In cell A16 insert the title Operating profit. Calculate the operating profit for the original budget, flexed budget and actual results.

(f)   Calculate the overall variance in cell F16.

(g)   Use conditional formatting in Column F to show all favourable variances in green and adverse variances in red.

(h)   Put an IF statement in cell F18 that will show 'Balanced' if the column totals balance and 'Check if they do not.

(i)   Colour cell F18 with a yellow background and black border.

(j)   Make sure all column headings are in bold.

(k) Copy the range A2 to F16 and paste into the new area of the worksheet called Williams restaurant Original budget for the quarter ended 31 March 20X5 (cost summary).

(l) Delete the row that contains the Revenue amounts.

(m) Produce subtotals for each of: consumables, labour, variable overheads and fixed overheads.

(n) Show subtotals in original budget, flexed budget, actual results and variances columns.

(o) Hide the detail to only show the subtotals and grand total, not the individual components.

(p) Return to the original budget, perform a spell check and ensure that all the contents of the cells can be seen.

(q) From the variances in cells F5 to F15 identify the most significant favourable variance and the most significant adverse variance. Insert appropriate text in Column G adjacent to each variance, for example 'Most significant favourable variance' and 'Most significant adverse variance'.

(r) Use the proforma email to do the following:

- Report the flexed budget, actual operating profit and total variance.

- Explain one possible cause for each of the two variances identified as most favourable and most adverse.

To:	Abby Hudson
From:	Ben Jackson
Date:	1 May 20X5
Subject:	Variances in quarter to 31 March 20X5

Task 4.14

You are Jamie McCrimmon, a part-qualified accounting technician. You work for Westside Hospital.

You cover all aspects of bookkeeping and accounting for the hospital. You report to Laura Wilde, the Finance Director.

Today's date is 11 June 20X6.

The hospital receives £180 per patient day from the government. It has some variable and fixed costs. Some of its staffing costs are stepped fixed costs, which are dependent on patient days. Its staffing costs are as follows:

Patient days per annum	Supervisors	Nurses	Assistants
Up to 20,000	5	8	22
20,000 – 24,000	5	10	26
Over 24,000	5	12	30

The salary for each supervisor is £30,000 each, nurse £23,000, assistant £16,000.

For the year ended 31 May 20X6 the hospital budgeted for 19,000 patient days, but there were actually 21,850 patient days.

Westside Hospital intends to open a new wing in May 20X7, which will allow it to accommodate more patients. For the year ended 31 May 20X8 it plans to budget for 25,000 patient days. However, the government has indicated that its total funding will be capped at £4 million.

Download the spreadsheet file **Question Task 4.14 Westside Hosp.xlsx** from www.bpp.com/aatspreadsheets. Save the spreadsheet file in the appropriate location and rename it in the following format: 'your initial-surname-AAT no-dd.mm.yy-Task4.14'. For example: H-Darch-123456-12.03.xx-Task4.14

A **high degree of accuracy** is required. You must **save your work as a .XLSX file** at regular intervals to avoid losing your work.

(a) **Open this renamed file. Calculate the percentage to flex the variable costs in this budget in line with the information about patient days and insert this percentage figure into cell D1.**

(b) **In cell D3 enter the title Flexed budget. Calculate the flexed budget for the relevant entries using absolute referencing where appropriate.**

(c) **In cell E3 enter the title Actual results. Use copy and paste to take the actual results from the information you've been given into the correct positions in Column E on the question worksheet.**

(d) **In cell F3 insert the title Variances. Calculate the variances for each revenue and each cost. Show these in Column F.**

(e) **In cell A15 insert the title Surplus/(Deficit). Calculate the operating profit for the original, flexed budget and actual results.**

(f) **Calculate the overall variance in cell F15.**

(g) **Put an IF statement in cell F17 that will show 'Balanced' if the column totals balance and 'Check' if they do not.**

(h) **Colour cell F17 with a yellow background and black border.**

(i) **Make sure all column headings are in bold.**

(j) **Copy the flexed budget figures for staff costs into cells C22–C24 in the area of the spreadsheet labelled Westside Hospital Staffing costs for the year ended 31 May 20X8.**

(k) **Calculate the staffing costs figures for 25,000 patient days and insert them in cells D22–D24.**

(l) **Calculate the difference between the budget figures for staffing costs using 21,850 patient days (current budget) and the budget figures for staffing costs using 25,000 patient days (new budget) figures for staffing costs and insert them in cells E22–E24, showing the total difference in cell E25.**

(m) **Return to the original budget and for each expense category (variable costs, staffing costs and fixed costs), highlight the biggest adverse variance by colouring the cell with a red background and putting a black border round the box.**

(n) **Perform a spell check and ensure that all the contents of the cells can be seen.**

(o) **Use the proforma email to do the following:**

- **Report the flexed budget, actual surplus and total variance.**

- **Report the biggest significant variances in each cost category and explain one possible cause for the biggest variance for a variable cost.**

- **Briefly discuss whether the hospital needs to be concerned about the cap in government funding, in the light of your calculations of the increases in staffing costs.**

To:	Laura Wilde
From:	Jamie McCrimmon
Date:	11 June 20X6
Subject:	Variances for year ended 31 May 20X6 and staff costs

Task 4.15

You are Victoria Waterfield, a part-qualified accounting technician. You work for Farrell Co, a firm of legal and tax consultants.

You cover all aspects of bookkeeping and accounting for the business. You report to Polly Urquhart, one of the partners in the firm.

Today's date is 21 July 20X7.

The figures for the year ended 30 June 20X7 have just become available. Polly wants you to provide an analysis of them. She has supplied you with the original budget, which was based on 15,000 annual chargeable consultant hours. However actual chargeable consultant hours were 16,500. Polly wants the most significant adverse variances in % terms highlighted for her to investigate.

Download the spreadsheet file **Question Task 4.15 Farrell Co.xlsx** from www.bpp.com/aatspreadsheets. Save the spreadsheet file in the appropriate location and rename it in the following format: 'your initial-surname-AAT no-dd.mm.yy-Task4.15'. For example: H-Darch-123456-12.03.xx-Task4.15

A **high degree of accuracy** is required. You must **save your work as a .XLSX file** at regular intervals to avoid losing your work.

(a)   **Open this renamed file. Calculate the percentage to flex this budget in line with the information about and insert this percentage figure into cell D1.**

(b)   **In cell D3 enter the title Flexed budget. Calculate the flexed budget for the relevant entries using absolute referencing where appropriate. Show these in Column D.**

(c)   **In cell E3 enter the title Actual results. Use copy and paste to take the actual results from the information you've been given into the correct positions in Column E on the question worksheet.**

(d)   **In cell F3 insert the title Variances £. Calculate the variances in £ for revenue and each cost. Show these in Column F.**

(e)   **In cell A14 insert the title Operating profit. Calculate the operating profit for the original budget, flexed budget and actual results.**

(f)   **Calculate the overall variance in £ in cell F14.**

(g)   **Put an IF statement in cell F16 that will show 'Balanced' if the column totals balance and 'Check' if they do not.**

(h)   **Colour cell F16 with a yellow background and black border.**

(i)   **In cell G3 insert the title Variances %. Calculate the variances in % for revenue and each cost. Show these in Column G. Note that adverse variances should be shown as negative.**

(j)   Calculate the overall variance in % in cell G14.

(k)   Make sure all column headings are in bold.

(l)   Copy the range A5–G13 and paste into the new area of the worksheet called Farrell Co Variance analysis for the year ended 30 June 20X7. Sort the data so that the items with the largest negative % variances are at the top of the list.

(m)   In the variances % column, highlight the three largest negative variances in red type with a yellow background and black border to their cells.

(n)   Return to the original budget, perform a spell check and ensure that all the contents of the cells can be seen.

(o)   Use the proforma email to do the following:

• Report the flexed budget, actual operating profit and total variance.

• State the three largest adverse variances in % terms.

• Give two reasons why it may be misleading to focus most on the largest adverse variances in % terms.

To:	Polly Urquhart
From:	Victoria Waterfield
Date:	21 July 20X7
Subject:	Variances for year ended 30 June 20X7

Task 4.16

You are Zoe Heriot, a part-qualified accounting technician. You work for Carter Co, a company that manufactures chairs for the home.

You cover all aspects of bookkeeping and accounting for the business. You report to Ken Masters, the Chief Executive.

Today's date is 24 July 20X8.

Ken would like the figures for the quarter ended 30 June 20X8 to be analysed. However a problem with the firm's computer system means that sales and production records are currently unavailable. The production department has estimated that Carter Co sold between 11,500 and 12,500 chairs in the quarter to 30 June 20X8. Ken therefore wants you to prepare budgets based on activity levels of 11,500 and 12,500 chairs, to provide yardsticks for measuring performance. The original budget was prepared on the assumption of making and selling 10,000 units.

Download the spreadsheet file **Question Task 4.16 Carter Co.xlsx** from www.bpp.com/aatspreadsheets. Save the spreadsheet file in the appropriate location and rename it in the following format: 'your initial-surname-AAT no-dd.mm.yy-Task4.16'. For example: H-Darch-123456-12.03.xx-Task4.16

A **high degree of accuracy** is required. You must **save your work as a .XLSX file** at regular intervals to avoid losing your work.

(a)   **Open this renamed file. Calculate the percentage to flex the original budget in line with sales being 11,500 and insert this percentage figure into cell D1.**

(b)   **In cell D3 enter the title Flexed budget 11,500. Calculate the flexed budget for the relevant entries using absolute referencing where appropriate.**

(c)   **In cell F3 enter the title Actual results. Use copy and paste to take the actual results from the information you've been given into the correct positions in Column F on the question worksheet.**

(d)   **In cell G3 insert the title Variances 11,500. Calculate the variances for each revenue and each cost. Show these in Column G.**

(e)   **In cell A15 insert the title Operating profit. Calculate the operating profit for the original budget, flexed budget and actual results.**

(f)   **Calculate the overall variance for 11,500 units in cell G15.**

(g)   **Use conditional formatting in Column G to show all favourable variances in green and adverse variances in red.**

(h)   **Put an IF statement in cell G17 that will show 'Balanced' if the column totals balance and 'Check' if they do not.**

(i)   **Colour cell G17 with a yellow background and black border.**

(j)   **Calculate the percentage to flex the original budget in line with sales being 12,500 and insert this percentage figure into cell E1.**

(k)   **In cell E3 enter the title Flexed budget 12,500. Calculate the flexed budget for the relevant entries using absolute referencing where appropriate.**

(l)   **In cell H3 insert the title Variances 12,500. Calculate the variances for revenue and each cost. Show these in column H.**

(m)   **Calculate the operating profit for the flexed budget at 12,500 chairs.**

(n)   **Calculate the overall variance for 12,500 units in cell H15.**

(o) Use conditional formatting in Column H to show all favourable variances in green and adverse variances in red.

(p) Put an IF statement in cell H17 that will show 'Balanced' if the column totals balance and 'Check' if they do not.

(q) Colour cell H17 with a yellow background and black border.

(r) Make sure all column headings are in bold.

(s) In the section of the worksheet labelled Carter Co Overhead summary for the quarter ended 30 June 20X8, copy and paste the column headers in cells C3–H3 into cells C20–H20.

(t) Under each header calculate total figures for each category of costs and total costs at the end.

(u) Return to the original budget, perform a spell check and ensure that all the contents of the cells can be seen.

(v) Use the proforma email to do the following:

- Compare the actual profit figure with the budgeted profit figure for 11,500 and 12,500 chairs.

- Discuss two concerns that your analysis has raised about the revenues and costs.

To:	Ken Masters
From:	Zoe Heriot
Date:	24 July 20X8
Subject:	Analysis of performance for quarter ended 30 June 20X8

Task 4.17

You are Liz Shaw, a part-qualified accounting technician. You work for Tarrant Co, which manufactures small boats.

You cover all aspects of bookkeeping and accounting for the business. You report to Bill Sayers, the Head of Accounts.

Today's date is 19 August 20X9.

The board of Tarrant Co is currently considering an investment in new plant and machinery, that will enable the company to improve the buoyancy of its boats, The board will make a decision about this next week and the investment will take place immediately afterwards if the board decides to go ahead.

You have been asked to produce an analysis for the board meeting of this investment, using the Internal rate of return (IRR) and payback methods of investment appraisal.

You have been given the following details about the investment:

- The investment appraisal should cover a time horizon of five years.

- Tarrant Co will need to make an immediate investment in plant and machinery of £150,000.

- Expected additional sales revenue in Year 1 will be £180,000 and expected variable costs will be £100,000.

- Sales revenue and costs are expected to rise by 5% in Years 2–5 compared with the previous year.

- Expected fixed costs will be £45,000 per year and will not change over the five year period.

Download the spreadsheet file **Question Task 4.17 Tarrant.xlsx** from www.bpp.com/aatspreadsheets. Save the spreadsheet file in the appropriate location and rename it in the following format: 'your initial-surname-AAT no-dd.mm.yy-Task4.17'. For example: H-Darch-123456-12.03.xx-Task4.17

A **high degree of accuracy** is required. You must **save your work as a .XLSX file** at regular intervals to avoid losing your work.

(a) **Open the renamed file. Calculate the revenues and variable costs for Years 1–5 using the information provided, showing variable costs as a negative figure.**

(b) **Enter the fixed costs for Years 1–5, showing them as a negative figure.**

(c) **In cell A6 enter the narrative Capital expenditure. Enter the amount of capital expenditure in the correct cell and show it as a negative figure.**

(d) **In cell A7 enter the narrative Cash flows and calculate the net cash flows for Years 0–5.**

(e) **In cell A9 enter the narrative Discounted cash flows and calculate the discounted cash flows for Years 0–5, using the cash flows you have calculated and the discount factors for 10% given in cells B8–G8.**

(f) **Calculate the NPV for 10% and inset it in cell B10.**

(g) **In cell A12 enter the narrative Discounted cash flows and calculate the discounted cash flows for Years 0–5, using the cash flows you have calculated and the discount factors given for 15% in cells B11–G11.**

(h) **Calculate the NPV for 15% and inset it in cell B13.**

(i) Tidy up the NPV calculation by showing all negative figures in brackets and all figures rounded to the nearest £, with comma for 000s.

(j) Use the NPV figures in cells B10 and B13 to calculate the IRR. Show your answer in cell B14, correct to 2 decimal places.

(k) For the payback calculation, copy and paste cells A7–G7 into A16–G16.

(l) Show the cumulative cash flows for each year as a running total in cells B17–G17.

(m) For the last negative cumulative cash flow, in the cell immediately beneath it in row 18, insert this figure as a positive number. Highlight this figure, the first positive cumulative cash flow and the year number in which the last negative cumulative cash flow occurs by placing a black border around the cells.

(n) Use the highlighted figures to carry out a payback calculation in cell B19, expressing your answer as a decimal rounded to two decimal places.

(o) Perform a spell check and ensure that the contents of all cells can be seen.

(p) Use the proforma email to do the following:

• Summarise the results of your calculations.

• Explain two problems with the results of the calculations that you have performed.

To:	Bill Sayers
From:	Liz Shaw
Date:	19 August 20X9
Subject:	Investment appraisal

Task 4.18

You are Jo Grant, a part-qualified accounting technician. You work for Trent Co, which manufactures garden barbecues.

You cover all aspects of bookkeeping and accounting for the business. You report to Vanessa Andenberg, the Finance Director.

Today's date is 24 September 20X0.

Vanessa has asked you to do some breakeven analysis, based on the budgeted figures for the next 12 months. Forecast sales are 25,000 units and sales price is £60.

Cost figures are as follows:

	£
Direct materials	500,000
Direct labour	350,000
Assembly	200,000
Packaging	280,000

40% of assembly costs and 25% of packaging costs are variable.

Vanessa has told you the company's target margin of safety is 20% and its target profit is £180,000.

Download the spreadsheet file **Question Task 4.18 Trent Co.xlsx** from www.bpp.com/aatspreadsheets. Save the spreadsheet file in the appropriate location and rename it in the following format: 'your initial-surname-AAT no-dd.mm.yy-Task4.18'. For example: H-Darch-123456-12.03.xx-Task4.18

A **high degree of accuracy** is required. You must **save your work as a .XLSX file** at regular intervals to avoid losing your work.

(a) **Open the renamed file. Calculate total revenue and enter it in cell B2.**

(b) **Enter total direct materials in cell B4 and total direct labour in cell B5.**

(c) **Calculate variable assembly and packaging costs and enter them in cells B6 and B7.**

(d) **Calculate total variable costs and enter them in cell B8.**

(e) **Calculate variable costs per unit, using the budgeted sales volume of 25,000, and enter it in cell B9.**

(f) **Calculate contribution per unit, using the budgeted sales price of £60, and enter it in cell B10.**

(g) **Calculate fixed assembly and packaging costs and enter them in cells B12 and B13.**

(h) **Calculate total fixed costs and enter them in cell B14.**

(i) Calculate the breakeven point in units and enter it in cell B15. Use conditional formatting to show this figure in green if it is less than the budgeted sales volume and red if it is more than the budgeted sales volume.

(j) Calculate the breakeven point in revenue terms and enter it in cell B16.

(k) Calculate the contribution/sales ratio and enter it in cell B17, showing it to 2 decimal places.

(l) Calculate the margin of safety in units and enter it in cell B18.

(m) Calculate the margin of safety in % terms and enter it in cell B19, showing it to 2 decimal places. Highlight this figure with a yellow background and black border. Put an IF statement in cell C19 to show HIGHER if it is greater than the target margin of safety of 20%, LOWER if it is less than the target margin of safety.

(n) Calculate the volume of sales needed to achieve the target profit of £180,000 and enter it in cell B20. Highlight this figure with a yellow background and black border. Put an IF statement in cell C20 to show LESS if the budgeted sales volume of 25,000 units is lower than the volume of sales needed to achieve the target profit, MORE if the budgeted sales volume Is higher.

(o) Perform a spell check and ensure that the contents of all cells can be seen.

(p) Use the proforma email to do the following:

- Comment on the results of your calculations.
- Give two problems with breakeven analysis.

To:	Vanessa Andenberg
From:	Jo Grant
Date:	24 September 20X1
Subject:	Breakeven analysis

Task 4.19

You are working on a set of accounts for a newspaper publisher that pays its advertising sales employees a bonus dependent on the number of adverts sold during the year.

These employees are expected to sell at least 100 adverts before any bonus is paid. The bonus is paid at a rate of 2.5% based on the individual basic salary for each employee.

The following information is available.

Staff employee number	Basic salary £	Adverts sold during the year
123	20,000	85
124	22,000	150
125	28,000	70
126	25,000	165
127	20,000	50
128	18,000	210

Required

Open a new spreadsheet and use the IF Function calculate any bonuses payable to each employee.

Your analysis also needs to show each employee's total pay and an overall figure to go into the statement of profit or loss.

Task 4.20

Eisenhower Ltd had originally budgeted to make and sell 14,000 widgets in the quarter to 30 September 20X8. However, it actually made and sold 17,600 widgets in the quarter.

The original budget for the quarter to 31 March 20X8 is in the 'Original Budget' worksheet of this spreadsheet.

Today's date is 15 October 20X9.

The directors have been looking at the various different variable costs and have noticed that the direct labour costs seem high.

(a)   In the worksheet marked 'Original Budget', in Column D you will need to calculate the following ratios to understand where the main differences are occurring. Use absolute referencing in your formulas to enable you to click and drag the formula into cells D7:D11.

- Budgeted selling price per unit

- Budget cost per unit for materials, direct labour and variable overheads

- Copy cells D5:D11

(b)   Go to worksheet 'Actual Results', and paste the copied cells as data only in cells D5:D12.

- In cell D3 type "Budget costs per unit" and wrap the data in the cell so it is fully visible

- In cell E3 insert a heading 'Actual costs per unit' and wrap the text in the cell too.

- Using absolute referencing in your formulas, calculate the actual costs per unit in cells E5:D11.

- In cells F7:F11 use the ROUNDDOWN function so that the costs per unit are rounded to the nearest tenth of a pound. Format these cells in italics.

- Insert a new row before line 11. Make row 12 a total with the contents in bold font.

- In line 14, calculate the contribution for the year (total) using a suitable formula and insert in cell C14. Make row 12 bold font.

- In column C, give the numbers thousand separators and no decimal places.

(c)   Highlight the direct labour row in yellow. In cell G3, insert a title 'Variance' and calculate using a suitable formula, the different in cost per unit for the direct labour costs.

The directors are planning on sending their skilled labour force on a course that aims to improve their efficiency. From further analysis, the directors have realised that the budgeted direct labour cost per unit was understated, and they aim to revise the costs.

(d) Copy the Actual results worksheet and rename this duplicated worksheet 'Revised budget'

- Update the title in row 2 to reflect the worksheet title amendment

- Hide column F

- In column H, give it a title of 'Flexed budget'. In cell H4, put in the revised budgeted units figure of 18,000.

- Change the year of the budget for the period ending 30 September 20Y0.

- Using the actual costs per unit, calculate the expected flexed budgeted costs in cells H7:H10, using suitable formulas.

- Calculate the total costs and the total contribution for the year using these revised figures.

- Format the numbers in column H, so they have thousand separators and rounded to the nearest whole pound.

(e) In cell I14, calculate the percentage contribution against revenue for the flexed budget results against budgeted revenue.

The accountants have calculated that the company must make a contribution of £1.3million next year. The directors have revised the budgeted costs, so can only flex the budgeted revenue accordingly. To be able to answer their question, you will need to use the Goal Seek function, but you must capture the evidence of this in the worksheet called 'Screen Print' before accepting the Goal Seek answer.

(f) Copy the actual results from cells H4:H10 and paste their values only in cells J4:J10.

- Using the goal seek function, find out what the revenue figure needs to be in order for the contribution to £1,300,000 next year.

- Take a screenshot of your results from the goal seek function prior to accepting them.

- Once you have the revised revenue figure, calculate the revised selling price per unit, based on the budgeted units of 18,000 for the year. Put your answer in cell K5.

Assessment objective 5 – Spreadsheets for Accounting/Advanced Bookkeeping/Final Accounts Preparation

Task 5.1

The Pivotal Partnership has 3 partners; Jeff, Gary and Fran.

The partnership wishes to make use of spreadsheet capabilities to analyse how much the 3 partners have extracted from the partnership.

The following information has been taken from the partnership current accounts.

Item	Jeff £	Gary £	Fran £
Drawings	3,000	500	4,000
Interest on capital	90	160	120
Profit share	12,750	12,750	25,500

Required

Open a new spreadsheet and insert a pivot table to analyse the above information.

- **Sort your pivot table on the value of most money taken out of the partnership.**

- **Use light blue infill to show the highest value in each category.**

Task 5.2

Ivan E Nuff, a sole trader needs to calculate his closing capital account balance for inclusion in his statement of financial position as at 31 January 20X6. Ivan started trading on 1 January 20X6.

1   Capital introduced as at 1 January 20X6 £7,500.

2   Owner purchased fixtures and fittings with a value of £1,678 from his own personal bank account.

3   During the year he put £1,500 into the business to help with cash flow.

4   Ivan withdrew £500 per month as drawings over the 12 month period.

5   £1,000 was taken out of this account to pay for a laptop for his own personal use.

6   Net profit for the year was £8,600.

Required

Open a new spreadsheet and construct a capital account for Ivan showing carried down and brought down amounts. Ignore any VAT implications.

Apply the following formatting to your spreadsheet:

- **Account heading in bold, italics using size 12 font**

- **Heading merged and centred over respective columns**

- **Figures to be presented with thousand separators and no decimals**

- **Insert currency (£) symbols where relevant**

- **Use top and double bottom borders on account totals**

....

Task 5.3

Mr I Jones needs assistance in the completion of his statement of profit or loss.

He has supplied the following trial balance for the year ended 31 May 20X6.

	£	£
Accruals		350
Bank	23,700	
Capital account		33,200
Closing inventory	9,000	9,000
General expenses	63,800	
Drawings	20,000	
Administration costs	3900	
IT Equipment depreciation expense	850	
IT Equipment accumulated depreciation		3,400
IT Equipment at cost	8,500	
Opening inventory	7,800	
Prepayments	530	
Purchases	150,800	
Purchase ledger control account		16,170

	£	£
Sales		280,480
Sales ledger control account	14,720	
VAT		3,000
Wages	42,000	
	345,600	345,600

Required

(a) **Open a new spreadsheet and prepare a statement of profit or loss for the year ended 31 May 20X6.**

Your statement must use appropriate formulas where relevant and be formatted in a style suitable to meet your client's needs.

- **Merge and centre the title of the spreadsheet, the client details and the year the statement of profit or loss relates to.**

- **Use formula for the costs of sales, gross profit, total expenses and the net profit figures.**

(b) Your client has requested for security purposes he would like add security to the numeric cells of the statement of profit or loss.

Use cell protection to lock the numeric data on your prepared statement. Use the password 'doom' to lock the cells.

Task 5.4

Karen, Jake and Saffron are in partnership. You have the following information about the business.

The financial year ends on 31 August 20X6.

Partners' annual salaries:

Karen – £11,400
Jake – £14,400
Saffron – £9,600

Partners' interest on capital:

Karen – £1,000 per full year
Jake – £1,200 per full year
Saffron – £600 per full year

Profit share:

Karen – 20%
Jake – 65%
Saffron – 15%

Profit during the year ended 31 August 20X6 was £180,000.

The partners have requested your assistance in calculating the profit available for distribution between the partners.

Required

(a) **Open a new spreadsheet and prepare the appropriation account for the partnership for the year ended 31 August 20X6.**

   Your statement must use appropriate formulas where relevant and be formatted in a style suitable to meet the partnership's needs.

   Apply the following formatting to your spreadsheet:

   • **Headings to be formatted in bold.**

   • **Figures to be presented with thousand separators and no decimals.**

   • **Insert currency (£) symbols where relevant.**

   • **Use top and double bottom borders totals.**

   • **Interest paid formatted in red font.**

(b) **As an accuracy check use an IF Function to test whether profit for distribution equals total profit distributed. Your function should be able to indicate whether the entries are 'Correct' or 'Incorrect'.**

Task 5.5

A trader has lost his sales records in a flood. You have been asked to reconstruct the sales figures along with a gross profit figure for his statement of profit or loss.

The following information is available:

• Inventory at the start of the year £1,500
• Inventory at the end of the year £1,800
• Purchases during the year £7,600
• The business operates on a profit margin of 20%

Required

(a) **Open a new spreadsheet and using appropriate formulas calculate the missing sales and gross profit information.**

(b) **A company adds a 60% mark-up to cost of sales to arrive at a sales figure and intends to use a spreadsheet function to quickly calculate how much cost of sales will be.**

Open a spreadsheet and enter the following information and formula in cell B3.

	A	B
1	Mark-up factor	1.60
2	Cost of sales	100
3	Sales	=B1*B2

(c) **Using the Goal Seek function calculate how much the cost of sales will be if sales are £3,200.**

Task 5.6

You have been allocated the task of calculating the depreciation charge and carrying values of a company's non-current assets for the year ended 31 December 20X6.

You have been given the following information:

Property – depreciated on a straight-line basis over a 50 year period
Motor vehicles – depreciated on a reducing balance method – at a rate of 30%
Fixtures and fittings – depreciated on a reducing balance – at a rate of 10%

Details as at 31 December 20X5:

	Cost £	Accumulated depreciation £
Property	650,000	195,000
Motor vehicles	45,000	22,950
Fixtures and fittings	27,000	5,130

Required

Open a new spreadsheet and using appropriate formulas calculate the following for the year ended 31 December 20X6.

- **Individual depreciation charges to be entered in the statement of profit or loss**
- **Individual carrying amounts**
- **A total carrying amount to be entered into the statement of financial position**

....

Answer Bank

Assessment objective 1 – Ethics for Accountants

Task 1.1

(a)

Statement	True	False
'I know I act ethically as I have never broken the law and always comply with regulations.'		✓
'The AAT *Code of Professional Ethics* is legally binding if you are a member of the AAT.'		✓

(b)

Familiarity	✓
Self-interest	
Advocacy	

(c)

Integrity	
Objectivity	✓
Confidentiality	

(d)

Action	✓
Resign from RMS Accountancy	
Inform RMS Accountancy of his link with Carmichael Ltd	✓
Inform the AAT of his link with Carmichael Ltd	

(e)

Leaders of the firm have issued clear policies on the ethical behaviour expected at RMS Accountancy.	
Leaders of the firm demonstrate the importance of compliance with the fundamental principles.	✓
Leaders of the firm require that any potential threat to the fundamental principles is communicated to them in order for the most appropriate action to be taken.	

(f)

| Transparency | can be assessed by considering whether or not the decision maker would mind other people knowing the decision that they have taken.

(g)

Statement	True	False
Disciplinary procedures are an example of safeguard.	✓	
Safeguards always eliminate threats of unethical behaviour from the organisation.		✓
Undertaking continuing professional development is considered to be one safeguarding measure.	✓	
The AAT *Code of Professional Ethics* makes the recommendation for breaches of ethical requirements to be reported.		✓
AAT only accept complaints of unethical behaviour from employers or members of the public.		✓

Safeguards cannot always eliminate threats of unethical behaviour and breaches of the AAT *Code of Professional Ethics*. Instead, where the threats cannot be fully eliminated, they should be reduced to an acceptable level.

The AAT *Code of Professional Ethics* makes it mandatory for breaches to be reported, it becomes 'an explicitly stated duty' (para. 100.16(ii)).

Complaints can also come from colleagues or any other source (para.100.16(i)).

(h) Charlotte should disclose confidential information on this matter directly to the ⌐firm's nominated officer⌐.

Even a small firm of accountants must have a nominated officer to deal with money laundering concerns. Employees must report their concerns to their nominated officer in the first instance.

Task 1.2

(a)

Statement	True	False
The AAT *Code of Professional Ethics* provides a set of rules to help accountants determine ethical behaviour.		✓
The accountancy profession has a responsibility to act in the public interest.	✓	

The AAT *Code of Professional Ethics* is not a set of rules, but a framework of principles to guide the ethical conduct of its members.

(b)

Action	Yes/No
Breach of contract	Yes
Negligence	Yes
Fraud	No

If an assignment is not completed with due care then this can result in a breach of contract through professional negligence. This means a failure to act with due skill and care, causing loss to another party and there may be a liability to pay the injured party compensation'. He may be liable to be charged with fraud if it can be proved that he acted with intent to defraud the client, however, the question states that he is surprised by the number of errors, so we can assume that it was unintentional in this case, hence 'no' for fraud.

(c)

Action	✓
Betsy should file the financial statements as the director has signed them.	
Betsy should report the company director to the National Crime Agency.	
Betsy should raise her concerns internally stating her concerns in an email to the Board of Directors.	✓

Considering the appropriate action to take, think of the consequences and what are your obligations? In this case, you have already stated your actions to one director, who has chosen to not take the advice. In this case, there is a Board of Directors who will have joint responsibility for the financial statements, so it would be recommended to ensure that all parties who are responsible for the financial statements should be made aware.

(d)

	✓
Operational risk	✓
Business risk	
Control risk	

(e)

Behaving ethically means acting with transparency, honesty, fairness and discretion in dealings with clients, suppliers, colleagues and others.

(f)

This is a potential self-interest threat on behalf of the junior and looking at the partner's file would be a breach of the confidentiality principle.

(g)

Statement	True	False
The principle of confidentiality must always be carefully abided by in all situations.		✓
In some situations it is entirely plausible that the principle of integrity could be over-ridden as a result of the circumstances.		✓

Task 1.3

(a)

It is required by law that they do so	
To maintain public confidence in the profession	✓
To prevent dishonest individuals from entering the profession	

(b)

	True	False
'The AAT *Code of Professional Ethics* does not apply to me yet as I am only a student accounting technician.'		✓
'Ethical codes provide advice as to how to comply with the law.'	✓	

(c) If you have an ethical concern at work, usually the most appropriate first course of action would be to raise this with ⟨your immediate supervisor⟩ or ⟨employee helpline⟩ .

(d)

Action	
Are customer due diligence procedures only required for new clients?	No
Is it always acceptable for accountants to pay a referral fee to obtain a new client?	No
Is it acceptable to offer a commission to employees for bringing in a new client?	Yes

You may offer commissions to employees for introducing new clients. To clarify the point regarding referral fees, these are only acceptable if the client is aware of the third party being paid for the referral. The third party should be similarly bound by professional ethical standards and should be relied upon to maintain their integrity and professional standards.

(e)

5 years	✓
7 years	
Indefinitely	

(f)

	True	False
Whistleblowing should occur as soon as illegal activity is suspected.		✓
Employees are protected under the Public Information Disclosure Act to ensure they cannot be dismissed for whistleblowing.	✓	
If the disclosure is in the public interest, then the fundamental principle of confidentiality is not breached.	✓	
If the employee is bound by a confidentiality clause in their contract, or has signed a non-disclosure agreement, then the employee could still face dismissal.		✓

Task 1.4

(a) The UK accountancy profession as a whole is regulated by the

| FRC |

and global ethical standards are set by the

| IESBA |

.

(b)

Statement	True	False
The duty to comply with the fundamental principles is more relevant to accountants working in practice than accountants working in business.		✓
Compliance with the law, as well as the policies and procedures of the organisation for which you work will ensure that you never break the five fundamental principles.		✓

(c)

Familiarity	✓
Self-interest	
Intimidation	

(d)

Integrity	✓
Professional competence and due care	
Confidentiality	

(e)

Action	
Familiarity	
Self-interest	✓
Intimidation	✓
Self-review	

(f)

Change the accounts as requested	
Refuse and explain her reasons for doing so with Andrew	✓
Refuse and inform the media as it is in the public interest to disclose the matter	

Task 1.5

(a)

Statement	True	False
Under the AAT *Code of Professional Ethics*, as a minimum you are expected to comply with the laws and regulations of the country in which you live and work.	✓	
The ethical code exists primarily to enhance the public image of accountancy and increase public confidence in the profession.		✓

(b)

Ensuring all work is carried out in the public interest	
Having no previous or current links, financial or otherwise, with a client	
Carrying out work objectively and with integrity	✓

(c)

Self-review	
Self-interest	
Familiarity	✓

(d)

She should accept the gift as it is insignificant and will not influence her audit.	
She should reject the gift as it may appear to others to compromise her objectivity.	✓
She should reject the gift as it may appear to others to compromise her integrity.	

(e) Accountants should not accept significant gifts or preferential treatment from a client. This is because it represents a self-interest threat to the fundamental principles.

(f)

Action	
The skills required to carry out the engagement	Could be taken into account
The outcome of the engagement	Must not be taken into account
The value of the service to the client	Could be taken into account

A contingent fee is a fee calculated on a predetermined basis relating to the outcome of a transaction or the result of the work performed. Contingent fees are used widely for certain types of non-assurance engagements, for example debt recovery work. There is a risk that they give rise to threats to compliance with the fundamental principles. Therefore, it would not appropriate for an assurance engagement as in this question.

(g)

Statement	True	False
Tipping off is an offence which may be carried out by accountants.	✓	
Accountants can go to jail if they are found guilty of having been involved in money laundering.	✓	

Task 1.6

(a)

Statement	True	False
There are no disadvantages to professional accountants of complying with the AAT *Code of Professional Ethics*.		✓
Accountants are required under the AAT *Code of Professional Ethics* to comply with all relevant laws and regulations.	✓	
Accountants are required to uphold the reputation of the accounting profession in both their professional and private lives.	✓	

By complying with the AAT *Code of Professional Ethics*, it may mean that the member must resign from an assignment or an employment (para.100.9, AAT *Code of Professional Ethics*). Therefore, there is a risk that in order to comply with the AAT *Code of Professional Ethics*, the accountant may have to lose business (resign from the engagement).

Also, it is stated that 'a client...receives competent professional service based on current developments in practice, legislation and techniques...(a) member shall act diligently and in accordance with applicable technical and professional standards...' (para.100.5). The accountant should ensure they are competent and understand the latest laws and regulations.

(b)

	✓
Transparency	
Effect	
Fairness	✓

(c)

	✓
When it is in the public interest to do so	
When it is required by law to do so	
An accountant should never breach the objectivity principle	✓

Objectivity is not one of the principles that can ever be breached, the other options would be more applicable to breaches of confidentiality.

(d)

	✓
Johnson has not compromised his professional ethics; everyone embellishes a little to get a job.	
Johnson has acted irresponsibly and has therefore breached the professional ethic of self-interest.	
Johnson has misled a potential employer and has therefore breached the professional ethic of integrity.	✓
Johnson has misled a potential employer and has therefore breached the professional ethic of confidentiality.	

He has behaved in an unethical manner by embellishing his CV, so he will have breached at least one of the fundamental principles of the AAT *Code of Professional Ethics*. By fabricating some of the content on his CV he is not behaving in an honest and professional manner and is therefore breaching the principle of integrity.

Self-interest is a threat to the fundamental principles, but not one of the fundamental principles itself.

(e)

Statement	True	False
It is fine for Johnson to use these skills, knowledge and experience as the new firm would expect a degree of insider knowledge to be obtained as a perk of employing a former employee of the competition.		✓
It is fine for Johnson to use these skills, knowledge and experience provided he does not disclose any confidential information.	✓	
It is fine for Johnson to use these skills, knowledge and experience, but only after a reasonable amount of time has elapsed to prevent conflicts of interest arising.		✓

(f)

Statement	True	False
This is an ethical principle.	✓	
This is a legal obligation.	✓	

Task 1.7

(a)

	✓
The shareholders or other key investors	
The employees of the organisation	
Society as a whole (including shareholders and employees)	✓

(b)

	✓
Providing working papers to a new firm who is taking on a former client	✓
As a result of an enquiry by AAT	✓
To a financial institution who has requested the information directly to your firm of accountants	
To protect a member's professional interest in a court of law	✓

(c)

	✓
Senior management set clear policies and procedures that are cascaded down through the organisation.	
Senior management lead by example.	✓
Senior management establish a clear disciplinary procedure to ensure ethical breaches are escalated to be dealt with at the top of the organisation.	

(d)

	✓
No, she was unaware of being involved in money laundering and withdrew from the engagement as soon as she suspected wrong doing.	
No, the money laundering scheme was very small scale and would therefore be below the threshold for criminal conviction.	
Yes, if she has been part of the scheme, even unknowingly, she could still be guilty of money laundering.	✓

(e)

Statement	True	False
Rita has tipped off the client.		✓
If Rita does fail to disclose her suspicions of money laundering she may face additional charges.	✓	
If Rita was to make a protected disclosure she may have a defence against any money laundering charges brought against her.		✓
If Rita was to make an authorised disclosure she may have a defence against any money laundering charges brought against her.	✓	

(f) When unethical or illegal behaviour is uncovered, whistleblowing should be carried out as a last resort. External whistleblowing should take place following internal discussion with management.

Task 1.8

(a) The AAT requires its members to behave in a way that maintains its reputation, maintains public confidence and protects the public interest .

(b)

Action	Yes/No
Failing to comply with the AAT's CPD requirements	Yes
Failing to reply to an item of correspondence from the AAT	No

(c)

Action	Economic/Social/Environmental
Carrying out a conference call between various members of regional staff	Economic OR Environmental
Holding an away day for members of the finance department	Social
Reducing the future cost of electricity by investing in solar panels	Economic OR Environmental

Note. Both Economic and Environmental are valid answers for the first and third requirements of this question. Marks would be awarded for either of these choices.

(d)

Statement	True	False
Christie should not accept this engagement as the large fee compromises her integrity.		✓
It would be acceptable practice for Christie to include a disclaimer or liability in the written reference.	✓	
Christie should not accept this engagement as the length of the relationship with the client compromises her objectivity.		✓
Christie should not accept this engagement as a safeguard against the threat of intimidation presented by this situation.		✓

(e) If Christie gives the reference, even though she knows that Alpha limited has no means of paying the rent, she would be committing fraud by false representation .

BPP
LEARNING MEDIA

(f)

Statement	True	False
When a member in practice submits a tax return on behalf of a client the responsibilities of the member should be made clear in a letter of engagement.	✓	
When a member in practice submits a tax return on behalf of the client, the member assumes all responsibility for the return and computations.		✓

Task 1.9

(a)

Fundamental principle	Yes	No
Confidentiality		✓
Integrity	✓	

(b)

Action	✓
Internal auditing	
Insolvency practice	✓
Taxation services	

(c)

	✓
Corporate Social Reporting (CSR)	
Ethical business practices	
Sustainability	✓

(d)

Action	✓
Integrity	
Objectivity	✓
Confidentiality	✓
Professional competence and due care	
Professional behaviour	

(e) The AAT *Code of Professional Ethics* says that 'a member providing professional tax services has a duty to put forward the best position in favour of a client or employer . '(para.160.3)

(f)

	✓
Escalate the matter to her line manager	
Report Mo to the AAT	
Discuss the situation with Mo and encourage him to make his phone calls outside normal working hours	✓

Task 1.10

(a)

	✓
IFAC	✓
IESBA	
CCAB	

(b)

	✓
Honesty	✓
Confidentiality	
Accountability	✓
Discretion	

(c)

Action	✓
Breach of contract	✓
Breach of trust	✓
Professional negligence	✓
Fraud accusations	✓

(d)

Report the electrician to his trade regulatory body	
Cease to work on behalf of the electrician	✓
Disclose the matter publically as the matter is one of public interest	

(e)

Statement	True	False
If Alfred does not disclose his suspicions of money laundering, then he himself will have committed a criminal offense.	✓	
Failure to disclose money laundering suspicions can result in a fine up to £10,000.		✓
Alfred must ensure that he makes François aware that the relevant disclosures have been made.		✓

(f)

Protected disclosure	✓
Authorised disclosure	
Anonymous disclosure	

Task 1.11

(a)

Statement	True	False
An accountant who is employed by an organisation is more likely to face an advocacy threat than an accountant working in practice.		✓
A dominant individual attempting to influence your decisions is an example of a threat of advocacy.		✓
The fundamental principle most likely to be compromised as the result of an advocacy threat is objectivity.	✓	

(b)

	✓
Professional behaviour	
Professional competence and due care	✓
Integrity	

(c)

Action	
Misappropriation of assets	Criminal
Money laundering	Criminal
Negligence	Civil
Fraud	Criminal

(d)

Internal fraud	
External fraud	✓
Systems failure	

(e)

Go to the festival, it is a once in a lifetime opportunity and she knows that she carried out her work in accordance with the AAT *Code of Professional Ethics*.	
Inform her manager that the offer has been made to her.	✓
Refuse the tickets and report the matter to AAT.	

(f)

Action	True	False
Peter could be found guilty of money laundering.	✓	
Peter could be found guilty of the offense of tipping off.		✓
Peter could be found guilty of prejudicing the investigation.	✓	

Assessment objective 2 – Ethics for Accountants/ Advanced Bookkeeping/Final Accounts Preparation

Task 2.1

(a)

£	48,700

Workings

	£
Cost of sales (from question part (ix)	24,350
Total sales (× 2) (gross profit margin 50%)	48,700

(b)

Cash account

Account	£	Account	£
Sales (from (a))	48,700	Bank account (Cash banked from sales)	32,000
		Purchases of materials (per part iv)	3,200
		General expenses (per part iv)	490
		Drawings (balancing figure)	12,910
		Bal c/d (float) per part iv	100
	48,700		48,700

This is the cash account and therefore will not include items which have been paid through the bank account, such as the purchases through the bank.

(c)

£	27,280

Workings

	£
Bank account	14,370
Cash account (from (d))	12,910
Total drawings	27,280

(d)

	✓
Integrity	✓
Selflessness	
Honesty	
Objectivity	✓

Selflessness is one of the Nolan principles not one of the ethical principles from the AAT *Code of Professional Ethics*. Objectivity is stated in the Code as a member ' shall not allow bias, conflict of interest or undue influence of others to override professional or business judgements' (AAT, 2017: p.9) Integrity is stated in the Code as that a member shall 'be straightforward and honest in all professional and business relationships' (AAT, 2017:p.9). Honesty is therefore included within the principle of integrity but is not a stand alone principle under the *Code of Professional Ethics*.

(e)

	✓
Maintain the reputation of the accountancy profession	✓
Increase opportunities for AAT members	
Act in the public interest	✓
Ensure protection from negligence claims	
Ensure professional knowledge and skill of AAT members and students	✓

The AAT *Code of Professional Ethics* requires its members (including students) to behave in a way that maintains the reputation of professional accountants and the accountancy profession (*Code*, s.150.1) ensures professional knowledge and skill of AAT members and students and ensures they act in a diligent and professional manner (*Code*, s.100.5).

It cannot ensure protection against negligence claims (although if an accountant has followed the principles and the Code, then it will assist and support the accountant).The purpose of the Code is not to increase the opportunities per se, however, by ensuring the professionalism of its members, it will add credibility to the AAT as a whole.

Task 2.2

(a)

Workings

	Carrying amount £	£
Aygosh	100,000 × 0.25 = 25,000	25,000
Scrawler B	25,000 × 0.25 = 6,250	6,250
Total depreciation expense		31,250

Note: No depreciation is charged on Masher A as it was disposed of during the year and company policy is to charge a full year in the year of acquisition and none in the year of disposal.

(b)

	Debit £	Credit £
Bank and cash	20,000	
Non-current assets – cost		85,000
Non-current asset – accumulated depreciation	70,000	
Profit and loss account		5,000

(c) Year 1: 45,480 × 25% = 11,370.00

Year 2: (45,480-11,370) × 25% = 8,527.50

Year 3: (45,480-11,370-8,527.50) × 25% = 6,395.62

(d)

	True	False
An error of commission does not cause an imbalance in the trial balance.	✓	
The suspense account can appear in the financial statements.		✓
An error of principle causes an imbalance in the trial balance.		✓
A trial balance is prepared before the financial statements.	✓	

An error of commission would not cause an imbalance in the trial balance because debits=credits (it is an error because the figures have been posted to the wrong account).

The suspense account is a temporary differences account and should be cleared prior to completion of the final trial balance. It should never be shown in the financial statements.

An error of principle does not cause an imbalance because debits=credits (it is an error because the figures have been posted to the wrong type of account).

A trial balance is always prepared prior to completion of the financial statements.

(e)

	✓
Integrity	✓
Honesty	
Selflessness	
Professional competence and due care	

Of the options stated, only two are fundamental principles in line with the AAT *Code of Professional Ethics*: Integrity and professional confidence and due care. As the issue is one of self-interest and self-review, the principle being breached is that of integrity. The ethical principle most at risk here is the integrity principle as it may be possible that expenses claims have been made dishonestly.

Selflessness and Honesty are Nolan principles. Professional competence is not the most appropriate (even though the accounting individual has acted unethically) as there is no evidence to suggest they have acted beyond their accounting skillset.

(f) This issue should be reported to a supervisor or line manager. If this is not reported or disclosed then the accounting professional will be implicating themselves in the fraud.

....

Task 2.3

(a)

£	2,480

Workings: $\dfrac{(16,200-3,800)}{5} = 2,480$

(b)

Details	£	Debit ✓	Credit ✓
Vehicle cost	16,200	✓	
Bank	16,200		✓

(c)

Details	£	Debit ✓	Credit ✓
Depreciation expense	2,480	✓	
Accumulated depreciation	2,480		✓

(d)

Account	Ledger balance Debit £	Ledger balance Credit £	Adjustments £	Trial balance Debit £	Trial balance Credit £
Bank	22,450		(17,000)	5,450	
Capital		13,200			13,200
Purchase ledger control account		4,095			4,095
Sales ledger control account	6,725		900	7,625	
Sales		45,200	(1,700)		46,900
Purchases	32,570			32,570	
Administration costs	750			750	
Drawings			1,600	1,600	
Vehicles – Cost			16,200	16,200	
Vehicles Accumulated depreciation			(2,480)		2,480
Depreciation expense			2,480	2,480	
Totals	62,495	62,495	0	66,675	66,675

Task 2.4

(a)

Details	Debit £	Credit £
Irrecoverable debt expense	950	
Sale ledger control account		950

(b)

£	1,000

Workings

£5,000/5 years = £1,000 per annum, full year's charge in the year of acquisition.

(c)

Details	Debit £	Credit £
Depreciation expense	1,000	
Accumulated depreciation		1,000

(d) The four enhancing qualitative characteristics are comparability, verifiability, timeliness and understandability.

(e)

Details	£	Details	£
Balance b/d	660	Drawings	750
Office Expenses	90	Balance c/d	0
Total	750	Total	750

The rent error will not be reflected in the suspense account as it is a reversal of entries error, and will still allow the trial balance to balance.

Task 2.5

(a)

Suspense account

Details	£	Details	£
Balance b/f	2,500	Drawings	2,000
Sales	500	Insurance	1,000
		Balance c/d	0
	3,000		3,000

(b)

£	1,500

Workings

(£8,000 – £500)/ 5 years

(c)

	Initial trial balance			Revised trial balance	
	Debit £	Credit £	Adjustments £	Debit £	Credit £
Sales		265,500	(500)		266,000
Purchases	143,250			143,250	
Opening inventory	10,000			10,000	
Closing inventory	13,500	13,500		13,500	13,500
Office expenses	750			750	
Insurance	1,400		1,000	2,400	
Drawings	24,000		2,000	26,000	
Trade receivable	1,200			1,200	
Trade payable		1,350			1,350
Accruals		3,200			3,200

	Initial trial balance		Adjustments £	Revised trial balance	
	Debit £	Credit £		Debit £	Credit £
Prepayments	900			900	
Capital	70,000			70,000	
Cash at bank	16,050		(8,000)	8,050	
Suspense	2,500		(2,500)		
Motor vehicle			8,000	8,000	
Depreciation expense			1,500	1,500	
Accumulated depreciation			(1,500)		1,500
	283,550	283,550	0	285,550	285,550

(d)

£	126,250

Workings

Sales	266,000
Less	
Opening Inventory	10,000
Purchases	143,250
Less: Closing inventory	(13,500)
	(139,750)
Gross profit	126,250

Assessment objective 3 – Ethics for Accountants/Final Accounts Preparation

Task 3.1

(a)

Current accounts

	Andrew £	Brown £	Carter £	Account	Andrew £	Brown £	Carter £
Drawings W1	30,000	38,000	45,000	Balance b/d	1,160	420	5,570
Balance c/d	25,892	10,054	14,204	Salaries	15,000	18,000	24,000
				Interest on capital	2,860	1,980	1,980
				Share of profit or loss	36,872	27,654	27,654
				Balance c/d	0	0	
Total	55,892	48,054	59,204		55,892	48,054	59,204

Working

Drawings:

Andrew: £2,500 × 12 months = £30,000

Drawings for Brown and Carter taken from question.

(b) Who would, usually be the most appropriate first person to raise this with [your immediate supervisor] or [employee helpline] .

(c) **Are these statements relating to whistleblowing true or false?**

Statement	True	False
Employees are protected under the Public Information Disclosure Act provided that they have acted in good faith and the belief is that the environment is being damaged	✓	
You should start the whistleblowing process as soon as illegal activity is suspected.		✓
The fundamental principle of confidentiality is not breached, if the disclosure is in the public interest.	✓	
If the organisation has an ethics committee, this should be approached before getting to the whistleblowing stage.	✓	

Task 3.2

(a)

	Cost £	Accumulated depreciation £	Carrying amount £
Non-current assets			
Fixtures & Fittings	24,500	8,550	15,950
Motor vehicles	48,000	29,800	18,200
Current assets			
Cash and cash equivalents	11,950		
Trade receivables (W1)	32,250		
Prepayments	1,250		
Inventory	43,500		
		88,950	

	Cost £	Accumulated depreciation £	Carrying amount £
Current liabilities			
Trade payables	40,800		
VAT	3,050		
Accruals	1,000		
		44,850	
Net current assets			44,100
Net assets			**78,250**
Financed by:			
Capital			74,300
Profit for the year			22,950
Less:			
Drawings			(19,000)
			78,250

Workings

35,450 – 3,200 = 32,250

(b)   **The two fundamental qualitative characteristics of financial information, according to the IASB's *Conceptual Framework* are:**

     | relevance | and | faithful representation |

(c)

	✓
The effect of transactions being recognised when they occur	
That the business will continue in operation for the foreseeable future	✓
To ensure similar businesses can be compared to allow for investors to assess them	
To ensure the financial statements have been prepared on time	

Task 3.3

(a)

	£	£
Sales revenue		171,800
Less:		
Opening inventory	20,100	
Purchases	122,500	
Less: Closing inventory	(21,750)	
Cost of goods sold		(120,850)
Gross profit		50,950
Less:		
Depreciation expense	5,125	
Irrecoverable debt expense (from additional information)	475	
Electricity	1,025	
Insurance	900	
Motor expenses	1,550	
Miscellaneous expense	750	

	£	£
Rent	1,700	
Telephone	975	
Repairs and maintenance	1,250	
Total expenses		13,750
Profit/loss for the year		37,200

(b) **Any THREE of the following reasons**

1 The LLP must be registered with the Registrar of Companies. A sole trader does not need to be registered.

2 Formation documents must be signed by at least two members. A sole trader requires no formal documentation in terms of its formation.

3 The partnership must file annual returns and financial statements. A sole trader prepares financial statements, however, these are not filed with the Registrar of Companies.

4 The partnership may require an audit. Sole traders do not require audits.

5 The LLP is a separate legal entity. This is not the case with sole traders.

6 Members liability is limited to an amount stated in the partnership agreement. A sole trader has unlimited liability for any debts incurred in the business.

7 As the financial statements are filed with the Registrar of Companies, the business is now open to scrutiny and the figures can be viewed by any interested party. As a sole trader, the financial statements of a business are private (unless specifically requested by an interested party such as a bank or investor). The accounts of an LLP are in the public domain, whereas this is not the case for a sole trader.

8 The preparation of the financial statements must be completed in line with Generally Accepted Accounting Principles and Accounting Standards. Accounting Standards are not required to be followed in the preparation of sole trader financial statements.

Task 3.4

(a) Goodwill is the excess of the value of a business over its individual assets and liabilities. Goodwill may arise as a result of a number of factors, such as the reputation of the business or the skills of its management. As goodwill is intangible it can be very difficult to value and therefore is normally excluded from assets in the statement of financial position.

(b) The objectivity principle is most at risk when valuing goodwill as there can be a temptation for the valuer to be biased and place a too high figure for the goodwill figure. A possible safeguard here can be to have an independent valuer who should not be influenced when arriving at a valuation

(c)

To: Maria Lemieux
From: An Accountant
Date: Today
Subject: Becoming a partnership

Dear Maria

Thank you for your question regarding partnerships, I have addressed the key points below:

Advantages

- An opportunity for you to bring additional capital and expertise into the business

- Having a partnership arrangement can also help to expand the business by taking on new clients or customers

- You may be able to diversify into new areas of business, such as designing the sportswear rather than just acting as a retailer of existing brands.

Disadvantages

- Increased potential for disagreements between partners over business strategy and decision making

- Any profits from the business must be shared between the partners, which initially may reduce the money you receive from your existing, established business.

- A partnership also has the same status as a sole trader with unlimited liability and this can be seen as disadvantage for the partners as they can become liable for the activities of the other partner or partners.

Potential safeguards and next steps

- Draw up a partnership agreement which sets out the terms and conditions, including any salaries, capital invested at the outset and the profit sharing proportions.

- Consider looking at becoming an LLP (Limited liability partnership) as this can offer additional safeguards like those of a limited company.

If you have any further questions, please let me know

An Accountant

Task 3.5

(a) The ethical principle most at risk in these circumstances is professional competence and due care. The professional competence and due care principle states that members must possess the required level of knowledge and skills to complete tasks in hand.

(b) The most robust and immediate safeguard Jemima can put in place here is not to complete this task until she has developed the necessary skills and knowledge to complete it to the standard expected.

The skills and knowledge can be obtained by a combination of the following examples of continuing professional development methods:

(i)   College and online courses
(ii) Internal training
(iii) Professional body seminars
(iv) Professional journals
(v)   Peer learning
(vi) Internet research

(c) The key differences between companies and sole traders can be outlined as follows (select any FIVE from the following)

- There are specific accounting standards that apply to companies and not to sole traders.

- For Companies, the formats of the statement of profit or loss and statement of financial position are standardised with required headings and terminology. Sole traders have some flexibility on layouts that can be used.

- Companies are obliged to produce additional statements. An example is the cash flow statement. There is no legislative obligation for a sole trader to produce a cash flow.

- There are strict public filing rules and deadlines for companies to adhere to.

- Tax on profit is included in a company's financial statements but does not appear in a sole traders financial statements.

- Non-current assets are shown net of depreciation on the face of a company's financial statements. This is not normally the case for sole traders.

- Companies are required to prepare notes to the accounts so that accounting policies and other information can be disclosed to users. Sole traders do not have a requirement for this additional disclosure.

(d)

Statements	✓
If a company goes into liquidation, the maximum amount that the shareholder lose is the amount of capital they have agreed to invest in the company	✓
The information provided in the financial statements is strictly limited.	
All directors are shareholders in a company limited by liability.	
If a company goes into liquidation, each of the shareholders need only pay an amount equal to their investment plus any additional taxes as required by HMRC.	

Employees may receive or be offered shares, however, shareholders are not automatically employees. Directors may be offered shares, but all shareholders do not become directors of the company. All limited liability companies must prepare their financial statements in accordance with the Companies Act 2006 and using recognised accounting standards, however, if the directors wish to add further information to the financial statements in order to make the information more relevant or to faithfully represent the performance of a company, this is allowed. The nature of share capital means that the shareholders' liabilities are restricted to the par value of the share upon the liquidation of a company

(e)

£	5,500

Workings

Cash at bank

Account	£	Account	£
Balance b/d	10,000	Motor expenses	650
Receipts from customers	36,000	Drawings (balancing figure)	5,500
		Payments to suppliers	25,000
		Balance c/d	14,850
Total	46,000	Total	46,000

(f)

£	28,800

Workings

Receipts from customers £36,000 Mark up on sales is 25%, therefore $100/125 \times £36,000 = £28,800$ cost of sales in the period

....

Task 3.6

(a) The threats most involved here are self-interest and self-review. This is because there can be a self-interest in making claims for non-existent expenses and a self-review threat as the same person is effectively reviewing his or her expense claim.

(b) A simple safeguard would be to reintroduce two members to staff to raise and review expense claims. There is less risk when two individuals have to be in collusion to facilitate a fraud. Another safeguard can be to rotate staff who are responsible for accounting for expense claims. This can reduce the risk of one person to have total control over a function and can help to identify any discrepancies when new staff take over responsibility.

(c) The contents of a partnership agreement can include the following:

The capital that each partner is required to initially invest into the business. This may include a minimum balance to be retained in the business.

BPP
LEARNING MEDIA

If any interest is payable on balances on the partners' capital accounts. The agreement will also state the rate of interest and when to be received.

How profits are to be shared among partners. This profit share ratio will need to be updated when there is a change of partners or if it is agreed that the profit share should be amended.

Agreement on whether drawings can be made from the partnership. If drawings can be made then there may also be agreement on the date when drawings can be made.

Whether interest is chargeable on any drawings made by the partners. The agreement will also state the rate of interest and when to be charged.

The agreement will need to specify the salaries to be paid to partners. There can be differences in the amount of salaries paid to partners due to experience, qualifications or the amount of work put into the partnership business.

Task 3.7

(a) Materiality is a concept that provides a cut-off value on how transactions are to be treated in the financial statements. An example can be when identifying whether an expenditure should be capitalised as a non-current asset in the statement of financial position or written-off as an expense in the statement of profit or loss. A materiality policy may set the materiality level at £500 so office expenditure under this amount would be an expense and anything over this threshold treated as a non-current asset. Different businesses will have a different level of materiality. What is material for a small business may not be for a larger business. A useful rule to keep in mind is if a misstatement or omission of an item changes a user's view of results then this item is likely to be material.

(b) The colleagues' statement is incorrect as materiality levels do not apply to criminal acts of money laundering. The Latin term for this is that there is no de minimis rule to exempt **from** the law. In this instance this matter should be reported to the business's Nominated Officer. The colleague appears to have an interest in not pursuing this issue further so may be involved in the fraud in some way. In which case care needs to be taken not to tip-off that this being reported.

(c) The ethical principle most at risk here is confidentiality as any information must not be disclosed without proper authority. Not only does Amy have a professional responsibility to keep information confidential but also there is a legal requirement under the data protection regulations to keep individual information secure.

The threat most evident is intimidation as the customer is threatening to withdraw his custom if Amy does not comply with his request.

(d) Amy must refuse this request and to maintain complete confidentiality regarding customer details.

If Amy was to contact each customer and ask for specific authorisation to release information about them in this way then it can be acceptable. Other times when information can be disclosed is when it is in the public interest and if there is a legal requirement to do so.

Task 3.8

(a) A conflict of interest is where an individual's objectivity may become threatened due to the circumstances of an assignment or relationship. An example can be where an accountant is acting on behalf of two clients whose business interests overlap.

(b) The accountant will need to identify if any conflict of interest threats exist. If threats do exist and are considered to be significant then safeguards need to be put in place to reduce those threats to an acceptable level.

(c) There is a clear conflict of interest here as Jaz is preparing the accounts for both parties and is aware of sensitive information that is relevant to the loan A has made to B. In these circumstances Jaz must remain independent and complete any work with objectivity and without bias. A principle at threat here is confidentiality and Jaz needs to be very careful in not disclosing confidential information to either party.

The safeguards that Jaz can put in place may include:

- Inform both clients that she is acting for both clients
- Obtain written consent to act on behalf of both clients. This may include confidentiality agreements.
- Investigate whether a colleague may be able to handle the work of one of the clients
- Have a senior partner to independently review Jaz's work to ensure independence and confidentiality is being observed
- Ensure that any information is kept confidential within Jaz's office by having a 'Chinese Wall' to keep information secure or a code of conduct on access.
- In the last resort if all other safeguards are still not adequate resign from one of the assignments.

Task 3.9

(a) Capital represents the long-term investment into the business by its owner. When a business is started the owner may inject cash into business and this can be used to purchase non-current assets such as motor vehicles and current assets, for example inventories.

Over a period of time the amount of capital that is owed to the owner by the business will fluctuate due to profits and losses made by the business and drawings taken out of the business by the owner.

The capital of the business will be shown in the capital section of the statement of financial position.

(b)

£	68,000

Workings

Opening capital	56,730
Profit for the year	38,920
	95,650
Less drawings (24,650 + 3,000)	27,650
Closing capital	68,000

(c) The laptop Y has taken should be recorded as drawings and needs to reduce the balance of Y's partnership current account accordingly to the value of the laptop. Withdrawals of capital from a business are treated as drawings whether taken as cash or in other assets.

Y has been dishonest in not disclosing his actions to X and is in breach of the ethical principle of integrity.

The appropriate double entry will be:

Dr: Y's Current account   £x

Cr: Purchases in the journal entry   £x

£x = the value of the laptop

Task 3.10

(a) A limited company is financed by equity and this can be made up of share capital where shares have been issued and also accumulated profits that have been added to the reserves of the company.

Normally the owners of the business, the shareholders, will extract money from the company in the form of dividends paid from accumulated profits made by the company.

This is different to a sole trader or partnership arrangement where the owner or owners invest capital into the business and subsequently withdraw capital in the form of drawings.

(b) The two ethical principles most affected here are professional competence and due care and professional behaviour. The accountant did not take due care when not checking the equity figure was correct. Professional behaviour is also threatened as reports in the financial press and other media will bring disrepute to the accountancy profession.

Observing that equity had increased by 80 times from the previous year the accountant may have had some doubts over the accuracy of this increase.

(c) Professional scepticism is where a professional person may question the accuracy or validity of any information or evidence that is made available to them in the completion of their work. As the equity figure is a material amount in the financial statements the accountant should have initially questioned whether the £2m figure was correct and should have planned his work to obtain evidence to substantiate this figure.

Task 3.11

(a) The two relevant accounting standards here are:

IAS 2 *Inventories*

IAS 16 *Property, plant and equipment*

(b) The ethical principle most at risk when being out of date in knowledge and skills is professional competence and due care.

(c) An accountant can keep their skills and knowledge up to date by completing regular continuing professional development (CPD). Evidence of complying with the professional competence and due care can be achieved by keeping a CPD Log to record and explain any CPD activities completed. It is important to note that professional bodies do require completing of CPD and if a member is found to be in non-compliance then it is likely the body will take disciplinary action against the member.

If it is found that a member's work has been completed without all the necessary skills required this may also result in breach of contract with the risk of being sued for negligence by an injured party who may have suffered a loss due to sub-standard work.

Assessment objective 4 – Spreadsheets for Accounting/Management Accounting: Costing

Task 4.1

(a)

	Trainer	Course	Unit price	Units
April	Alex	Level 1	79	15
April	Alex	Level 2	99	8
April	Alex	Level 3	129	4
April	Alex	Complete	269	22
April	Janine	Level 1	79	29
April	Janine	Level 2	99	11
April	Janine	Level 3	129	2
April	Janine	Complete	269	18
April	Simone	Level 1	79	24
April	Simone	Level 2	99	7
April	Simone	Level 3	129	3
April	Simone	Complete	269	15
April	Karesh	Level 1	79	15
April	Karesh	Level 2	99	12
April	Karesh	Level 3	129	11
April	Karesh	Complete	269	19
May	Alex	Level 1	79	13
May	Alex	Level 2	99	12
May	Alex	Level 3	129	9
May	Alex	Complete	269	11
May	Janine	Level 1	79	22
May	Janine	Level 2	99	4

Sales | Price structure | Total Values | Bonus

(b)

	Trainer	Course	Unit price	Units	Total value
May	Karesh	Level 3	129	11	1,419
May	Karesh	Complete	269	14	3,766
June	Alex	Level 1	79	13	1,027
June	Alex	Level 2	99	11	1,089
June	Alex	Level 3	129	15	1,935
June	Alex	Complete	269	12	3,228
June	Janine	Level 1	79	4	316
June	Janine	Level 2	99	1	99
June	Janine	Level 3	129	1	129
June	Janine	Complete	269	19	5,111
June	Simone	Level 1	79	18	1,422
June	Simone	Level 2	99	3	297
June	Simone	Level 3	129	6	774
June	Simone	Complete	269	14	3,766
June	Karesh	Level 1	79	24	1,896
June	Karesh	Level 2	99	12	1,188
June	Karesh	Level 3	129	5	645
June	Karesh	Complete	269	18	4,842
					90,982

Sales | Price structure

(c)

Create a pivot table and pivot chart showing the total value of sales, broken down by course, made by each of Alex, Janine, Simone and Karesh.

– Place the pivot table and pivot chart on a new sheet, and rename this sheet 'Total Values'.

– Add a chart title 'Total sales value Apr–Jun'.

BPP LEARNING MEDIA

If any of the trainers manage to recruit 20 or more individuals on to any of the courses in a month, that trainer will receive a bonus of £5 per individual booked on that course.

(d) Give Column G the heading 'Bonus' and use an IF function to show the amount of bonus payments due.

- Total all bonuses to be paid.

	Trainer	Course	Unit price	Units	Total value	Bonus
32 May	Karesh	Level 3	129	11	1,419	0
33 May	Karesh	Complete	269	14	3,766	0
34 June	Alex	Level 1	79	13	1,027	0
35 June	Alex	Level 2	99	11	1,089	0
36 June	Alex	Level 3	129	15	1,935	0
37 June	Alex	Complete	269	12	3,228	0
38 June	Janine	Level 1	79	4	316	0
39 June	Janine	Level 2	99	1	99	0
40 June	Janine	Level 3	129	1	129	0
41 June	Janine	Complete	269	19	5,111	0
42 June	Simone	Level 1	79	18	1,422	0
43 June	Simone	Level 2	99	3	297	0
44 June	Simone	Level 3	129	6	774	0
45 June	Simone	Complete	269	14	3,766	0
46 June	Karesh	Level 1	79	24	1,896	120
47 June	Karesh	Level 2	99	12	1,186	0
48 June	Karesh	Level 3	129	5	645	0
49 June	Karesh	Complete	269	18	4,842	0
50					90,982	835

- Create a pivot table in a new tab which shows the total bonus to be paid to each trainer.

- Sort the data in this pivot table to arrange the trainers in ascending order in terms of the bonus payment due to them for the quarter.

- Rename the tab 'Bonuses'.

(e) Password protect the entire workbook and using the password Better123.

Task 4.2

(a) Open the renamed spreadsheet and open the subs worksheet.

– Format the data on this page as a table, include the headings.

– On the finance team worksheet, use a VLOOKUP function to complete the subs column.

The first screenshot shows an Excel spreadsheet "Task - 5.2 - Excel" with formula bar showing `=VLOOKUP(F2,Table2.2,PALSE)` for cell H2.

Employee Number	Name	Age	Years Service	Qualification	Country	Status	Subs	Paid
123456	Josey Ann Daley	45	20	ACCA	Cayman Isles	Part Qualified	60	Y
123457	May June Yong	30	2	CIMA	Malaysia	Qualified	55	N
123458	Larissa Gross	36	5	ICAS	Russia	Part Qualified	65	N
123459	Ashweeni Basanoo	56	15	ACCA	Luxembourg	Qualified	60	N
123460	Shuk Kiun Chin	40	4	CIMA	Malaysia	Part Qualified	55	Y
123461	Mary Buckley	52	23	ACCA	United Kingdom	Part Qualified	60	N
123462	Malena Kerpechova	25	3	ICAS	Bulgaria	Part Qualified	65	Y
123463	Kah Yan Fu	28	1	CIMA	United Kingdom	Qualified	55	N
123464	Andrew Charteris	25	2	AAT	United Kingdom	Part Qualified	45	Y
123465	Shraddha Patel	24	5	ACCA	United Kingdom	Part Qualified	60	Y
123466	Lucy Jones	53	14	AAT	United Kingdom	Qualified	45	N
123467	Claire Tyler	37	9	AAT	United Kingdom	Qualified	45	N
123467	Benjamin Davies	31	6	CIMA	France	Qualified	55	Y
123468	Adrienne Wilson	29	4	AAT	United Kingdom	Qualified	45	Y

Tabs: Finance Team, Subs

- Format the subs figures in a red font colour.

(b) Use conditional formatting to highlight all employees aged 40 and over.

The second screenshot shows an Excel spreadsheet "Task - 5.2 - Excel" with cell M19 selected.

Employee Number	Name	Age	Years Service	Qualification	Country	Status	Subs	Paid
123456	Josey Ann Daley	45	20	ACCA	Cayman Isles	Part Qualified	60	Y
133426	May June Yong	30	2	CIMA	Malaysia	Qualified	55	N
149726	Larissa Gross	36	5	ICAS	Russia	Part Qualified	65	N
122234	Ashweeni Basanoo	56	15	ACCA	Luxembourg	Qualified	60	N
143212	Shuk Kiun Chin	40	4	CIMA	Malaysia	Part Qualified	55	Y
123461	Mary Buckley	52	23	ACCA	United Kingdom	Part Qualified	60	N
172685	Malena Kerpecheva	25	3	ICAS	Bulgaria	Part Qualified	65	Y
168063	Kah Yan Fu	28	1	CIMA	United Kingdom	Qualified	55	N
132425	Andrew Charteris	25	2	AAT	United Kingdom	Part Qualified	45	Y
123465	Shraddha Patel	24	5	ACCA	United Kingdom	Part Qualified	60	Y
184256	Lucy Jones	53	14	AAT	United Kingdom	Qualified	45	N
123467	Claire Tyler	37	9	AAT	United Kingdom	Qualified	45	N
123468	Benjamin Davies	31	6	CIMA	France	Qualified	55	Y
123470	Adrienne Wilson	29	4	AAT	United Kingdom	Qualified	45	Y
123479	Daniel Booth	44	12	CIMA	United Kingdom	Qualified	55	N

Tabs: Finance Team, Subs

- Sort the data based on employee number, from lowest to highest.

First spreadsheet (Task 5.2 – Excel), cell K16 selected:

Employee Number	Name	Age	Years Service	Qualification	Country	Status	Subs	Paid
122234	Ashweeni Basanoo	58	15	ACCA	Luxembourg	Qualified		60 N
123456	Josey Ann Daley	45	20	ACCA	Cayman Isles	Part Qualified		60 Y
123461	Mary Buckley	52	23	ACCA	United Kingdom	Part Qualified		60 N
123465	Shraddha Patel	24	5	ACCA	United Kingdom	Part Qualified		60 Y
123467	Claire Tyler	37	9	AAT	United Kingdom	Qualified		45 N
123468	Benjamin Davies	31	6	CIMA	France	Qualified		55 Y
123470	Adrienne Wilson	29	4	AAT	United Kingdom	Qualified		45 Y
123479	Daniel Booth	44	12	CIMA	United Kingdom	Qualified		35 N
132425	Andrew Charteris	25	2	AAT	United Kingdom	Part Qualified		45 Y
133426	May June Yong	30	2	CIMA	Malaysia	Qualified		55 N
134256	Lucy Jones	55	14	AAT	United Kingdom	Qualified		45 N
143212	Shuk Kiun Chin	40	4	CIMA	Malaysia	Part Qualified		55 Y
149726	Larissa Gross	36	5	ICAS	Russia	Part Qualified		65 N
172635	Malena Kerpecheva	25	3	ICAS	Bulgaria	Part Qualified		65 Y
188963	Kah Yan Fu	28	1	CIMA	United Kingdom	Qualified		35 N

(c) Rename Column J as 'holiday'.

- Use an IF statement to complete the data in this column to show how many days holiday per year to which each individual is entitled.

Second spreadsheet (Task 5.2 – Excel), cell J2 with formula =IF(D2<5,25,30):

Employee Number	Name	Age	Years Service	Qualification	Country	Status	Subs	Paid	Holiday
122234	Ashweeni Basanoo	58	15	ACCA	Luxembourg	Qualified		60 N	30
123456	Josey Ann Daley	45	20	ACCA	Cayman Isles	Part Qualified		60 Y	30
123461	Mary Buckley	52	23	ACCA	United Kingdom	Part Qualified		60 N	30
123465	Shraddha Patel	24	5	ACCA	United Kingdom	Part Qualified		60 Y	30
123467	Claire Tyler	37	9	AAT	United Kingdom	Qualified		45 N	30
123468	Benjamin Davies	31	6	CIMA	France	Qualified		55 Y	30
123470	Adrienne Wilson	29	4	AAT	United Kingdom	Qualified		45 Y	25
123479	Daniel Booth	44	12	CIMA	United Kingdom	Qualified		35 N	30
132425	Andrew Charteris	25	2	AAT	United Kingdom	Part Qualified		45 Y	25
133426	May June Yong	30	2	CIMA	Malaysia	Qualified		55 N	25
134256	Lucy Jones	55	14	AAT	United Kingdom	Qualified		45 N	30
143212	Shuk Kiun Chin	40	4	CIMA	Malaysia	Part Qualified		55 Y	25
149726	Larissa Gross	36	5	ICAS	Russia	Part Qualified		65 N	30
172635	Malena Kerpecheva	25	3	ICAS	Bulgaria	Part Qualified		65 Y	25
188963	Kah Yan Fu	28	1	CIMA	United Kingdom	Qualified		35 N	25

(d) Format the data as a table with light blue shading.

– Use the filter function to display only individuals who are members or students of the AAT who have not yet paid their subs.

Task 4.3

(a) Open the renamed spreadsheet.

– Use find and replace to update any cells which refer to 'Cater co' to show the name of the new company.

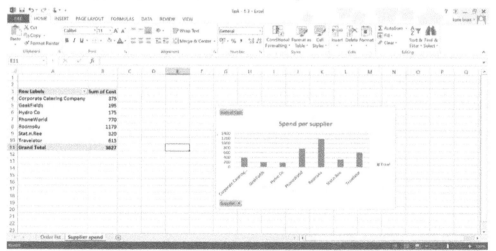

– Rename the worksheet 'order list'.

(b) Create a pivot table and pivot chart in a new worksheet to represented the amount spent with each supplier.

– Rename the chart as 'Spend per supplier'.

– Rename the worksheet 'Supplier spend' and ensure the order of the worksheets is such that the order list worksheet is on the left and the supplier spend worksheet is on the right.

Ensure the conditional formatting has been correctly completed, ensuring that it is over £350.

	A	B	C	D	E	F	G	H	I	J	K	L
1	**Row Labels** ▾	**Sum of Cost**										
2	Corporate Catering Company	375										
3	GeekFields	195										
4	Hydro Co	175										
5	PhoneWorld	770										
6	Rooms4u	1179										
7	Stat.n.Ree	320										
8	Travelator	613										
9	**Grand Total**	**3627**										

Sum of Cost

Spend per supplier

Greater Than

Format cells that are GREATER THAN:

| 350 | | with | Light Red Fill with Dark Red Text ▾ |

OK   Cancel

Supplier ▾

The amended pivot chart with the suppliers with the biggest spend should look like this:

	A	B	C	D	E	F	G	H	I	J	K
1	**Row Labels** ⊤	**Sum of Cost**									
2	Corporate Catering Company	375									
3	PhoneWorld	770									
4	Rooms4u	1179									
5	Travelator	613									
6	**Grand Total**	**2937**									

Sum of Cost

Spend per supplier

Corporate Catering Company   PhoneWorld   Rooms4u   Travelator

■ Total

Supplier ▾

Detail on the average function required, don't forget to click on the Show Formulas in the ribbon to make it visible (tip: unclicking the option will hide the formula again).

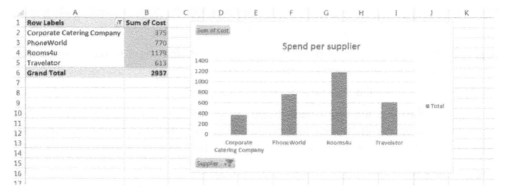

	A	B	C	D	E
1	**Row Labels**	⊤ **Sum of Cost**			
2	Corporate Catering Company	375			
3	PhoneWorld	770			
4	Rooms4u	1179			
5	Travelator	613			
6	**Grand Total**	**2937**			
7					
8		=AVERAGE(B2:B5)			

Sum of Cost

Corporate Catering Company

Supplier ▾

(c) Copy the Order List worksheet and rename this duplicate tab "Department spend".

- Insert a new pivot table for this data, this needs to be positioned on the existing worksheet to the right of the data

- Sort the pivot table to show the spend per department

- Insert a 3D pie chart, label it 'Total spend by department'

The second pivot table will need building like this:

Order no.	Department	Supplier	Description	Cost	Date
12345	Finance	Stat.n.Ree	Envelopes	£15.00	Jan
12346	Marketing	Stat.n.Ree	Paper	£25.00	Jan
12347	Sales	PhoneWorld	Mobile phone	£350.00	Jan
12348	HR	Stat.n.Ree	Paperclips	£4.00	Feb
12349	IT	GeekFields	Cables	£45.00	Feb
12350	Finance	Hydro Co	Water cooler refils	£35.00	Feb
12351	Finance	Travelator	Train tickets	£75.00	May
12352	IT	Stat.n.Ree	Post-it notes	£20.00	May
12353	Finance	Rooms4u	Hotel room	£129.00	May
12354	Marketing	Stat.n.Ree	Pens	£12.00	June
12355	Sales	Corporate Catering Company	Hospitality	£60.00	June
12356	Finance	Stat.n.Ree	Pens	£12.00	June
12357	Sales	Hydro Co	Water cooler refils	£35.00	June
12358	Sales	Travelator	Train tickets	£109.00	June
12359	Sales	Travelator	Air fare	£380.00	June
12360	Sales	Rooms4u	Hotel rooms	£1,050.00	June
12361	HR	Corporate Catering Company	Lunch for meeting room	£70.00	June
12362	Marketing	Hydro Co	Water cooler refils	£35.00	July
12363	HR	Stat.n.Ree	Headed paper	£200.00	July
12364	IT	GeekFields	External hard drive	£150.00	July
12365	IT	Hydro Co	Water cooler refils	£35.00	July
12366	Finance	PhoneWorld	mobile phone	£420.00	Aug
12367	Marketing	Stat.n.Ree	Post-it notes	£20.00	Aug
12367	HR	Hydro Co	Water cooler refils	£35.00	Sep
12367	Finance	Corporate Catering Company	Hospitality	£150.00	Nov
12367	HR	Travelator	Train tickets	£49.00	Nov
12367	Sales	Corporate Catering Company	Hospitality	£95.00	Dec
12367	IT	Stat.n.Ree	Pens	£12.00	Dec

Create PivotTable
Choose the data that you want to analyse
Select a table or range
Table/Range: Department spend'!$A$2:$F$30
Use an external data source
Choose Connection...
Connection name:
Choose where you want the PivotTable report to be placed
New Worksheet
Existing Worksheet
Location: Department spend'!$I$6
Choose whether you want to analyse multiple tables
Add this data to the Data Model
OK   Cancel

Row Labels	Sum of Cost
Finance	836
HR	358
IT	262
Marketing	92
Sales	2079
Grand Total	3627

Sum of Cost

Total spend by department

Department
- Finance
- HR
- IT
- Marketing
- Sales

Ensure the pie chart is correctly labelled and is a 3D pie chart (Go to the ribbon across the top, click on Insert/Charts and select 3D pie chart).

Task 4.4

(a) Open the renamed spreadsheet and go into the location tab.

– Add the header 'location code' to Column E and format the cell to be the same as the others in this row.

– Create a location code in cell E2 comprising of the aisle, location and bin number, eg 1A3.

– Apply this formula to all relevant cells in Column E.

(b) Open the inventory list worksheet and use lookup functions to complete.

– The location information in Column B.

– The unit price information in Column C.

Formula bar: `=VLOOKUP('Inventory List'!$A3,PriceList,2,FALSE)`

Inventory ID	Location	Unit Price	Quantity in Stock	Inventory value	Reorder Level	Order Required	Discontinued?	Reorder quantity
Inventory List								
MK1425	1A3	1.99	0		600		Yes	
MK1426	1A7	1.99	750		600		Yes	
MK1427	1B2	1.99	500		500			200
MK1428	1B3	2.99	520		500			200
MK1429	1C5	2.99	480		500			200
MK1430	1C1	2.99	401		400			150
MK1431	2A4	3.99	248		250			100
MK1432	2A12	4.99	251		250			100
MK1433	2D8	4.99	300		200			100
MK1434	2B6	5.99	164		150			80
MK1435	2G5	5.99	150		150			80
MK1436	3B1	6.99	99		100			50
MK1437	3B2	7.99	0		100		Yes	
MK1438	3B3	7.99	84		80			40
MK1439	3D16	8.49	112		80			40
MK1440	3E14	8.49	44		50			20
MK1441	3F5	8.99	63		40			20
MK1442	3H9	8.99	3		40		Yes	
MK1443	4C2	9.99	19		30			15
MK1444	4G18	19.99	25		20			10

Tabs: Inventory List | Locations | Price List | Order June 20X6

– Insert a formula to calculate the value of each item of inventory in Column E.

Formula bar: `='Inventory List'!$C3*'Inventory List'!$D3`

Inventory ID	Location	Unit Price	Quantity in Stock	Inventory value	Reorder Level	Order Required	Discontinued?	Reorder quantity
Inventory List								
MK1425	1A3	1.99	0	0	600		Yes	
MK1426	1A7	1.99	750	1492.5	600			
MK1427	1B2	1.99	500	995	500			200
MK1428	1B3	2.99	520	1554.8	500			200
MK1429	1C5	2.99	480	1435.2	500			200
MK1430	1C1	2.99	401	1198.99	400			150
MK1431	2A4	3.99	248	989.62	250			100
MK1432	2A12	4.99	251	1252.49	250			100
MK1433	2D8	4.99	300	1497	200			100
MK1434	2B6	5.99	164	982.36	150			80
MK1435	2G5	5.99	150	898.8	150			80
MK1436	3B1	6.99	99	692.01	100			50
MK1437	3B2	7.99	0	0	100		Yes	
MK1438	3B3	7.99	84	671.16	80			40
MK1439	3D16	8.49	112	950.88	80			40
MK1440	3E14	8.49	44	373.56	50			20
MK1441	3F5	8.99	63	566.37	40			20
MK1442	3H9	8.99	3	26.97	40		Yes	
MK1443	4C2	9.99	19	189.81	30			15
MK1444	4G18	19.99	25	499.75	20			10

Tabs: Inventory List | Locations | Price List | Order June 20X6

(c) Insert an IF function to determine whether or not items are due to be re-ordered in Column G.

- If the item is above the re-order level, this should return the value 0. If the item is on or under the re-order level, this should return the value 1.

(d) Format the data contained in cells B1:I22 as a table, using Table style medium 14.

- Format cells A1:I1 using font Arial 12, in bold. Merge and centre the title across the top of the table. Select a suitable purple shade of background.

- Hide the gridlines to improve the look of the worksheet.

- Sort the data by using the filter on Column H to remove all items that have been discontinued.

	A	B	C	D	E	F	G	H	I
1					Inventory List				
2	Inventory ID	Location		Unit Price	Quantity in Stock	Inventory value	Reorder Level	Order Required	Discontinued	Reorder quantity
5	MK1427	1B2		1.99	500	995	500	1		200
6	MK1428	1B3		2.99	520	1554.8	500	0		200
7	MK1429	1C5		2.99	480	1435.2	500	1		200
8	MK1430	1C1		2.99	401	1198.99	400	0		150
9	MK1431	2A4		3.99	248	989.52	250	1		100
10	MK1432	2A12		4.99	251	1252.49	250	0		100
11	MK1433	2D8		4.99	300	1497	200	0		100
12	MK1434	2E6		5.99	164	982.36	150	0		80
13	MK1435	2G5		5.99	150	898.5	150	1		80
14	MK1436	3B1		6.99	99	692.01	100	1		50
16	MK1438	3B3		7.99	84	671.16	80	0		40
17	MK1439	3D16		8.49	112	950.88	80	0		40
18	MK1440	3E14		8.49	44	373.56	50	1		20
19	MK1441	3F5		8.99	63	566.37	40	0		20
11	MK1443	4C2		9.99	19	189.81	30	1		15
12	MK1444	4G18		19.99	25	499.75	20	0		10

- Hide Column H.

	A	B	C	D	E	F	G	I	J
1					Inventory List				
2	Inventory ID	Location		Unit Price	Quantity in Stock	Inventory value	Reorder Level	Order Required	Reorder quantity
4	MK1426	1A7		1.99	750	1492.5	500	0	
5	MK1427	1B2		1.99	500	995	500	1	200
6	MK1428	1B3		2.99	520	1554.8	500	0	200
7	MK1429	1C5		2.99	480	1435.2	500	1	200
8	MK1430	1C1		2.99	401	1198.99	400	0	150
9	MK1431	2A4		3.99	248	989.52	250	1	100
10	MK1432	2A12		4.99	251	1252.49	250	0	100
11	MK1433	2D8		4.99	300	1497	200	0	100
12	MK1434	2E6		5.99	164	982.36	150	0	80
13	MK1435	2G5		5.99	150	898.5	150	1	80
14	MK1436	3B1		6.99	99	692.01	100	1	50
16	MK1438	3B3		7.99	84	671.16	80	0	40
17	MK1439	3D16		8.49	112	950.88	80	0	40
18	MK1440	3E14		8.49	44	373.56	50	1	20
19	MK1441	3F5		8.99	63	566.37	40	0	20
21	MK1443	4C2		9.99	19	189.81	30	1	15
22	MK1444	4G18		19.99	25	499.75	20	0	10

(e) Use the filter function to show only those items that need to be reordered (Column G).

	A	B	C	D	E	F	G	I	J
					Inventory List				
	Inventory ID	Location		Unit Price	Quantity in Stock	Inventory value	Reorder Level	Order Required	Reorder quantity
	MK1427	1B2		1.99	500	995	500	1	200
	MK1429	1C5		2.99	480	1435.2	500	1	200
	MK1431	2A4		3.99	248	989.52	250	1	100
	MK1435	2G5		5.99	150	898.5	150	1	80
	MK1436	3B1		6.99	99	692.01	100	1	50
	MK1440	3E14		8.49	44	373.56	50	1	20
	MK1443	4C2		9.99	19	189.81	30	1	15

- Copy and paste the values onto the 'Order June 20X6' worksheet to create an order list.

- Ensure you do not copy over the table format to the new order list.

	A	B	C	D	E	F	G	H	I
6	**Order - June 20X6**								
7									
8	**Inventory Item**	**Quantity Required**							
9	MK1427	200							
10	MK1429	200							
11	MK1431	100							
12	MK1435	80							
13	MK1436	50							
14	MK1440	20							
15	MK1443	15							
16									
17									
18									
19									

Teaching note: When pasting your order in here, make sure you use Paste Special - Values Only, so that the table format is not copied across

Task 4.5

(a) Open the renamed spreadsheet.

- Add a formula to cell C31 to calculate the amount of flexi-time earned or used on Monday. Apply this formula to the rest of the days of the week.

– Add a formula to cell C32 to calculate the current balance of flexitime on Monday. Apply this formula to the rest of the days of the week.

– Replace the formulas in cells I25 and I28 with more robust formulas to check for errors in the summing of data.

BPP
LEARNING MEDIA

	A	B	C	D	E	F	G	H	I	J	K	L	M	N	O	P	Q	R	S
	Project 4								0										
9	MANAGEMENT																		
10	Supervision of others			2					2										
11	Review of work								0										
12	Training staff								0										
14	OTHER																		
15	Attending training					7			7										
16	Admin			2			1	1	4										
17	Miscellaneous				0.5		1	1	3.5										
19	ABSENCE																		
20	Sickness								0										
21	Annual								0										
22	Flexi-day								0										
23	Other								0										
25	TOTALS																		
26	Total hours worked			8	7	7	8	5	35										
27	Total absence			0	0	0	0	0	0										
28																			
29	TOTAL			8	7	7	8	5											
30																			
31	Flexihours earned			0.5	-0.5	-0.5	0.5	-2.5											
32	Current flexihours balance			0	0.5	0	-0.5	0	-2.5										

Week 1

(b) Use a data validation function in cells C29:G29 to identify any days where less than six hours are worked.

– Set the data validation to circle in red any days where fewer than six hours have been worked.

	A	B	C	D	E	F	G	H	I	J	K	L	M	N	O	P	Q	R	S
5	Project 2			4	1.5				5.5										
6	Project 3				3		5	1	9										
7	Project 4								0										
9	MANAGEMENT																		
10	Supervision of others			2					2										
11	Review of work								0										
12	Training staff								0										
14	OTHER																		
15	Attending training					7			7										
16	Admin			2			1	1	4										
17	Miscellaneous				0.5		1	1	3.5										
19	ABSENCE																		
20	Sickness								0										
21	Annual								0										
22	Flexi-day								0										
23	Other								0										
25	TOTALS																		
26	Total hours worked			8	7	7	8	5	35										
27	Total absence			0	0	0	0	0	0										
28																			
29	TOTAL			8	7	7	8	5	44										
30																			

Week 1

(c) Use a data validation function to prevent more than two hours of admin being charged on any given day.

– Attempt to change the admin charge on Monday to three hours.

(d) Insert two new worksheets.

– Change the name of the new worksheets to 'Week 2' and 'Week 3'

– Copy the format and formulas used on Week 1 to Week 2 and Week 3 and populate the spreadsheets with the information given above.

– Link the formula related to flexi-time to ensure the balance from week 1 is carried over to Week 2 and so on.

(e) Insert a new worksheet and rename it 'Summary'.

  – Use the data from Weeks 1–3 to produce a summary sheet which collates the total number of hours charged to each activity per week.

  – Format the summary sheet in the same style as the weekly worksheets.

  – Use the split function to keep the header rows in place.

	A	B	C	D	E
1			Week 1	Week 2	Week 3
4	Project 1		5	0	7
5	Project 2		5.5	0	3
6	Project 3		9	0	7
7	Project 4		0	0	0
9	MANAGEMENT				
10	Supervision of others		2	0	3
11	Review of work		0	0	0
12	Training staff		0	0	0
14	OTHER				
15	Attending training		7	0	16
16	Admin		4	0	5
17	Miscellaneous		2.5	0	0
19	ABSENCE				
20	Sickness		0	0	0
21	Annual		0	37.5	0
22	Flexi-day		0	0	0
23	Other		0	0	0
25	TOTALS				
26	Total hours worked		35	0	41
27	Total absence		0	37.5	0
28					
29	TOTAL		35	37.5	41
30					
31					
32					
33					
34					
35					

Week 1 | Week 2 | Week 3 | **Summary** | ⊕

Task 4.6

(a) Open the renamed spreadsheet and go into the Record tab.

— Use a lookup function to complete the employee name column.

(b) Use an IF statement in Column I along with a lookup function in Column E to determine whether or not a certificate is required.

— The IF statement should return the values 0 for no and 1 for yes and the lookup should refer to the table in Columns J and K.

– **Hide Columns I, J and K.**

BPP
LEARNING MEDIA

(c) Insert a pivot table on a new worksheet which summarises the total number of sickness days taken by each employee.

– Rename this worksheet 'Summary'.

(d) Return to the 'Record' worksheet and sort the data by employee number.

– Use a subtotal function to count the instances of sickness taken by each individual.

– Highlight the entire worksheet and apply conditional formatting to highlight the employee number of any individuals who are at risk of falling into the frequent sickness category.

	A	B	C	D	E	F	G	H	I	J	
1	Date of leave	Employee Ref	Employee Name	Number of days	Certificate required?	Reason			Certificate lookup		
2	9th March	111234	ACAROGLU, D	3 No		Infection			0	1	Yes
3		111234 Count		1							
4	18th March	111235	ALLEN, G	3 No		Injury			0	0	No
5		111235 Count		1							
6	7th April	111238	BASS, L	1 No		Nausea			0		
7		111238 Count		1							
8	3rd March	111239	CHEN, Y	1 No		Nausea			0		
9		111239 Count		1							
10	16th April	111241	COLEMAN, O	1 No		Medical problem			0		
11		111241 Count		1							
12	21st March	111242	D'ONOFRIO, N	25 Yes		Accident			1		
13		111242 Count		1							
14	21st March	111243	EADIE, L	1 No		Blood test			0		
15		111243 Count		1							
16	3rd March	111244	EGERTON, J	1 No		Migraine			0		
17	15th March	111244	EGERTON, J	2 No		Tummy bug			0		
18	25th March	111244	EGERTON, J	1 No		Headache			0		
19	10th April	111244	EGERTON, J	1 No		Flu			0		
20	20th April	111244	EGERTON, J	1 No		Cold			0		
21	27th April	111244	EGERTON, J	2 No		48 hour bug			0		
22		111244 Count		6							
23	17th March	111247	FOBEL, P	2 No		Pregancy related illness			0		
24		111247 Count		1							
25	12th March	111248	GARVEY, J	1 No		24 hour bug			0		
26		111248 Count		1							
27	15th March	111249	GARVEY, M	1 No		Headache			0		
28		111249 Count		1							
29	11th March	111252	HUBBARD, Phine	7 Yes		Medical problem			1		
30		111252 Count		1							
31	4th March	111254	JOSSERAND, A	3 No		Lower back			0		
32		111254 Count		1							
33	23rd April	111255	KUMAR, T	1 No		Joint pain			0		
34		111255 Count		1							
35	24th April	111256	LISTER, B	1 No		Doctors appointment			0		
36		111256 Count		1							
37	27th March	111257	LOGAN, T	1 No		Stomach pain			0		
38		111257 Count		1							
39	29th March	111258	LOVETT, W	4 No		Hypertension			0		
40		111258 Count		1							
41	29th March	111259	MCDERMID, A	3 No		Tooth abscess			0		

Record (2)   Summary   Record   Employee names

Task 4.7

(a) Open the renamed spreadsheet.

    –   Run a data validation test to remove any duplicate entries.

	A	B	C	D	E	F	G
1	Surname	Initial	TEST 1	TEST 2	TEST 3	TEST 4	OVERALL SCORE
2	ALLEN	T	151	120	120	94	118
3	KOBRIN	J	121	150	124	121	141
4	BARING	R	123	137	135	125	133
5	NASATYR	A	144	146	124	121	
6	LEVY	J	122	190	132	91	
7	SAUNDERS	J	130	139	135	93	
8	SMITH	B	134	125	142	91	
9	ROBERTSON	F	121	123	88	91	
10	JENSEN	U	113	137	130	91	
11	KIRKPATRICK	L	137	142	127	91	
12	HUGHES	G	126	123	158	91	
13	BASDEN	G	121	123	112	120	124
14	RATIU	T	111	118	108	108	119
15	PETERS	F	136	143	138	106	145
16	ENGLISH	P	132	144	150	127	142
17	RICHARDS	A	146	149	132	139	150
18	POLYCHRONOPOULOS	H	120	169	122	139	137
19	BRETTLE	R	146	146	127	131	143
20	FEVRIER	L	131	137	135	114	137
21	GLADWIN	N	103	142	138	106	141
22	TOWNSEND	G	138	138	130	111	141

Sheet1

Microsoft Excel

2 duplicate values found and removed; 45 unique values remain.

OK

Was this information helpful?

Calculate the average score for each student

		Function Library			Time ▾ Reference ▾ Trig ▾ Functions ▾	Manager ▭ Create...	Defined Name

nction ▾   Used ▾   ▾   ▾   ▾

2   ▾ : ✕ ✓ *fx* =AVERAGE(C2:F2)

	A	B	C	D	E	F	G	H
	Surname	Initial	TEST 1	TEST 2	TEST 3	TEST 4	OVERALL SCORE	Average score
	ALLEN	T	111	122	120	96	118	112
	KOBRIN	J	121	150	124	131	141	
	BARING	R	123	137	135	125	133	
	NASATYR	A	144	146	124	125	150	
	LEVY	J	122	150	132	106	140	
	SAUNDERS	Y	130	139	135	121	138	

Formatting the cells with conditional formatting so that any who have failed the pass mark (70% of 150 is 105, so 105 is the pass mark required in the conditional formatting).

Clipboard ▾   Font ▾   Alignment

I7   ▾ : ✕ ✓ *fx* =IF(H7<120, "Refer"," ")

	A	B	C	D	E	F
1	Surname	Initial	TEST 1	TEST 2	TEST 3	TEST 4
2	HAY	S	106	118	108	102
3	RATIU	T	111	116	108	108
4	ROBERTSON	F	121	123	98	103
5	ALLEN	T	111	122	120	96
6	WEBSTER	S	124	101	142	104
7	HERVEY	F	125	128	116	107
8	BASDEN	G	121	123	112	129
9	FULLONE	B	119	126	124	125
10	HUGHES	G	126	123	138	107
11	BERGMAN	B	134	125	142	96
12	CLARKE	Q	115	143	127	113
13	JOHNSON	W	128	143	130	106

Insert a new column H and create an IF statement where the average scores below 120 are required to be referred. Ensure table is correctly formatted and the tab is renamed to 'referrals'.

	A	B	C	D	E	F	G	H	I	J	K	L	M
1	Surname	Initial	TEST	TEST	TEST	TEST	Average scor	Comments					
2	HAY	S	106	118	108	102	109	Refer					
3	RATIU	T	111	116	108	96	108	Refer					
4	ROBERTSON	F	121	123	99	103	111	Refer					
5	ALLEN	T	111	122	120	96	112	Refer					
6	WEBSTER	S	124	101	142	104	118	Refer					

=IF(G3<120, "Refer"," ")

Conditional Formatting Rules Manager

Show formatting rules for: This Table

New Rule... | Edit Rule... | Delete Rule

Rule (applied in order shown)	Format	Applies to	Stop If True
Cell Value = 105	AaBbCcYyZz	=$H$1	
Cell Value < 105	AaBbCcYyZz	=$H$1:$A$1:$G$6	

OK | Close | Apply

(b) Return to worksheet 'test results' and format the data as a table using table style medium 2.

FILE HOME INSERT PAGE LAYOUT FORMULAS DATA REVIEW VIEW

Arial — 10 — A A ... Wrap Text ... General

B I U ... Merge & Center — % , ... Conditional Format as Ce Formatting ▾ Table ▾ Style

Clipboard | Font | Alignment | Number | Styles

A1 — fx Surname

	A	B	C	D	E	F	G	H	I	J	K
1	Surname	Initial	TEST 1	TEST 2	TEST 3	TEST 4	OVERALL SCORE				
2	ALLEN	T	111	122	120	96	118				
3	KOBRIN	J	121	150	124	131	141				
4	BARING	R	123	137	135	125	133				
5	NASATYR	A	144	146	124	125	150				
6	LEVY	J	122	150	132	106	140				
7	SAUNDERS	Y	130	139	135	121	138				

(c) Add a column called 'outcome' in Column H.

    – Insert the text 'Scholarship' in this column next to the top 5 students, and 'Interview' against the remaining students.

    – Remove the filters, and rename this worksheet "scholarship"

    – Use the filters within the table to identify only those students who will be offered an interview for the scholarship program. Reorder the data using the filter to rank the potential scholarship candidates from highest scoring to lowest scoring.

Surname	Initial	TEST	TEST	TEST	TEST	AVERAGE SCOR	Outcon
BARING	R	123	137	135	125	130	Interview
BRETTLE	R	132	146	127	131	134	Interview
CHOHHAN	S	125	136	124	142	132	Interview
ENGLISH	P	132	144	130	127	133	Interview
GARZARELLI	C	136	135	135	117	131	Interview
KOBRIN	J	121	150	124	131	132	Interview
KURGAN	L	125	141	135	127	132	Interview
LAVINGTON	F	138	143	138	105	131	Interview
MORAS	T	124	149	132	117	130	Interview
OUDKERK	J	143	150	101	140	134	Interview
POLYCHRONOPOULOS	H	120	150	122	139	133	Interview
RYLEY	K	125	145	138	128	134	Interview
SAUNDERS	Y	130	139	135	121	131	Interview

Insert the text 'Scholarship' in this column next to the top 5 students, and 'Interview' against the remaining students.

	A	B	C	D	E	F	G	H
1	Surname	Initial	TEST	TEST	TEST	TEST	AVERAGE SCOR	Outcon
10	CRAMSIE	J	142	150	138	120	137	Scholarship
18	HORSELL	B	131	144	130	146	138	Scholarship
32	NASATYR	A	144	146	124	125	135	Scholarship
37	RICHARDS	A	148	149	132	139	142	Scholarship
42	SHAI	D	138	145	138	142	141	Scholarship
47								
48								

	A	B	C	D	E	F	G	H
1	Surname	Initial	TEST 1	TEST 2	TEST 3	TEST 4	AVERAGE SCORE	Outcome
2	ALLEN	T	111	122	120	96	112	
3	BARING	R	123	137	135	125	130	Interview
4	BASDEN	G	121	123	112	129	121	
5	BERGMAN	B	134	125	142	96	125	
6	BRETTLE	R	132	146	127	131	134	Interview
7	CHING	Y	126	134	124	132	129	
8	CHOHHAN	S	125	136	124	142	132	Interview
9	CLARKE	Q	115	143	127	113	125	
10	CRAMSIE	J	142	150	138	120	137	Scholarship
11	ENGLISH	P	132	144	130	127	133	Interview
12	FENNER	L	131	137	135	114	129	
13	FULLONE	B	119	126	124	125	123	
14	GARZARELLI	C	136	135	135	117	131	Interview
15	GLADWIN	M	133	142	138	104	129	
16	HAY	S	106	118	108	102	109	
17	HERVEY	F	125	128	118	110	120	
18	HORSELL	B	131	144	130	146	138	Scholarship
19	HUGHES	G	126	123	138	107	124	
20	JENSEN	U	113	137	130	127	127	
21	JOHNSON	W	128	143	130	106	127	
22	JOYCE	J	115	144	135	122	129	
23	KIRKPATRICK	L	137	142	127	112	129	
24	KLEIN WASSINK	L	133	146	118	120	129	
25	KOBRIN	J	121	150	124	131	132	Interview
26	KURGAN	L	125	141	135	127	132	Interview
27	LAVINGTON	F	138	143	138	105	131	Interview
28	LEVY	J	122	150	132	106	128	
29	MILLWARD	T	136	127	124	122	127	
30	MORAS	T	124	149	132	117	130	Interview

scholarship | referrals | (+)

(d) Password protect the entire workbook and using the password Test123.

There are two options here. One is to protect the entire workbook from any access at all, which means that the contents cannot be viewed. Alternatively, you can allow access, but prevent any changes to the worksheets (such as changing results). In the real assessment, you will be advised which option to take. Here, we have used the second option, which protects the integrity of the results.

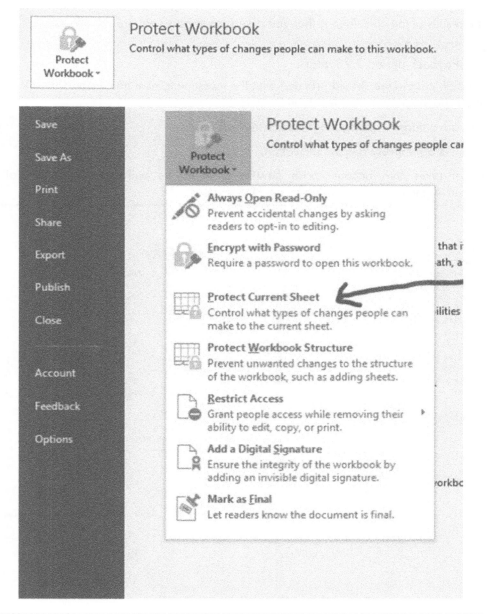

Task 4.8

To:	Tom Howard
From:	Ian Chesterton
Date:	3 January 20X0
Subject:	Investment in plant and machinery

Hi Tom

The results of the calculations that you asked me to carry out are as follows:

- NPV £52,997
- Payback period 2.73 years

On both criteria we should proceed with the investment, as it has a positive NPV and a payback period of less than 3 years.

Two advantages of using the payback method are:

- It is a relatively simple calculation.

- It takes into account cash flow and when we will recover our initial investment.

	A	B	C	D	E	F	G	H	I
1	NPV								
2	Year	0	1	2	3	4			
3	Revenues		200,000	220,000	231,000	237,930			
4	Variable costs		(100,000)	(110,000)	(115,500)	(118,965)			
5	Fixed costs		(20,000)	(20,000)	(20,000)	(20,000)			
6	Capital expenditure	(240,000)							
7	Cash flows	(240,000)	80,000	90,000	95,500	98,965			
8	Present value factor 9%	1.0000	0.9174	0.8417	0.7722	0.7084			
9	Discounted cash flows	(240,000)	73,392	75,753	73,745	70,107			
10	Net present value	52,997	ACCEPT				=IF(B10>0, "ACCEPT","REJECT")		
11	Payback								
12	Cash flows	(240,000)	80,000	90,000	95,500	98,965			
13	Cumulative cash flows	(240,000)	(160,000)	(70,000)	25,500	124,465			
14				70,000					
15	Payback calculation	2.73	ACCEPT						
16					=IF(B15<3, "ACCEPT","REJECT")				
17									
18		The spell check will pick up							
19		the error on the spelling here							
20									
21									
22									

Task 4.9

Setting the print area, ensure to select the icon as highlighted, after having highlighted the correct cells A1:G16:

	A	B	C	D	E	F	G
1	NPV						
2	Year	0	1	2	3	4	
3	Revenues		250,000	275,000	297,000	311,850	
4	Variable costs		(150,000)	(159,000)	(165,360)	(170,321)	
5	Fixed costs		(40,000)	(40,000)	(40,000)	(40,000)	
6	Capital expenditure	(300,000)					
7	Cash flows	(300,000)	60,000	76,000	91,640	101,529	
8	Present value factor 11%	1.0000	0.9009	0.8116	0.7312	0.6587	
9	Discounted cash flows	(300,000)	54,054	61,682	67,007	66,877	
10	Net present value	(50,380)	REJECT				
11	Payback						
12	Cash flows	(300,000)	60,000	76,000	91,640	101,529	
13	Cumulative cash flows	(300,000)	(240,000)	(164,000)	(72,360)	29,169	
14					72,360		
15	Payback calculation	3.71	ACCEPT				
16							

The header and footer for the print area can be selected by either:

File/Print/Page set up

Or by going to the ribbon and selecting Page Layout/Print titles and opening the Page Setup tab.

fx =IF(B15<4,"ACCEPT","REJECT")

Page Setup

Page | Margins | Header/Footer | Sheet

Riley NPV Calculation

Header:

Riley NPV Calculation

Custom Header... | Custom Footer...

Footer:

27/04/201917:00

27/04/201917:00

☐ Different odd and even pages
☐ Different first page
☑ Scale with document
☑ Align with page margins

Print... | Print Preview | Options...

OK | Cancel

	A	B	C	D	E	F	G	H	I	J	K
1	NPV Riley calculation										
2	Year	0	1	2	3	4	Don't forget new title and format				
3	Revenues		250,000	275,000	297,000	311,850					
4	Variable costs		(150,000)	(159,000)	(165,360)	(170,321)					
5	Fixed costs		(40,000)	(40,000)	(40,000)	(40,000)					
6	Capital expenditure	(300,000)									
7	Cash flows	(300,000)	60,000	76,000	91,640	101,529	Print layout border will be visible once set				
8	Present value factor 11%	1.0000	0.9009	0.8116	0.7312	0.6587					
9	Discounted cash flows	(300,000)	54,054	61,682	67,007	66,877					
10	Net present value	(50,380)	REJECT								
11	Payback										
12	Cash flows	(300,000)	60,000	76,000	91,640	101,529					
13	Cumulative cash flows	(300,000)	(240,000)	(164,000)	(72,360)	29,169					
14					72,360		=IF(B10<0,"REJECT","ACCEPT")				
15	Payback calculation	3.71	ACCEPT								
16											
17											
18				=IF(B15<4,"ACCEPT","REJECT")							
19											
20											
21	Spellcheck will correct the spelling of "Revenues"										
22											
23											
24											

172

To:	Lynne Dupont
From:	Barbara Wright
Date:	25 January 20X1
Subject:	Investment in machinery

Hi Lynne

The results of the calculations that you asked me to carry out are as follows:

- NPV −£50,380
- Payback period 3.71 years

The NPV is negative, so on that criteria we should not proceed with the investment. The payback period is however less than our maximum period, so according to the payback criteria we should proceed with the investment.

It would be better to use the NPV result to determine our decision, as NPV is a better method than payback for the following reasons:

- It takes into account the time value of money.

- It considers all the cash flows related to the investment, not just those occurring within the payback period.

Task 4.10

Ensure that when setting up the formatting for cell B11, that only the font is coloured and not the cell fill. This can be done by the following steps:

Conditional formatting, select New Formatting Rule. Go to 'use a formula to determine which cells to format', and edit the rule description. Here we have highlighted the cell and set the parameters to be greater than the 11% IRR required by the management. By then clicking on the Format button, the colour of the font can be changed. Add green font for results greater 11, and red font for those below 11. You will have to add two separate rules, see second screenshot below:

	A	B	C	D	E	F	G	H
1	NPV							
2	Year	0	1	2	3	4		
3	Revenues		400,000	450,000	510,000	590,000		
4	Variable costs		(180,000)	(207,000)	(231,840)	(255,024)		
5	Fixed costs		(40,000)	(42,000)	(44,100)	(46,305)		
6	Capital expenditure	(675,000)						
7	Cash flows	(675,000)	180,000	201,000	234,060	288,671		
8	Present value factor 14%	1.0000	0.8772	0.7695	0.6750	0.5921		
9	Discounted cash flows	(675,000)	157,896	154,670	157,991	170,922		
10	Net present value	(33,522)	REJECT					
11	IRR	11.84						
12								

New Formatting Rule

Select a Rule Type:
- Format all cells based on their values
- Format only cells that contain
- Format only top or bottom ranked values
- Format only values that are above or below average
- Format only unique or duplicate values
- ► Use a formula to determine which cells to format

Edit the Rule Description:

Format values where this formula is true:

=$B$11>11

Preview: AaBbCcYyZz   Format...

OK   Cancel

Conditional Formatting Rules Manager

Show formatting rules for: Current Selection

New Rule...   Edit Rule...   Delete Rule

Rule (applied in order shown)	Format	Applies to	Stop If True
Formula: =$B$11<11	AaBbCcYyZz	=$B$11	
Formula: =$B$11>11	AaBbCcYyZz	=$B$11	

OK   Cancel   Apply

Ensure that when entering the comment that it is visible (not hidden when the cell is not selected) by right clicking on the cell, and select view/hide comments.

	A	B	C	D	E	F	G	H	I	J
1	NPV									
2	Year	0	1	2	3	4				
3	Revenues		400,000	450,000	510,000	590,000				
4	Variable costs		(180,000)	(207,000)	(231,840)	(255,024)				
5	Fixed costs		(40,000)	(42,000)	(44,100)	(46,305)				
6	Capital expenditure	(675,000)								
7	Cash flows	(675,000)	180,000	201,000	234,060	288,671				
8	Present value factor 14%	1.0000	0.8772	0.7695	0.6750	0.5921				
9	Discounted cash flows	(675,000)	157,896	154,670	157,991	170,922				
10	Net present value	(33,522)	REJECT							
11	IRR	11.84								
12										
13										
14										
15										
16										
17										
18										
19										

Author:
For the IRR to >11 the criteria set by Kingsley Co is valid

Make sure the comment box is visible and not hidden

=IF(B10>0,"ACCEPT","REJECT")

To:	Charles Frere
From:	Susan Foreman
Date:	29 February 20X2
Subject:	Investment in new technology

Hi Charles

The results of the calculations that you asked me to carry out are as follows:

- NPV −£33,522
- IRR 11.84%

The NPV is negative, so on that criteria we should not proceed with the investment. The IRR is however more than our target IRR, so according to the IRR criteria we should proceed with the investment.

It would be better to use the NPV result to determine our decision, as NPV is a better method than IRR for the following reasons:

- It takes into account the absolute value of the investment.
- It is not distorted by unusual patterns of cash flows.

Task 4.11

To:	Avril Rolfe
From:	Steven Taylor
Date:	14 March 20X3
Subject:	Investment in machinery

Hi Avril

The results of the calculations that you asked me to carry out are as follows:

- NPV £10,265
- IRR 9.30%

On both criteria we should proceed with the investment, as it has a positive NPV and an IRR that is more than our target IRR of 9%.

Two advantages of using the IRR method are:

- It takes into account the time value of money.
- It gives a clear % answer.

	A	B	C	D	E	F
1	NPV					
2	Year	0	1	2	3	4
3	Sales units		60,000	70,000	80,000	90,000
4	Sales price per unit		5.00	5.50	6.00	6.60
5	Variable cost per unit		(3.00)	(3.40)	(3.80)	(4.30)
6	Revenues		300,000	385,000	480,000	594,000
7	Variable costs		(180,000)	(238,000)	(304,000)	(387,000)
8	Fixed costs		(60,000)	(60,000)	(60,000)	(60,000)
9	Capital expenditure	(320,000)				
10	Cash flows	(320,000)	60,000	87,000	116,000	147,000
11	Present value factor 8%	1	0.9259	0.8573	0.7938	0.7350
12	Discounted cash flows	(320,000)	55,554	74,585	92,081	108,045
13	Net present value	10,265	ACCEPT			
14	IRR	9.30				

Task 4.12

To:	Kate Harvey
From:	Dodo Chaplet
Date:	11 April 20X4
Subject:	Variances in quarter to 31 March 20X4

Hi Kate

The operating profit variance from the flexed budget was £9,800 favourable. This arose because the budgeted profit when flexed to the actual volume of 45,000 units was £311,500, whereas we made an actual profit of £321,300.

The single most significant variance was aloe vera, which was £27,000 favourable. This could have been achieved by changing suppliers.

The single most significant adverse variance was quality control expenses, which was £6,975 adverse. This could have been due to problems with the materials being supplied – possibly linked to the favourable variance for aloe vera.

	A	B	C	D	E	F	G
1				12.50%			
2	Maxwell Co Original budget for the quarter ended 31 March 20X4						
3			Original budget	Flexed budget	Actual results	Variances	
4							
5	Revenue		920,000	1,035,000	1,040,000	5,000	
6	Materials	Silk powder	264,000	297,000	300,000	-3,000	
7	Materials	Silk amino acids	32,000	36,000	37,500	-1,500	
8	Materials	Aloe vera	224,000	252,000	225,000	27,000	Most significant favourable variance
9	Direct labour	Skilled	30,000	33,750	37,100	-3,350	
10	Direct labour	Unskilled	15,000	16,875	17,500	-625	
11	Variable overheads	Supervision	30,000	33,750	36,200	-2,450	
12	Variable overheads	Quality control	25,000	28,125	35,100	-6,975	Most significant adverse variance
13	Fixed overheads	Sales and distribution	18,000	18,000	22,400	-4,400	
14	Fixed overheads	Administration	8,000	8,000	7,900	100	
15	Operating profit		274,000	311,500	321,300	9,800	
16							
17						Balanced	
18							
19	Maxwell Co Original budget for the quarter ended 31 March 20X4 (cost summary)						
20			Original budget	Flexed budget	Actual results	Variances	
21							
25	Materials total		520,000	585,000	562,500	22,500	
28	Direct labour total		45,000	50,625	54,600	-3,975	
31	Variable overheads total		55,000	61,875	71,300	-9,425	
34	Fixed overheads totals		26,000	26,000	30,300	-4,300	
35	Costs		646,000	723,500	718,700	4,800	
36							

Task 4.13

To:	Abby Hudson
From:	Ben Jackson
Date:	1 May 20X5
Subject:	Variances in quarter to 31 March 20X5

Hi Abby

The operating profit variance from the flexed budget was £115 adverse. This arose because the budgeted profit when flexed to the actual volume of 3,825 meals sold was £82,195, whereas we made an actual profit of £82,080.

The biggest single favourable variance was revenue, which was £7,000 favourable. This could have arisen because customers chose a more expensive mix of food and drink than we budgeted for in an average meal.

The biggest single adverse variance was kitchen staff wages, which was 2,750 adverse. The adverse variance for waiters' wages was almost as high, suggesting that that we employed staff for more hours than the business needed them.

	A	B	C	D	E	F	G	H	I	J
1				-15%						
2	Williams restaurant Original budget for the quarter ended 31 March 20X5									
3			Original budget	Flexed budget	Actual results	Variances				
4										
5	Revenue		220,000	187,000	194,000		Most significant favourable variance			
6	Consumables	Food	18,000	15,300	16,100	-800				
7	Consumables	Drink	7,800	6,630	6,850	-220				
8	Labour	Waiter wages	13,000	11,050	13,650	-2,600				
9	Labour	Kitchen staff wages	14,000	11,900	14,650	-2,750	Most significant unfavourable variance			
10	Variable overheads	Energy	9,500	8,075	7,770	305				
11	Variable overheads	Administration	1,000	850	900	-50				
12	Fixed overheads	Manager's salary	13,500	13,500	13,500					
13	Fixed overheads	Chef's salary	12,000	12,000	12,900	-900				
14	Fixed overheads	Rent, rates and depreciation	13,000	13,000	12,700	300				
15	Fixed overheads	Financial and administration	12,500	12,500	12,900	-400				
16	Operating profit		105,700	82,195	82,080	-115				
17										
18						Balanced				
19	Williams restaurant Original budget for the quarter ended 31 March 20X5 (Cost summary)									
20			Original budget	Flexed budget	Actual results	Variances				
21										
24	Consumables total		25,800	21,930	22,950	-1,020				
27	Labour total		27,000	22,950	28,300	-5,350				
30	Variable overheads total		10,500	8,925	8,670	255				
35	Fixed overheads total		51,000	51,000	52,000	-1,000				
36	Total costs		114,300	104,805	111,920	-7,115				

Task 4.14

To:	Laura Wilde
From:	Jamie McCrimmon
Date:	11 June 20X6
Subject:	Variances for year ended 31 May 20X6 and staff costs

Hi Laura

The operating profit variance from the flexed budget was £94,000 adverse. This arose because the budgeted profit when flexed to the actual number of 21,850 patient days was £239,000, whereas we made an actual surplus of £145,000.

The most significant adverse overhead variances in each cost category were a variance of £5,000 in catering costs (variable costs), a variance of $14,000 for nurse costs (staff costs) and a variance of £40,000 in administration costs (fixed costs). The catering costs could have been higher than expected due to a general increase in food prices.

The increase of £110,000 in costs for staff needed to cope with 25,000 patient days will be a concern to our hospital. The maximum amount of funding that the hospital will receive when it is able to take 25,000 patient days is $4 million, which is an increase of only £67,000 on current funding, leaving a shortfall of £43,000. The £4 million will also need to cover an increase in variable costs, increasing the risks that the hospital will run a deficit.

	A	B	C	D	E	F	G
1					15%		
2	Westside Hospital Original budget for the year ended 31 May 20X6						
3			Original budget	Flexed budget	Actual results	Variances	
4							
5	Revenue		3,420,000	3,933,000	3,933,000	0	
6	Variable costs	Catering	440,000	506,000	511,000	(5,000)	
7	Variable costs	Laundry	120,000	138,000	142,000	(4,000)	
8	Variable costs	Pharmacy	560,000	644,000	638,000	6,000	
9	Staff costs	Supervisors	150,000	150,000	160,000	(10,000)	
10	Staff costs	Nurses	184,000	230,000	244,000	(14,000)	
11	Staff costs	Assistants	352,000	416,000	421,000	(5,000)	
12	Fixed costs	Administration	750,000	750,000	790,000	(40,000)	
13	Fixed costs	Security	80,000	80,000	82,000	(2,000)	
14	Fixed costs	Rent and property	780,000	780,000	800,000	(20,000)	
15	Surplus/(Deficit)		4,000	239,000	145,000	(94,000)	
16							
17						Balanced	
18							
19	Westside Hospital Staffing costs for the year ended 31 May 20X8						
20			Current budget	New budget	Increase		
21							
22	Staff costs	Supervisors	150,000	150,000	-		
23	Staff costs	Nurses	230,000	276,000	46,000		
24	Staff costs	Assistants	416,000	480,000	64,000		
25	Increase				110,000		

Task 4.15

To:	Polly Urquhart
From:	Victoria Waterfield
Date:	21 July 20X7
Subject:	Variances for year ended 30 June 20X7

Hi Polly

The operating profit variance from the flexed budget was £145,700 adverse. This arose because the budgeted profit when flexed to the actual volume of 16,500 chargeable consultant hours was £980,200, whereas we made an actual surplus of £834,500.

In % terms the three largest adverse variances were the casual wages (13.64%), printing, postage and stationery (12.50%) and telephone (8.59%). Whilst we might be concerned that these are adverse variances, the three highest adverse cost variances in £ terms are completely different and we may be more worried about these.

The largest adverse variance of all in £ terms was for revenue and we may wish to examine the reasons for this separately.

	A	B	C	D	E	F	G
1				10%			
2	Farrell Co Original budget for the year ended 30 June 20X7						
3			Original budget	Flexed budget	Actual results	Variances $	Variances %
4							
5	Revenue		2,000,000	2,200,000	2,100,000	(100,000)	(4.55)
6	Fixed overheads	Administration staff salaries	100,000	100,000	105,000	(5,000)	(5.00)
7	Fixed overheads	Consultants' salaries	960,000	960,000	990,000	(30,000)	(3.13)
8	Variable overheads	Casual wages	14,000	15,400	17,500	(2,100)	(13.64)
9	Fixed overheads	Motor and travel costs	75,000	75,000	80,000	(5,000)	(6.67)
10	Fixed overheads	Telephone	8,000	8,000	8,200	(200)	(2.50)
11	Variable overheads	Telephone	18,000	19,800	21,500	(1,700)	(8.59)
12	Variable overheads	Printing, postage and stationery	16,000	17,600	19,800	(2,200)	(12.50)
13	Fixed overheads	Premises and equipment	24,000	24,000	23,500	500	2.08
14	Operating profit		785,000	980,200	834,500	(145,700)	(14.86)
15							
16						Balanced	
17							
18	Farrell Co Variance analysis for the year ended 30 June 20X7						
19			Original budget	Flexed budget	Actual results	Variances $	Variances %
20							
21	Variable overheads	Casual wages	14,000	15,400	17,500	(2,100)	(13.64)
22	Variable overheads	Printing, postage and stationery	16,000	17,600	19,800	(2,200)	(12.50)
23	Variable overheads	Telephone	18,000	19,800	21,500	(1,700)	(8.59)
24	Fixed overheads	Motor and travel costs	75,000	75,000	80,000	(5,000)	(6.67)
25	Fixed overheads	Administration staff salaries	100,000	100,000	105,000	(5,000)	(5.00)
26	Revenue		2,000,000	2,200,000	2,100,000	(100,000)	(4.55)
27	Fixed overheads	Consultants' salaries	960,000	960,000	990,000	(30,000)	(3.13)
28	Fixed overheads	Telephone	8,000	8,000	8,200	(200)	(2.50)
29	Fixed overheads	Premises and equipment	24,000	24,000	23,500	500	2.08

Task 4.16

To:	Ken Masters
From:	Zoe Heriot
Date:	24 July 20X8
Subject:	Analysis of performance for quarter ended 30 June 20X8

Hi Ken

I have compared the actual results with what the budget would have been for 11,500 units and 12,500 units. Rather worryingly, the actual profit of £297,900 is less than both of the budgeted profits. At 11,500 units the actual profit is £13,900 less than the budgeted profit of £311,800 and at 12,500 units the actual profit is £45,100 less than the budgeted profit of £343,000.

It is clear from the figures that the fixed costs and costs of Material B were over-budget whatever the level of sales.

The other figures show conflicting pictures about what the level of production and sales was. The actual revenue is much closer to the budgeted revenue for 11,500 units, but the other cost figures are closer to the budgeted figures for 12,500 units. This suggests either that we did not achieve the level of revenue we expected on what we sold, or that there was a general problem controlling costs.

	A	B	C	D	E	F	G	H
1				15%	25%			
2	Carter Co Original budget for the quarter ended 30 June 20X8							
3			Original budget	Flexed budget 11,500	Flexed budget 12,500	Actual results	Variances 11,500	Variances 12,500
4								
5	Revenue		600,000	690,000	750,000	700,000	10,000	-50,000
6	Materials	A	40,000	46,000	50,000	49,000	-3,000	1,000
7	Materials	B	44,000	50,800	55,000	56,000	-5,400	-1,000
8	Materials	C	32,000	36,800	40,000	39,200	-2,400	800
9	Direct labour	Skilled	72,000	82,800	90,000	87,000	-4,200	3,000
10	Direct labour	Unskilled	36,000	41,400	45,000	44,000	-2,600	1,000
11	Variable overheads	Supervision	42,000	48,300	52,500	51,000	-2,700	1,500
12	Variable overheads	Production planning	22,000	25,300	27,500	26,700	-1,400	800
13	Fixed overheads	Sales and distribution	25,000	25,000	25,000	26,500	-1,500	-1,500
14	Fixed overheads	Finance and administration	22,000	22,000	22,000	22,700	-700	-700
15	Operating profit		265,000	311,800	343,000	297,900	-13,900	-45,100
16								
17							Balanced	Balanced
18								
19	Carter Co Overhead summary for the quarter ended 30 June 20X8							
20			Original budget	Flexed budget 11,500	Flexed budget 12,500	Actual results	Variances 11,500	Variances 12,500
21								
22	Materials	summary	116,000	133,400	145,000	144,200	-10,800	800
23	Direct labour	summary	108,000	124,200	135,000	131,000	-6,800	4,000
24	Variable overheads	summary	64,000	73,600	80,000	77,700	-4,100	2,300
25	Fixed overheads	summary	47,000	47,000	47,000	49,200	-2,200	-2,200
26	Cost summary		335,000	378,200	407,000	402,100	-23,900	4,900

Task 4.17

To:	Bill Sayers
From:	Liz Shaw
Date:	19 August 20X9
Subject:	Investment appraisal

Hi Bill

I've carried out the investment appraisal that you wanted. The results are that the payback period on in the investment is 3.69 years and the IRR is 12.87%.

Two problems with the results of the calculations are:

- I have not been given any benchmarks against which to assess whether the figures for payback period and IRR are satisfactory.

- Net present value is considered to be a better method of investment appraisal than payback or IRR, as it uses discounted cash flows (which payback period does not) and provides a clear measure in absolute terms of whether a project is acceptable (which IRR does not).

	A	B	C	D	E	F	G
1	IRR						
2	Year	0	1	2	3	4	5
3	Revenues		180,000	189,000	198,450	208,373	218,791
4	Variable costs		(100,000)	(105,000)	(110,250)	(115,763)	(121,551)
5	Fixed costs		(45,000)	(45,000)	(45,000)	(45,000)	(45,000)
6	Capital expenditure	(150,000)					
7	Cash flows	(150,000)	35,000	39,000	43,200	47,610	52,241
8	Present value factor 10%	1.0000	0.9091	0.8264	0.7513	0.6830	0.6209
9	Discounted cash flows	(150,000)	31,819	32,230	32,456	32,518	32,436
10	Net present value	11,458					
11	Present value factor 15%	1.0000	0.8696	0.7561	0.6575	0.5718	0.4972
12	Discounted cash flows	(150,000)	30,436	29,488	28,404	27,223	25,974
13	Net present value	(8,475)					
14	IRR	12.87					
15	Payback						
16	Cash flows	(150,000)	35,000	39,000	43,200	47,610	52,241
17	Cumulative cash flows	(150,000)	(115,000)	(76,000)	(32,800)	14,810	67,051
18					32,800		
19	Payback calculation	3.69					

Task 4.18

To:	Vanessa Andenberg
From:	Jo Grant
Date:	24 September 20X1
Subject:	Breakeven analysis

Hi Vanessa

I've carried out the breakeven calculations that you asked me to carry out. They show that the breakeven sales volume is 16,500 units and the breakeven sales revenue is £990,000. We should achieve a contribution/sales ratio of 0.33. The margin of safety in units is 8,500, in % terms 34%, which is greater than our target of 20%. However our budgeted sales are 500 units short of the sales needed to achieve our target profit of £180,000.

Two problems with breakeven analysis are:

- It assumes fixed costs are constant.
- It assumes variable costs per unit are constant.

	A	B	C
1		**Breakeven calculations**	
2	**Revenue**	1,500,000	
3	**Variable costs**		
4	Direct materials	500,000	
5	Direct labour	350,000	
6	Assembly	80,000	
7	Packaging	70,000	
8	Total variable costs	1,000,000	
9	Variable costs per unit	40	
10	Contribution per unit	20	
11	**Fixed costs**		
12	Assembly	120,000	
13	Packaging	210,000	
14	Total fixed costs	330,000	
15	Breakeven point in units	16,500	
16	Breakeven point in revenue	990,000	
17	Contribution/Sales ratio	0.33	
18	Margin of safety in units	8,500	
19	Margin of safety in %	34.00	HIGHER
20	Target profit volume	25,500	LESS

Task 4.19

	A	B	C	D	E	F
1	Adverts	100				
2	Bonus rate	2.5%				
3						
4	Staff employee number	Basic salary	Adverts sold during the year	Bonus	Total pay	
5	123	£20,000	85	£0	£20,000	
6	124	£22,000	150	£550	£22,550	
7	125	£28,000	70	£0	£28,000	
8	126	£25,000	165	£625	£25,625	
9	127	£20,000	50	£0	£20,000	
10	128	£18,000	210	£450	£18,450	
11	Total pay for all employees				£134,625	
12						

Suggested formulae

	A	B	C	D	E
1	Adverts	100			
2	Bonus rate	0.025			
3					
4	Staff employee number	Basic salary	Adverts sold during the year	Bonus	Total pay
5	123	20000	85	=IF(C5>B$1,B5*B$2, 0)	=(B5+D5)
6	124	22000	150	=IF(C6>B$1,B6*B$2, 0)	=(B6+D6)
7	125	28000	70	=IF(C7>B$1,B7*B$2, 0)	=(B7+D7)
8	126	25000	165	=IF(C8>B$1,B8*B$2, 0)	=(B8+D8)
9	127	20000	50	=IF(C9>B$1,B9*B$2, 0)	=(B9+D9)
10	128	18000	210	=IF(C10>B$1,B10*B$2, 0)	=(B10+D10)
11	Total pay for all employees				=SUM(E5:E10)
12					
13					

Task 4.20

(a) Calculation of the costs per unit as budgeted:

| D10 | ▾ | : | × | ✓ | fx | =C10/$C$4 |

	A	B	C	D	E	F	G	H	I
1									
2	Eisenhower Ltd: original budget for quarter ended 30 September 20X9								
3	Item		Original Budget £	Ratios					
4	Units		14000						
5	Revenue		2800000	200					
6									
7	Materials:	Direct materials 1	472500	33.75					
8	Materials:	Direct materials 2	315000	22.5					
9	Direct labour:	Skilled	710500	50.75					
10	Variable overheads:	Supervision	182000	13					
11	Costs		1680000	120					
12									

Absolute referencing will 'freeze' the units, but pull the formula down the page. Therefore saving you typing out or amending the formula each time.
Suggested formula: C7/$C$4

When copying the cells across to Actual Results ensure that you use the correct version of paste:

| Calibri ▾ | 11 ▾ | A A | 🔲 ▾ % , | 🔲 |

B I ≡ ◊ ▾ A ▾ 🔲 ▾ .0 .00 🖌

✂ Cut

📋 Copy

📋 Paste Options:

📋 📋 📋 📋 📋 📋

Paste Special... ▸

Insert Copied Cells...

Delete...

Clear Contents

📊 Quick Analysis

Filter ▸

Sort ▸

🗨 Insert Comment

🔲 Format Cells...

Pick From Drop-down List...

(b) and (c) Actual results including the variance in column G, with the correct highlighting of the direct labour and the totals and calculated contribution for the year:

	A	B	C	D	E	F	G
1							
2	Eisenhower Ltd: Actual results for quarter ended 30 September 20X9						
3	Item		Actual results £	Budgeted costs per unit	Actual costs per unit		Variance
4	Units		17,600				
5	Revenue		3,520,000	200	200		
6							
7	Materials:	Direct materials 1	594,000	33.75	33.75	33.7	
8	Materials:	Direct materials 2	396,000	22.5	22.5	22.5	
9	Direct labour:	Skilled	1,159,136	50.75	65.86	65.8	15.11
10	Variable overheads:	Supervision	228,800	13	13	13	
11							
12	Costs		2,377,936	120	135.11	135.1	
13							
14	Contribution for the year		1,142,064				
15							
16							

(d) and (e)

	A	B	C	D	E	F	G	
1								
2	Eisenhower Ltd: Revised budget for quarter ended 30 September 20Y0							
3	Item		Actual results £	Budget costs per unit	Actual costs per unit	Variance	Flexed Budget	
4	Units		17,600				18,000	
5	Revenue		3,520,000	200	200		3,600,000	
6								
7	Materials:	Direct materials 1	594,000	33.75	33.75		607,500	
8	Materials:	Direct materials 2	396,000	22.5	22.5		405,000	
9	Direct labour:	Skilled	1,159,136	50.75	65.86	15.11	1,185,480	
10	Variable overheads:	Supervision	228,800	13	13		234,000	
11								
12	Costs		2,377,936	120	135.11		2,431,980	
13								
14	Contribution for the year		1,142,064				1,168,020	32%
15								
16								
17								
18								
19								
20								

Actual results   **Revised budget**   Original budget   ⊕

(f) Goal seek results should look like this, with the status update as follows:

	A	B	C	D	E	H	I	J	K	L	M	N	O	P
1	Eisenhower Ltd: Revised budget for quarter ended 30 September 20Y0													
				Budgeted costs	Actual costs per									
	Item		Actual results £	per unit	unit	Flexed budget		Goal seek						
	Units		17,600			18,000			18000					
	Revenue		3,520,000	200	200	3,600,000			3,731,980					
	Materials:	Direct materials 1	594,000	33.75	33.75	607,500			607,500					
	Materials:	Direct materials 2	396,000	22.5	22.5	405,000			405,000					
	Direct labour:	Skilled	1,159,136	50.75	65.86	1,185,480			1,185,480					
	Variable overheads:	Supervision	228,800	13	13	234,000			234,000					
	Costs		2,377,936	120	135.11	2,431,980			2,431,980					
	Contribution for the year		1,142,064			1,168,020	32%		1,300,000					

Goal Seek Status

Goal Seeking with Cell J14 found a solution.

Target value: 1300000
Current value: 1,300,000

Step | Pause | OK | Cancel

Goal Seek Status

Goal Seeking with Cell J14 found a solution.

Target value: 1300000
Current value: 1,300,000

Step
Pause
OK   Cancel

Revised budget needs to show the goal seek calculation including the revised sale price per unit to get the correct revenue figure, giving a revised sale price of £207 per unit.

				Budgeted costs	Actual costs per				
2	Eisenhower Ltd: Revised budget for quarter ended 30 September 20Y0								
3	Item		Actual results £	per unit	unit	Flexed budget		Goal seek	
4	Units		17,600			18,000		18000	
5	Revenue		3,520,000	200	200	3,600,000		3,731,980	207.33
6									
7	Materials:	Direct materials 1	594,000	33.75	33.75	607,500		607,500	
8	Materials:	Direct materials 2	396,000	22.5	22.5	405,000		405,000	
9	Direct labour:	Skilled	1,159,136	50.75	65.86	1,185,480		1,185,480	
10	Variable overheads:	Supervision	228,800	13	13	234,000		234,000	
11									
12	Costs		2,377,936	120	135.11	2,431,980		2,431,980	
13									
14	Contribution for the year		1,142,064			1,168,020	32%	1,300,000	
15									
16									
17									

Assessment objective 5 – Spreadsheets for Accounting/Advanced Bookkeeping/Final Accounts Preparation

Task 5.1

	A	B	C	D	E	F
1	Item	Jeff	Gary	Fran		
2	Drawings	3,000	500	£4,000		
3	Interest on capital	90	£160	120		
4	Profit share	£12,750	£12,750	£25,500		
5						
6						
7		Column Labels				
8	Values	Drawings	Interest on capital	Profit share	Grand Total	
9	Sum of Fran	4000	120	25500	29620	
10	Sum of Jeff	3000	90	12750	15840	
11	Sum of Gary	500	160	12750	13410	
12						
13						
14						

PivotTable Fields ▾ ✕

Choose fields to add to report:

☑ Item
☑ Jeff
☑ Gary
☑ Fran

MORE TABLES...

Drag fields between areas below:

▼ FILTERS

▥ COLUMNS

Item ▼

▥ ROWS

Σ Values ▼

Σ VALUES

Sum of... ▼
Sum of... ▼

☐ Defer Layout Upda... | UPDATE

Task 5.2

	A	B	C	D	E	F	G
1			*Capital account*				
2			£			£	
3		Drawings	6,000	01/01/X6	Capital introduced	7,500	
4		Laptop	1,000		Fixtures and fitings	1,678	
5					Cash	1,500	
6	31/01/X6	Balance c/d	12,278		Profit	8,600	
7			19,278			19,278	
8				01/01/X7	Balance b/d	12,278	
9							
10							

Suggested formulae

	B	C	D	E	F	G
1		*Capital account*				
2		£			£	
3	Drawings	6000	01/01/X6	Capital introduced	7500	
4	Laptop	1000		Fixtures and fitings	1678	
5				Cash	1500	
6	Balance c/d	=SUM((F7-(C3+C4)))		Profit	8600	
7		=F7			=SUM(F3:F6)	
8			01/01/X7	Balance b/d	=C6	
9						
10						
11						

Task 5.3

(a)

	A	B	C	D	E	F	G	I
1				Mr I Jones				
2				Statement of Profit or Loss				
3				For the year ended 31 May 20X6				
4								
5					£		£	
6	Sales revenue						280,480	
7	Opening inventory				7,800			
8	Purchases				150,800			
9	Closing inventory				9,000			
10	Cost of sales						149,600	
11	Gross profit						130,880	
12								
13	Less expenses							
14	General expenses				63,800			
15	Administration costs				3,900			
16	IT equipment depreciation				850			
17	Wages				42,000			
18							110,550	
19	Net profit						20,330	
20								

Suggested formulae

	Mr I Jones			
	Statement of Profit or Loss			
	For the year ended 31 May 20X6			
		£		£
Sales revenue				280480
Opening inventory	7800			
Purchases	150800			
Closing inventory	9000			
Cost of sales				=E7+E8-E9
Gross profit				=G6-G10
Less expenses				
General expenses	63800			
Administration costs	3900			
IT equipment depre	850			
Wages	42000			
				=SUM(E14:E17)
Net profit				=G11-G18

(b)

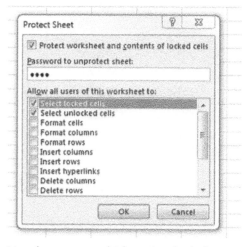

| | HOME | INSERT | PAGE LAYOUT | FORMULAS | DATA | REVIEW | VIEW |

Proofing | Language | Comments

fx | Mr I Jones

	A	B	C	D	E	F	G	H	I	J	K
				Mr I Jones							
				Statement of Profit or Loss							
				For the year ended 31 May 20X6							
				£		£					
Sales revenue						280,480					
Opening inventory				7,800							
Purchases				150,800							
Closing inventory				9,000							
Cost of sales						149,600					
Gross profit						130,880					
Less expenses											
General expenses				63,800							
Administration costs				3,900							
IT equipment depreciation				850							
Wages				42,000							
						110,550					
Net profit						20,330					

Protect Sheet

☑ Protect worksheet and contents of locked cells

Password to unprotect sheet:

••••

Allow all users of this worksheet to:

☑ Select locked cells
☑ Select unlocked cells
☐ Format cells
☐ Format columns
☐ Format rows
☐ Insert columns
☐ Insert rows
☐ Insert hyperlinks
☐ Delete columns
☐ Delete rows

OK | Cancel

Use the password 'doom' to lock the spreadsheet.

When trying to amend the cells, the following warning will show:

> **Microsoft Excel** ✕
>
> ⚠ The cell or chart you're trying to change is on a protected sheet.
>
> To make changes, click Unprotect Sheet in the Review tab (you might need a password).
>
> [OK]

Task 5.4

(a) & (b)

	A	B	C	D
1	**Partnership appropriation account**			
2	**For the year ended 31 August 20X6**			
3			£	
4	**Profit for the year**		180,000	
5	**Salaries:**			
6	Karen		11,400	
7	Jake		14,400	
8	Saffron		9,600	
9	**Interest on capital**			
10	Karen		1,000	
11	Jake		1,200	
12	Saffron		600	
13	Totals		38,200	
14	**Profit available for distrubution**		141,800	
15	Profit share			
16	Karen	20%	28,360	
17	Jake	65%	92,170	
18	Saffron	15%	21,270	
19	**Total profit distributed**	100%	141,800	
20				
21		**Accuracy check**	Correct	
22				

Suggested formulae

	A	B	C	D
1	**Partnership appropriation account**			
2	**For the year ended 31 August 20X6**			
3			£	
4	**Profit for the year**		180000	
5	**Salaries:**			
6	Karen		11400	
7	Jake		14400	
8	Saffron		9600	
9	**Interest on capital**			
10	Karen		1000	
11	Jake		1200	
12	Saffron		600	
13	Totals		=SUM(C6:C12)	
14	**Profit available for distrubution**		=(C4-C13)	
15	Profit share			
16	Karen	0.2	=C14*B16	
17	Jake	0.65	=C14*B17	
18	Saffron	0.15	=C14*B18	
19	**Total profit distributed**	=SUM(B16:B18)	=SUM(C16:C18)	
20				
21		**Accuracy check**	=IF(C14=C19,"Correct","Incorrect")	
22				

Task 5.5

(a)

	A	B	C	D	E
1		£		£	
2	**Sales**			**9,125**	
3	Opening inventory	1,500			
4	Add purchases	7,600			
5	Less closing inventory	-1,800			
6	Cost of sales			7,300	
7	**Gross proft**			1,825	
8					
9	**Alternative G.P. calculation**			1,825	
10					
11					
12					
13	**Profit profile**	%			
14	Sales	100			
15	Cost of sales	80			
16	Profit	20			
17					
18					

Suggested formulae

	A	B	C	D	E
1		£		£	
2	**Sales**			=D6*100/80	
3	Opening inventory	1500			
4	Add purchases	7600			
5	Less closing inventory	-1800			
6	Cost of sales			=SUM(B2:B5)	
7	**Gross proft**			=D2-D6	
8					
9	**Alternative G.P. calculation**			=D6*20/80	
10					
11					
12					
13	**Profit profile**	%			
14	Sales	100			
15	Cost of sales	80			
16	Profit	20			
17					
18					

(b)

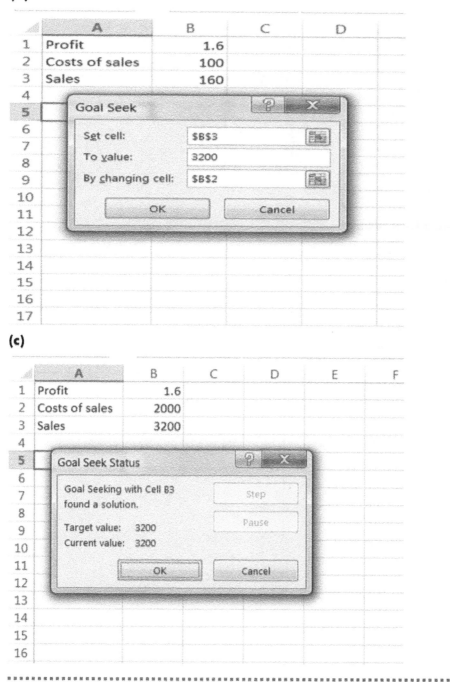

	A	B	C	D
1	Profit	1.6		
2	Costs of sales	100		
3	Sales	160		
4				
5				

Goal Seek

Set cell: $B$3

To value: 3200

By changing cell: $B$2

OK   Cancel

(c)

	A	B	C	D	E	F
1	Profit	1.6				
2	Costs of sales	2000				
3	Sales	3200				
4						
5						

Goal Seek Status

Goal Seeking with Cell B3 found a solution.

Target value: 3200
Current value: 3200

Step

Pause

OK   Cancel

Task 5.6

	A	B	C	D	E	F
1	Property	50				
2	Motor vehicles	30%				
3	Fixtures and fittings	10%				
4						
5			20X5		20X6	
6		Cost	Accumulated depreciation	Depreciation charge	Accumulated depreciation	Carrying amount
7		£	£	£	£	£
8	Property	650,000	195,000	13,000	208,000	442,000
9	Motor vehicles	45,000	22,950	6,615	29,565	15,435
10	Fixtures and fittings	27,000	5,130	2,187	7,317	19,683
11						**477,118**
12						
13						

Suggested formulae

	A	B	C	D	E	F
1	Property	50				
2	Motor vehicles	0.3				
3	Fixtures and fittings	0.1				
4						
5			20X5		20X6	
6		Cost	Accumulated depreciation	Depreciation charge	Accumulated depreciation	Carrying amount
7		£	£	£	£	£
8	Property	650000	195000	=B8/B1	=C8+D8	=B8-E8
9	Motor vehicles	45000	22950	=(B9-C9)*B2	=C9+D9	=B9-E9
10	Fixtures and fittings	27000	5130	=(B10-C10)*B3	=C10+D10	=B10-E10
11						=SUM(F8:F10)
12						
13						
14						
15						

AAT AQ2016 ASSESSMENT 1
LEVEL 3 SYNOPTIC ASSESSMENT

**Time allowed: 2 hours and 45 minutes
(plus 15 minutes to upload your answers)**

AAT AQ2016 PRACTICE ASSESSMENT 1

The AAT may call the assessments on their website, under
Study support resources, either a 'practice assessment'
or 'sample assessment'.

Advanced Diploma Synoptic Assessment (AVSY) AAT practice assessment 1

Scenario

Task 1.1 is based on a workplace scenario separate to the rest of the assessment

Task 1.2 to 1.3 and 2.1 to 2.2 are based on the workplace scenario of BLM & Co

You are a part-qualified Accounting Technician. You work for BLM & Co, a business which manufactures and sells sinks. BLM & Co is owned and run by Brian and Lakmani Moore in partnership.

You cover all aspects of bookkeeping and accounting for the business, along with Jed Malone, who is responsible in particular for completing the VAT return.

BLM & Co also uses the services of Addo & Co, a firm of accountants. Keira Jackson is the accountant at Addo & Co who carries out tasks for BLM & Co.

Part 1

Task 1.1 (15 marks)

In the exam you will be able to access relevant extracts from the AAT *Code of Professional Ethics* via a pop-up window. This information is available in the Appendix which can be found at the back of this book.

This task is based on a workplace scenario separate to the rest of the assessment.

This task is about ethics for accountants.

(a) Are these statements true or false?

Statement	True	False
Accountants have no duty to act in the public interest provided that they act in the interests of their employer and the accountancy profession.'		
The Code of Professional Ethics provides detailed rules on how to act in every possible situation that an accountant might encounter at work.		

(2 marks)

Ethics are based on values, which are demonstrated in behaviour. Sometimes, there is conflict between personal and organisational values which needs to be resolved.

An accountant who is employed by a large organisation personally values loyalty and fairness highly.

(b) **In the table below, identify where there is a conflict between the organisation's behaviour and the accountant's personal values.**

Select 'Yes' or 'No' accordingly.

Organisation's behaviour	Accountant's personal value	Is there a conflict to resolve?
Gives long-standing employees an extra half day of holiday for every two years they remain with the organisation.	Loyalty	▼
Promotes employees on the basis of family or other close relationships	Fairness	▼

Drop-down list:

Yes
No

(2 marks)

An accountant has been offered gifts by the sales manager of one his employer's main suppliers. The accountant has known the sales manager for several years.

(c) **Complete the following statement by selecting the correct option below.**

Being offered gifts by the sales manager is_____ to the accountant's fundamental principle of _____

Options for gap 1	✓
An intimidation threat	
A familiarity threat	
Options for gap 2	**✓**
Objectivity	
Professional competence and due care	

(2 marks)

An accountant works for a large company. A potential customer of the company has asked the accountant to reveal confidential information about the company's cost structure and pricing strategy. The potential customer has offered to pay the accountant for his information.

(d) **Are the following statements true or false?**

Statement	True	False
The accountant may never disclose confidential information to any third party.		
The threat that the accountant is facing to her compliance with the fundamental principles is a self-interest threat.		
The accountant must resign immediately from the company as her integrity has been compromised by the offer from the potential customer.		

(3 marks)

An accountant is following the conflict resolution process in the Code of Professional Ethics in respect an ethical dilemma at work. He has collected evidence and documented the process carefully so he can seek guidance on the dilemma from another accountant.

(e) **Complete the following statement by selecting ONE of the options below.**

In relation to the evidence and documents, the accountant must be particularly careful to ensure the fundamental principle of _____ is not breached when seeking guidance.

	✓
Confidentiality	
Professional competence and due care	
Professional behaviour	

(2 marks)

An accountant has a client who has been involved in concealing criminal property. The accountant has reported the client to the relevant authority and has told the client this.

(f) Complete the following statement by selecting ONE of the options below.

The accountant has committed the criminal offence of_____.

	✓
Money laundering	
Failure to disclose	
Tipping off	

(2 marks)

An accountant is a sole practitioner. She has discovered that a client has been money laundering.

(g) Complete the following statement by selecting ONE of the options below.

	✓
The Nominated Officer	
The National Crime Agency	
HMRC	

(2 marks)

....

Task 1.2 (15 marks)

In the exam you will be able to access relevant extracts from the AAT *Code of Professional Ethics* via pop-up windows. This information is available in the Appendix which can be found at the back of this book.

This task is based on the workplace scenario of BLM & Co.

Today's date is 15 April 20X7.

BLM & Co' VAT control account at 31 March is as follows

VAT control account

		£			£
06/02	Cash book	60,880.98	01/01	Balance b/d	60,880.98
31/03	Purchases day book	99,120.25	31/03	Sales day book	161,728.27
31/03	Sales returns day book	3,529.57	31/03	Purchase returns day book	2,403.68
31/03	Balance c/d	61,482.13			
		225,012.93			225,012.93

On reviewing BLM & Co's day books, you have found two errors:

- VAT of £2,983.50 on a sales invoice was wrongly recorded as sales on 29 March

- A supplier had overstated VAT by £50 on an invoice received and posted by BLM on 27 March.

You prepare journals to correct these errors.

(a) **After the journals are processed, what will be the revised balance carried down on the VAT control account?**

£

(2 marks)

(b) **Complete the following sentence by selecting ONE of the options below.**

This balance will appear on the _____ side of the trial balance

	✓
Credit	
Debit	

(1 mark)

You discover that BLM & Co has been supplying sinks to Malone Ltd, a company owned and run by the brother of your fully-qualified colleague, Jed Malone. When you look at the relevant invoices you realise that Jed has been misrecording VAT so that BLM & Co's sales to Malone Ltd are overstated. As a result, Malone Ltd qualifies for a 15% trade discount on its future purchases from BLM & Co.

(c) **Applying the conceptual framework from the ethical code, which ONE of the following describes the situation faced by Jed Malone when recording sales to his brothers company?**

A self-review threat to professional competence and due care ☐

A familiarity threat to objectivity ☐

An intimidation threat to professional behaviour ☐

(2 marks)

You conclude that the deliberate misrecording of VAT is unethical behaviour by Jed Malone.

(d) **What should be your next action?**

Send a Suspicious Activity Report to the National Crime Agency ☐

Tell Brian and Lakmani about your concerns ☐

(1 mark)

On the morning of 16 April, Jed Malone is dismissed for misconduct by BLM & Co and leaves the office. You are temporarily BLM & Co's only accountant. A VAT officer will be coming to the office for a planned visit on the afternoon of 16 April. You are not prepared for this visit and do not believe you can answer any questions from the VAT officer effectively. Brian and Lakmani insist that you must be present and deal with the VAT officer without assistance.

(e) **Which of the following should be your next action?**

Resign from BLM & Co ☐

Request that the visit by the VAT officer is postponed ☐

Agree to deal with the VAT officer in line with your employers' instructions ☐

(2 marks)

As a resullt of Jed's misconduct, Brian and Lakmani have asked you to examine his recording of sales ledger transactions in the three months ended 31 March 20X7. You identify the following information:

Sales ledger control account balance at 1 January 20X7: £492,409

From 1 January to 31 March:

- Receipts from credit customers: £934,076
- Sales to credit customers, including VAT: £970,370
- Returns from credit customers, including VAT: £21,177
- Irrecoverable debts written off, including VAT: £4,330.

Amounts owed at 31 March 20X7, as confirmed by credit customers: £487,354.

(f) **Complete the sales ledger control account below, by including the four options in the appropriate column AND enter the totals to reconstruct the sales ledger control account for the three months ended 31 March 20X7.**

Sales ledger control account

	£		£
Balance b/d	492,409		
		Balance c/d	487,354
Total		**Total**	

Options:

Cash book	934,076

Sales day book	970,370

Sales return day book	21,177

Journal (irrecoverable debt)	4,330

(2 marks)

(g) **Calculate the missing figure in the sales ledger control account.**

£ [   ]

(1 mark)

(h) **Which of the following could the missing figure represent?**

Discounts allowed. ☐

Cheque from customer returned unpaid by the bank. ☐

Cash sales. ☐

(2 marks)

(i) **Complete the following statement about irrecoverable debts.**

The amount of an irrecoverable debt _____

	✓
...is calculated as a percentage of the total of trade receivables	
...always relates to a specified customer	
...increases the balance on the allowance for doubtful debts account.	

(2 marks)

Task 1.3 (15 marks)

In the exam you will be able to access relevant extracts from the AAT *Code of Professional Ethics* via a pop-up window. This information is available in the Appendix which can be found at the back of this book.

This task is based on the workplace scenario of BLM & Co.

Today's date is 28 February 20X8.

You are Sam Jones, a part-qualified Accounting Technician. You work for BLM & Co, a business which manufactures and sells sinks. BLM & Co is owned and run by Brian and Lakmani Moore in partnership.

Brian has asked you to prepare some financial statements, including a statement of cash flows, and some further documents, including a cash budget. He wants you to do this urgently. He needs to send these to the bank by the end of the week in support of a loan application. Brian tells you that obtaining the loan is very important for the survival of the business, and that the jobs of everyone in the business depend on this. So far, your studies have not covered statements of cash flows or cash budgets.

(a) **Explain the ethical issues that you face as a result of Brian's request. In your answer refer, to the conceptual framework of principles, threats and safeguards in the *Code of Professional Ethics* where relevant.**

(4 marks)

You have discussed the matter with Brian and Lakmani but they still wish you to carry out the tasks.

(b) **State the specific course of action you should take in order to remain ethical.**

(1 mark)

You receive the following email from Lakmani Moore:

To: Sam Jones <Sam.Jones@BLMCo.co.uk>

To: Sam Jones <Sam.Jones@BLMCo.co.uk>
From: Lakmani Moore <Lakmani.Moore@BLMCo.co.uk>
Date: 28/2/X8
Subject: BLM & Co: change in structure

Good morning Sam.

Brian and I are considering starting to operate the business as a limited company.

I would like you to tell me more about the advantages and disadvantages of a partnership becoming a limited company.

Please include these three sections in your response to me:

(1)   A brief description of a limited company

(2)   A summary of our position as owners if the business becomes a limited company

(3)   Explanations of one key advantage and one key disadvantage of operating as a limited company

Regards,

Lakmani

(c) **Reply to Lakmani, addressing all the points that have been raised.**

To:	
Subject:	

From: Sam Jones <Sam.Jones@BLMCo.co.uk>
Date: 28/2/X8

(10 marks)

Part 2

In this part of the assessment, you will be asked to download additional material from the internet. The material can be found at

www.bpp.com/aatspreadsheets

Task 2.1 (30 marks)

You are Sam Jones, a part-qualified accounting technician. You work for BLM & Co, a business which manufactures and sells sinks. BLM & Co is owned and run by Brian and Lakmani Moore in partnership.

You cover all aspects of bookkeeping and accounting for the business.

Today's date 27 April 20X8.

BLM & Co has suffered a computer crash. You have been asked to complete the half year sales spreadsheet for the six months ended 31 December 20X7 which was extracted immediately before the crash.

You have been given a spreadsheet which contains information relating to sales in the last six months of 20X7. It contains four worksheets: 'Invoices', 'Price list', 'Screen print' and 'BLM 1'.

Download this spreadsheet file ("Task 2.2 Assessment Data File.xls"). The spreadsheets referred to in this assessment are available for download either from the AAT website or type www.bpp.com/aatspreadsheets and follow the instructions provided. Save the spreadsheet file in the appropriate location and rename it using the following format: **'your initial-surname-AAT no – dd.mm.yy-Task2.2'**.

For example: J-Donnovan-123456-12.03xx-Task2.2

A **high degree of accuracy** is required. You **must save your work as an .XLS or .XLSX file** at regular intervals to avoid losing your work.

(a) **Open the worksheet called 'Invoices' which shows 20X7 sales invoices.**

  • **Use a Lookup function on the 'Item No' column to complete the net sales column for each invoice, using information from the 'Price List' worksheet.**

  • **Use absolute referencing to calculate the Gross Sales value of each invoice using the VAT figure provided in cell I2.**

(4 marks)

(b)   In the worksheet called 'Invoices':

- Apply the Remove Duplicates function to the whole of the completed Invoices table.

- When the Remove Duplicates dialogue box is showing – but BEFORE you the click the OK button – use the print screen function to capture evidence of your work. Then click OK in the Remove Duplicates dialogue box.

- In the 'Screen Print' worksheet paste the screenshot.

- Then return to the 'Invoices worksheet' and if there were any duplicates enter the number found in cell J2 (enter '0' if you found none).

Brian and Lakmani would like to know what the average value of their invoices were for the year.

- In cell J3 use a formula to calculate the average gross sales invoice value.

- Format the numerical data in the net and gross sales invoice columns to accounting style (two decimal places).

(5 marks)

(c)   From the 'Invoices' worksheet, produce a pivot chart and pivot table into a new worksheet of the number of 'Diamond' type sinks sold in each of the six months from July to December.

- Ensure the pivot table is sorted in chronological month order.

- Format the chart series to show highest sales for the period in black and lowest sales in red.

- Add a chart title 'Diamond Sink Sales'.

- Name this worksheet 'Diamond sinks sold'.

(6 marks)

You are now preparing the final accounts for BLM & Co for the year ended 31 December 20X7.

The statement of profit or loss for BLM & Co shows a profit for the year ended 31 December 20X7 of £250,000.

The business is still operated as a partnership.

You are given the following information arising from the partnership agreement:

- Lakmani is entitled to a salary of £25,000 per annum.

- Over the year, Brian has earned commission of £8,586 and Lakmani has earned commission of £8,500.

- Brian has taken drawings of £91,200 over the year, and Lakmani has taken £84,400.

- Interest on drawings has been calculated at £300 for Brian and £180 for Lakmani for the year ended 31 December 20X7

- The residual profit after adjustments is shared between Brian and Lakmani in the ratio 3:2.

You are required to prepare the appropriation account and current accounts for BLM & Co for the year ended 31 December 20X7.

(d) Complete the partnership appropriation statement and current accounts in the 'BLM 1' worksheet to share the profit for the year ended 31 December 20X7 between the two partners in accordance with the partnership agreement, by making the appropriate entries from the data given above.

(15 marks)

At the end of this task you should have one spreadsheet (saved as an .XLS or .XLSX file) to upload to the assessment environment. This should have six worksheets titled: 'Assessment tasks', 'Diamond sinks sold', 'Invoices', 'Price List', 'Screen print' and 'BLM 1' with information and data in them.

Below is a checklist for each task in this assessment.

As you complete each task, tick it off the list to show your progress.

Check boxes are provided for your assistance: using them does not constitute formal evidence that a task has been completed.

Completed

Lookup table and absolute referencing ☐

Duplicate removal and average values calculation ☐

Pivot chart and pivot table ☐

Partnership appropriation statement and current accounts ☐

Task 2.2 (25 marks)

You are Sam Jones, a part-qualified Accounting Technician. You work for BLM & Co, a business which manufactures and sells sinks. BLM & Co is owned and run by Brian and Lakmani Moore in partnership.

You cover all aspects of bookkeeping and accounting for the business.

You have been given a spreadsheet which contains information relating to the budgetary information for BLM & Co.

BLM & Co had originally budgeted to make and sell 5,000 sinks in the quarter to 31 March 20X8. Due to a marketing campaign, however, it actually made and sold 6,000 sinks in the quarter.

The original budget for the quarter to 31 March 20X8 is in the 'Original Budget' worksheet of the provided spreadsheet.

Today's date is 20 April 20X8.

> Download the spreadsheet file ("Task-2-1 Sample Assessment Question.xls"). The spreadsheet referred to in this assessment are available for download either from the AAT website or type www.bpp.com/aatspreadsheets and follow the instructions provided. Save the spreadsheet file in the appropriate location and rename it in the following format: **'your initial-surname-AAT no-dd.mm.yy-Task2.1'**.
>
> For example: J-Donnovan-123456-12.03.xx-Task2.1
>
> A **high degree of accuracy** is required. You **must save your work as a .XLS or .XLSX file** at regular intervals to avoid losing your work.

(a) **Open the worksheet called 'Original Budget'.**

- **In cell D1 use a formula to calculate the percentage by which to flex the original budget in light of actual activity in the quarter ended 31 March 20X8.**

- **Format cell D1 as a percentage to two decimal places (#.##%)**

- **In Column D to create a flexed budget, insert formulas to flex the revenue and costs where necessary, using absolute referencing to the percentage in cell D1.**

- **In Column E to update the actual results for the quarter use 'copy' and 'paste values' (do NOT paste link) to icopy the revenue and costs from the 'Actual Results' worksheet into the correct positions.**

(9 marks)

(b)   In the 'Original Budget' worksheet:

- Calculate the operating profit for the original, flexed budget, and actual results.

- In Column F, calculate the variances between the flexed budget and actual results, showing adverse variances as negative figures and favourable variances as positive figures.

- Insert a formula in cell F16 (the operating profit variance) to total cells F5 to F15.

(9 marks)

(c)   In the 'Original Budget' worksheet:

- Insert an IF statement in cell F18 that will show 'Agreed' if the figure for the operating profit variance is the same as the difference between the column totals for the flexed budget and actual results, and 'Check' if they do not.

- Freeze the worksheet so that the range A1:B16 always remains visible during scrolling.

(4 marks)

Brian and Lakmani have been told by the bank that their target profit for the next quarter must be £95,000. Brian wants to know by how much the cost of Direct materials 3 needs to be reduced in order to meet this target profit.

(d)   To be able to answer Brian's question, you will need to use the Goal Seek function, but you must capture the evidence of this in the worksheet called 'Screen Print' before accepting the Goal Seek answer.

- Copy all the data in the 'Original Budget' worksheet and paste (not paste-link) it into the 'Goal Seek' worksheet, starting in cell A1.

- In the 'Goal Seek' worksheet use the Goal Seek function to investigate what change in the actual Direct materials 3 cost figure (cell E8) would be required to generate an actual operating profit of £95,000 in cell E16.

- When the completed Goal Seek dialogue box is showing - but BEFORE you click the OK button - use the print screen function to capture evidence of your work and then accept the goal seek.

- In the 'Screen Print' worksheet paste the screenshot.

(3 marks)

At the end of this task you should have one spreadsheet (saved as an .XLS or .XLSX file) which in the live assessment, you will upload to the assessment environment. This should have five worksheets titled 'Original Budget', 'Assessment tasks', 'Actual Results', 'Goal seek', and 'Screen print' with information and data in them.

••

Below is a checklist for each task in this assessment.

As you complete each task, tick it off the list to show your progress.

Check boxes are provided for your assistance; using them does not constitute formal evidence that a task has been completed.

Completed

Percentage, flexed budget and actual ☐

Variances, operating profit and conditional formatting ☐

IF statement and formatting ☐

Copy values, goal function and screen print ☐

••

AAT AQ2016 ASSESSMENT 1
LEVEL 3 SYNOPTIC ASSESSMENT

ANSWERS

Advanced Diploma Synoptic Assessment (AVSY) practice assessment 1

Task 1.1

(a) Are these statements true or false?

Statement	True	False
Accountants have no duty to act in the public interest provided that they act in the interests of their employer and the accountancy profession.'		✓
The Code of Professional Ethics provides detailed rules on how to act in every possible situation that an accountant might encounter at work'.		✓

As per the AAT *Code of Professional Ethics* paragraph 100.1 accountants have 'the responsibility to act in the public interest'.

The ethical code 'provides guidance' rather than specific rules to apply in every scenario.

(b) In the table below, identify where there is conflict between the organisation's behaviour and the accountant's personal values.

Organisation's behaviour	Accountant's personal value	Is there a conflict to resolve?
Gives long-standing employees an extra half day of holiday for every two years they remain with the organisation.	Loyalty	Yes
Promotes employees on the basis of family or other close relationships	Fairness	No

The ethical code 'imposes a requirement on the member to comply with the specific provision.' (AAT *Code of Professional Ethics*: para 100.4). The accountant must provide a competent service following 'current developments in practice, legislation and techniques' (AAT *Code of Professional Ethics*: para.100.5(iii)). This latter point will mean that as a limited company must follow the legal requirements of the Companies Act 2006, and therefore,

the accountant should ensure they uphold and follows these regulations. They must comply with all regulations that affect the company.

Although the accountant is required to adopt professional behaviour, they are not required explicitly to promote the reputation, but they should 'avoid any action that brings our profession into disrepute' (AAT *Code of Professional Ethics*: para.100.5(v)), Therefore, the accountant should ensure they behave in a professional manner.

(c) Complete the following statement by selecting the correct option below.

Being offered gifts by the sales manager is _____ to the accountant's fundamental principle of _____

Options for gap 1	
An intimidation threat	
A familiarity threat	✓
Options for gap 2	
Objectivity	✓
Professional competence and due care	

(d) Are the following statements true or false?

Statement	True ✓	False ✓
The accountant may never disclose confidential information to any third party.		✓
The threat that the accountant is facing to her compliance with the fundamental principles is a self-interest threat.	✓	
The accountant must resign immediately from the company as her integrity has been compromised by the offer from the potential customer.		✓

(e) **Complete the following statement by selecting ONE of the options below.**

In relation to the evidence and documents, the accountant must be particularly careful to ensure the fundamental principle of _____is not breached when seeking guidance.

	✓
Confidentiality	✓
Professional competence and due care	
Professional behaviour	

(f) **Complete the following statement by selecting ONE of the options below.**

The accountant has committed the criminal offence of_____.

	✓
Money laundering	
Failure to disclose	
Tipping off	✓

(g) **Complete the following statement by selecting ONE of the options below.**

The accountant should disclose confidential information on this matter directly to_____

	✓
The Nominated Officer	
The National Crime Agency	✓
HMRC	

Under the Proceeds of Crime Act (2002) there is an obligation to disclose. A person may be committing a criminal offence if they fail to disclose as soon as is practical. In this case, making an authorised disclosure is the appropriate action to take. An authorised disclosure is when the person who has become involved makes the disclosure when they realise they have been or are going to be involved in money laundering.

Task 1.2

(a) **After the journals are processed, what will be the revised balance carried down on the VAT account?**

£	64,515.63

Workings

VAT control account

		£			£
06/02	Cash book	60,880.98	01/01	Balance b/d	60,880.98
31/03	Purchases day book	99,120.25	31/03	Sales day book	161,728.27
31/03	Sales returns day book	3,529.57	31/03	Purchases returns day book	2,403.68
				Purchases returns day book (journal)	**50.00**
31/03	Balance c/d	64,515.63		Sales day book (journal)	2,983.50
		228,046.43			228,046.43

(b) **Complete the following sentence by selecting ONE of the options below.**

This balance will appear on the _____side of the trial balance

	✓
Credit	✓
Debit	

(c) **Applying the conceptual framework from the ethical code, which ONE of the following describes the situation faced by Jed Malone when recording sales to his brothers company?**

A self-review threat to professional competence and due care. ☐

A familiarity threat to objectivity. ☑

An intimidation threat to professional behaviour. ☐

There is a risk that Jed may be put in a position whereby he can unduly influence the prices or service that another business may receive due to the close family connections between him and his brother's business.

(d) **What should be your next action?**

Send a Suspicious Activity Report to the National Crime Agency ☐

Tell Brian and Lakmani about your concerns. ☑

Internal reporting should always be the first step in any suspicion of unethical behaviour.

(e) **Which of the following should be your next action?**

Resign from BLM & Co. ☐

Request that the visit by the VAT officer is postponed. ☑

Agree to deal with the VAT officer in line with ☐
your employers' instructions.

The reasonable first step would be to request that the visit is postponed as you do not believe that you have the required level of knowledge and experience. Every member of the AAT should ensure that they have sufficient 'attainment of professional competence' (AAT *Code of Professional Ethics*: para. 130.2).

(f) **Complete the sales ledger control account below, by including the four options in the appropriate column AND enter the totals to reconstruct the sales ledger control account for the three months ended 31 March 20X7.**

Sales ledger control account

	£		£
Balance b/d	492,409	Cash book	934,076
Sales day book	970,370	Sales returns day book	21,177
		Journal (irrecoverable debt)	4,330
		Balance c/d	487,354
Total	1,462,779	**Total**	1,446,937

(g) **Calculate the missing figure in the sales ledger control account.**

£	15,842

Workings

	£		£
Balance b/d	492,409	Cash book	934,076
Sales day book	970,370	Sales returns day book	21,177
		Journal (irrecoverable debt)	4,330
		Balance c/d	487,354
		Balancing figure	15,842
Total	1,462,779	**Total**	1,462,779

(h) **Which of the following could the missing figure represent?**

Discounts allowed. ☑

Cheque from customer returned unpaid by the bank. ☐

Cash sales. ☐

Discounts allowed would be the only credit adjustment available here. Cash sales are not put through the sales ledger control account.

Cheque returned unpaid would increase the accounts receivable balance (therefore being a debit entry in the control account).

(i) **Complete the following statement about irrecoverable debts.**

The amount of an irrecoverable debt _____

	✓
...is calculated as a percentage of the total of trade receivables	
...always relates to a specified customer	✓
...increases the balance on the allowance for doubtful debts account.	

Task 1.3

(a) I do not have the experience, expertise (knowledge and skills), or time to complete the tasks properly.

It would be a breach of the principles of professional competence and due care, and integrity, to attempt to do so immediately.

I am facing familiarity, intimidation and self-interest threats because the partners of BLM & Co are trying to appeal to my loyalty to colleagues and fear of losing my job.

I need to apply relevant safeguards to bring the threat to my principles down to an acceptable level.

(b) I would tell Brian and Lakmani that I can only complete the tasks they have requested if I have additional training/qualified support/supervision to do so (which will take time).

OR

I would tell Brian and Lakmani that I cannot undertake the task competently so it should be given to someone else.

225

(c)

To: Lakmani Moore Lakmani.Moore@BLMCo.co.uk
Subject: BLM & Co: change in structure

Hello Lakmani

Thank you for your email of 28/2/X8.

(1)   **A limited company** is a business structure which is a separate legal entity distinct from its owners (known as shareholders). It needs to be registered at Companies House. A company's accounts and finances are separate from the personal finances of its owners.

(2)   A company is **owned by shareholders**, who have equity shares in the company. Persons acting as directors are responsible for running the company. A company must have at least one shareholder and at least one director. You and Brian can remain as the only owners if you own all the shares in the company between you; your ownership will be diluted if you include more shareholders. You can continue to run the company, acting as its only directors, or you may appoint additional directors.

Directors may be paid a salary by the company from its pre-tax profits. Shareholders may receive dividends paid from its after-tax profits. Any after-tax profits that are not paid out as dividends are reinvested in the company on the shareholders behalf.

(3)   The key **advantage** of operating as a limited company is that of limited liability for the owners. While you as partners in BLM & Co currently have unlimited liability for all the debts of the business, shareholders' liability for any unpaid debts of the company is limited and they only stand to lose their investment in shares. The company as a separate legal entity remains fully liable for its debts.

The key **disadvantage** of operating as a limited company is that companies are heavily regulated. There are a number of accounting regulations involved with running a limited company, and the statutory requirements of the Companies Act 2006 apply, as do accounting standards. This means that there is a much greater administrative burden than for a partnership. A company must file accounts each year before a certain date and it must file documents when it is set up. All this extra administration bears a cost.

I hope this is useful to you. Please contact me if you have any questions.

Kind regards

Sam

Task 2.1

Invoices worksheet:

BLM & Co

20X7 sales of sinks for the last 6 months of trading through various outlets

	VAT	20%		2
	Average Gross Invoice Value			£4,951.56

Assessors - this cell should show 2 duplicates

Assessors: this cell should show the formula =AVERAGE(I7:I390)

Type	Description	Item No	Quality Sol	When	Where	Invoice N	Net Sale		Gross sales	
Jade	1 Bowl & drainer	35698	46	July	Internet	281762	£	5,842.00	£	7,010.40
Jade	1 Bowl & drainer	35698	47	July	Direct	281763	£	5,969.00	£	7,162.80
Jade	1 Bowl & drainer	35698	34	July	Jones & Co	281764	£	4,318.00	£	5,181.60
Jade	1 Bowl & drainer	35698	42	July	Elders	281765	£	5,334.00	£	6,400.80
Jade	1 Bowl & drainer	35698	11	July	Brinks	281766	£	1,397.00	£	1,676.40
Jade	1 Bowl & drainer	35698	44	July	Ables	281767	£	5,588.00	£	6,705.60
Jade	1 Bowl & drainer	35698	39	July	Elways	281768	£	4,953.00	£	5,943.60
Jade	1 Bowl & drainer	35698	43	July	Zeebras	281769	£	5,461.00	£	6,553.20
Emerald	1 Bowl reversible drainer	28654	13	July	Internet	281722	£	1,612.00	£	1,934.40
Emerald	1 Bowl reversible drainer	28654	12	July	Direct	281723	£	1,488.00	£	1,785.60
Emerald	1 Bowl reversible drainer	28654	6	July	Jones & Co	281724	£	744.00	£	892.80
Emerald	1 Bowl reversible drainer	28654	49	July	Elders	281725	£	6,076.00	£	7,291.20
Emerald	1 Bowl reversible drainer	28654	12	July	Brinks	281726	£	1,488.00	£	1,785.60
Emerald	1 Bowl reversible drainer	28654	11	July	Ables	281727	£	1,364.00	£	1,636.80
Emerald	1 Bowl reversible drainer	28654	39	July	Elways	281728	£	4,836.00	£	5,803.20
Emerald	1 Bowl reversible drainer	28654	8	July	Zeebras	281729	£	992.00	£	1,190.40
Diamond	1 cubic bowl & drainer	28457	37	July	Internet	281730	£	6,105.00	£	7,326.00
Diamond	1 cubic bowl & drainer	28457	15	July	Direct	281731	£	2,475.00	£	2,970.00
Diamond	1 cubic bowl & drainer	28457	48	July	Jones & Co	281732	£	7,920.00	£	9,504.00
Diamond	1 cubic bowl & drainer	28457	24	July	Elders	281733	£	3,960.00	£	4,752.00
Diamond	1 cubic bowl & drainer	29457	16	July	Brinks	281734	£	2,640.00	£	3,168.00
Diamond	1 cubic bowl & drainer	28457	25	July	Ables	281735	£	4,125.00	£	4,950.00
Diamond	1 cubic bowl & drainer	28457	37	July	Elways	281736	£	6,105.00	£	7,326.00
Diamond	1 cubic bowl & drainer	28457	25	July	Zeebras	281737	£	4,125.00	£	4,950.00
Quartz	1 square reversible	28791	48	July	Internet	281745	£	6,528.00	£	7,833.60
Quartz	1 square reversible	28791	15	July	Direct	281747	£	2,040.00	£	2,448.00
Quartz	1 square reversible	28791	30	July	Jones & Co	281748	£	4,080.00	£	4,896.00
Quartz	1 square reversible	28791	21	July	Elders	281749	£	2,856.00	£	3,427.20
Quartz	1 square reversible	28791	43	July	Brinks	281750	£	5,848.00	£	7,017.60

Assessors - check this cell it should show =D17(VLOOKUP(C17,'Price list'!$A$5:$D$12,4,FALSE))*

*Assessors: ensure this cell contains an absolute reference formula e.g. =H17*$I$2+H17*

Screen print worksheet:

BLM & Co

20X7 sales of sinks for the last 6 months of trading through various outlets

Type	Description	Item No	Sold	When	Where	Invoice No	Net			VAT	20%	
Jade	1 Bowl & drainer	35698		46 July	Internet	281762	£					
Jade	1 Bowl & drainer	35698	9	47 July	Direct	281763						
Jade	1 Bo		9									
Jade	1 Bo		9									
Jade	1 Bo		9									
Jade	1 Bo											
Jade	1 Bowl & drainer	3569										
Jade	1 Bowl & drainer	3569										
Emerald	1 Bowl reversible drainer	2865										
Emerald	1 Bowl reversible drainer	2865										
Emerald	1 Bowl reversible drainer	2865										
Emerald	1 Bowl reversible drainer	2865										
Emerald	1 Bowl reversible drainer	2865										
Emerald	1 Bowl reversible drainer	2865										
Emerald	1 Bowl reversible drainer	2865										
Emerald	1 Bowl reversible drainer	2865										
Diamond	1 cubic bowl & drainer	28457		37 July	Internet	281730	£					
Diamond	1 cubic bowl & drainer	28457		15 July	Direct	281731	£					
Diamond	1 cubic bowl & drainer	28457		48 July	Jones & Co	281732	£					

Assessors this should show the "Select all" box highlighted

Remove Duplicates

To delete duplicate values, select one or more columns that contain duplicates.

Select All   Unselect All

☑ My data has headers

Columns
☑ Type
☑ Description
☑ Item No
☑ Sold
☑ When

OK   Cancel

Assessors- this should show all columns selected and the use of the "Remove Duplicates" dialogue box.

Diamonds sink sold worksheet:

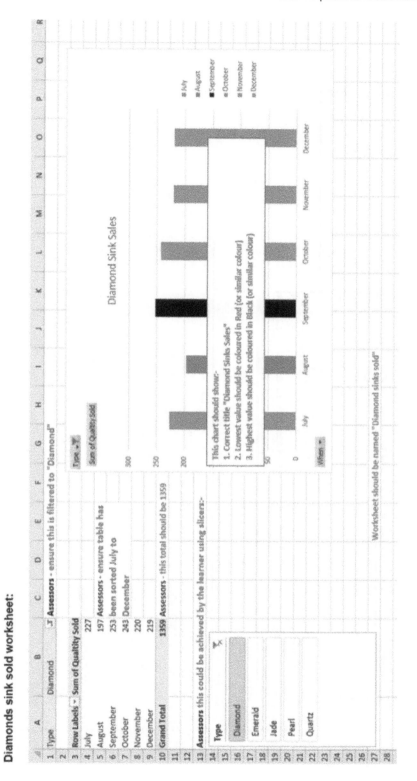

	A	B	C	D	E	F	G
1	Type	Diamond	**Assessors** - ensure this is filtered to "Diamond"				
2							
3	Row Labels	Sum of Quality Sold				Type	
4	July	227	**Assessors** - ensure table has			Sum of Quality Sold	
5	August	197					
6	September	253	been sorted July to				
7	October	243	December				
8	November	220					
9	December	219					
10	Grand Total	1359	**Assessors** - this total should be 1359				

Assessors this could be achieved by the learner using slicers:-

Type
- Diamond
- Emerald
- Jade
- Pearl
- Quartz

Diamond Sink Sales

This chart should show:-
1. Correct title "Diamond Sinks Sales"
2. Lowest value should be coloured in Red (or similar colour)
3. Highest value should be coloured in Black (or similar colour)

July   August   September   October   November   December

- July
- August
- September
- October
- November
- December

Worksheet should be named "Diamond sinks sold"

BLM 1 worksheet:

Partnership appropriation statement for year ended 31 December 20X7

	Brian	Lakmani	Total
Profit for the year			£250,000
Salary		£25,000	£25,000
Interest on drawings	£300	£180	£480
Commission	£8,586	£8,500	£17,086
Residual profit available for appropriation			£208,394
Profit share	£125,036	£83,358	£208,394
Total amount distributed to each partner	£133,322	£116,678	£250,000

Assessors: check that formulas have been used to provide totals.

Partnership current accounts for year ended 31 December 20X7

	Brian Debit	Lakmani Debit	Brian Credit	Lakmani Credit
Balance brought down			£1,200	£3,200
Salary				£25,000
Drawings	£91,200	£84,400		
Interest on drawings	£300	£180		
Commission			£8,586	£8,500
Profit share			£125,036	£83,358
Balance carried down	£43,322	£35,478		
	£134,822	£120,058	£134,822	£120,058

Assessors: check formula has been used for balancing figures

Task 2.2

Screen print worksheet:

Paste your Goal Seek screen print here

Assessor If Goal Seek is correctly applied BEFORE accepting the result you should see this screen print.

20.00%

BLM & Co: original budget for quarter ended 31 March 20X8

Item		Original Budget £	Flexed Budget £	Actual Results £	Variances £
Revenue		£800,000.00	£960,000.00	£975,000.00	£15,000.00
Materials:	Direct materials 1	£90,000.00	£108,000.00	£105,000.00	£3,000.00
Materials:	Direct materials 2	£110,000.00	£132,000.00	£125,000.00	£7,000.00
Materials:	Direct materials 3	£140,000.00	£168,000.00	£164,700.00	£3,300.00
Direct labour:	Skilled	£30,000.00	£36,000.00	£35,000.00	£1,000.00
Direct labour:	Unskilled	£70,000.00	£84,000.00	£81,500.00	£2,500.00
Variable overheads:	Supervision	£42,000.00	£50,400.00	£49,000.00	£1,400.00
Variable overheads:	Quality Control	£60,000.00	£72,000.00	£70,000.00	£2,000.00
Variable overheads:	Production planning	£55,000.00	£66,000.00	£60,000.00	£6,000.00
Fixed overheads:	Administration	£80,000.00	£80,000.00	£85,000.00	-£5,000.00
Fixed overheads:	Selling and distribution	£90,000.00	£90,000.00	£110,000.00	-£20,000.00
Operating Profit		£33,000.00	£73,600.00	£89,600.00	£16,200.00

Agreed

Goal Seek

Set cell: E16
To value: 95000
By changing cell: $E$6

OK   Cancel

If Screen Print taken AFTER Goal Seek - you should just see this screen print.

Goal Seek Status

Goal Seeking with Cell E16 found a solution.

Target value: 95000
Current value: £95,000.00

OK

Step   Pause   Cancel

Goal seek worksheet:

BLM & Co: original budget for quarter ended 31 March 20X8

		Original Budget £	Flexed Budget £ (20.00%)	Actual Results £	Variances £
Item					
Revenue		£800,000.00	£960,000.00	£975,000.00	£15,000.00
Materials:	Direct materials 1	£90,000.00	£108,000.00	£105,000.00	£3,000.00
Materials:	Direct materials 2	£110,000.00	£132,000.00	£125,000.00	£7,000.00
Materials:	Direct materials 3	£140,000.00	£168,000.00	£159,500.00	£8,500.00
Direct labour:	Skilled	£30,000.00	£36,000.00	£35,000.00	£1,000.00
Direct labour:	Unskilled	£70,000.00	£84,000.00	£81,500.00	£2,500.00
Variable overheads:	Supervision	£42,000.00	£50,400.00	£49,000.00	£1,400.00
Variable overheads:	Quality Control	£60,000.00	£72,000.00	£70,000.00	£2,000.00
Variable overheads:	Production planning	£55,000.00	£66,000.00	£60,000.00	£6,000.00
Fixed overheads:	Administration	£80,000.00	£80,000.00	£85,000.00	-£5,000.00
Fixed overheads:	Selling and distribution	£90,000.00	£90,000.00	£110,000.00	-£20,000.00
Operating Profit		£33,000.00	£73,600.00	£95,000.00	£21,400.00

Assessor if Goal Seek is correctly applied this cell should show £95,000.00 check screen print

Assessor - this cell should show £159,500.00 if Goal seek correctly applied - check Screen Print

Agreed

Original Budget worksheet:

Assessor - this cell should have a formula =(6000-5000)/5000 showing 20.00% or if different formula could show 120.00%

Assessor this value should be £15,000.00

Assessor - F6:F15 should all be calculated as eg D6-E6

Assessor - ensure the cells D5:D13 are absolute referenced to D1 (=C5*$D$1+C5)

Assessor - ensure this cell shows £966,000.00

Assessor - this cell should have a formula like =C5-(SUM(C6:C15)) and contain the value £33,000.00

Assessor - ensure the Fixed overheads are not flexed in cells D14 and D15

Assessor - this cell should show "Agreed" with an IF formula =IF((E16-D16)=F16,"Agreed","Check")

Assessor - you should not be able to scroll up into Rows 1:15. Or into Columns A or B

			D			
1						
2			20.00%			
3	**BLM & Co: original budget for quarter ended 31 March 20X8**					
4	Item		Original Budget £	Flexed Budget £	Actual Results £	Variances £
5	Revenue		£800,000.00	£960,000.00	£975,000.00	£15,000.00
6	Materials:	Direct materials 1	£90,000.00	£108,000.00	£105,000.00	£3,000.00
7	Materials:	Direct materials 2	£110,000.00	£132,000.00	£125,000.00	£7,000.00
8	Materials:	Direct materials 3	£140,000.00	£168,000.00	£164,700.00	£3,300.00
9	Direct labour	Skilled		£36,000.00	£35,000.00	£1,000.00
10	Direct labour	Unskilled		£84,000.00		£2,500.00
11	Variable overheads:	Supervision		£50,400.00		£1,400.00
12	Variable overheads:	Quality Control		£72,000.00		£2,000.00
13	Variable overheads:	Production planning	£55,000.00	£66,000.00	£60,000.00	£6,000.00
14	Fixed overheads:	Administration	£80,000.00	£80,000.00	£85,000.00	-£5,000.00
15	Fixed overheads:	Selling and distribution	£90,000.00	£90,000.00	£110,000.00	-£20,000.00
16	Operating Profit		£33,000.00	£73,600.00	£89,800.00	£16,200.00
17						
18					Agreed	

AAT AQ2016 ASSESSMENT 2
LEVEL 3 SYNOPTIC ASSESSMENT

You are advised to attempt the AAT Practice Assessments online from the AAT website. This will ensure you are prepared for how the assessment will be presented on the AAT's system when you attempt the real assessment. The assessments are called:
Practice CBT 1 *and* ***Practice CBT 2****, with the assessments using the AAT software and downloadable spreadsheet files for tasks 2.1 and 2.2. Please note that these are not marked, however, AAT provide pdf versions of the answers for you to review your responses.*
Please access the assessment using the address below:

https://www.aat.org.uk/training/study-support/search

The AAT may call the assessments on their website, under Study support resources, either a 'practice assessment' or 'sample assessment'.

AAT AQ2016 SAMPLE ASSESSMENT 2

BPP PRACTICE ASSESSMENT 1
LEVEL 3 SYNOPTIC ASSESSMENT

**Time allowed: 2 hours and 45 minutes
(plus 15 minutes to upload your answers)**

PRACTICE ASSESSMENT 1

BPP PRACTICE ASSESSMENT 1
LEVEL 3 SYNOPTIC ASSESSMENT

Time allowed: 3 hours and 45 minutes
(plus 15 minutes to upload your answers)

Advanced Diploma Synoptic Assessment (AVSY)
BPP practice assessment 1

Task 1.1 (15 marks)

The following statements have been made by trainee accountants in relation to the AAT *Code of Professional Ethics* and the fundamental principles.

(a) **Show whether the below statements are true or false?**

Statement	True	False
'It doesn't matter whether or not people might think my actions are unethical, it is whether or not I actually am that counts'.		
'As long as I comply with the principle of integrity, compliance with the other principles will be implied as a result'.		
'The ethical code applies to my role as a professional and my working life. My private life, on the other hand, is just that – private!'		
'As a professional accountant, it is more important for me to be ethical as I work in the public interest.'		

(4 marks)

Professional accountants are required to undertake continuing professional development (CPD).

(b) Show whether or not the *Code of Professional Ethics* specifically requires an AAT member to take each of the following actions in order to act in line with the principle of objectivity.

Statement	True	False
As an accountant in practice, if a member undertakes services for two clients working in the same industry, the member must always resign from one of the engagements.		
If a member has a family relative working in a managerial position at a company they provide services for, the member should alert their line manager.		
Your close friend, Jill, has become a director at one of the clients you work for. It is recommended that an alternative manager at your firm works with Jill's business instead.		

(3 marks)

Marion, a professional accountant in practice, gives Larch Ltd an opinion on the application of accounting principles to the company's specific transactions. Marion knew that she was forming her opinion on the basis of inadequate information.

(c) Which ONE of the following fundamental principles have been breached by Marion.

Action	
Confidentiality	
Professional competence and due care	
Fairness	

(2 marks)

Dipika is an accountant employed by Natural Beauty, a company which develops, manufactures and sells luxury bath and body products. One of the company's top selling products is a body polish which it claims uses all natural ingredients. The exfoliating quality of the polish is achieved using sea salt and fine sand.

During the course of her work, Dipika discovers that, in order to reduce costs, the company has begun to replace some of the sand with microbeads. Microbeads are tiny plastic beads which pollute both the ocean and the food chain for human consumption. The use of microbeads in banned in a number of countries, but they have not yet been banned by the country in which Natural Beauty operates. They are not 'natural' ingredients and the packaging has not been updated to reflect this.

(d)   Show whether the below statements are true or false?

Statement	True	False
Natural Beauty may have broken the law.		
Natural Beauty has acted unethically.		

(2 marks)

(e)   Which ONE of the below actions should Dipika now take?

Action	✓
Take the issue directly to the press as it is in the public interest to disclose this via the media	
She should do nothing, the issue is not of a financial nature and therefore outside the scope of her expertise and ethical requirements	
Discuss the findings with her immediate manager and share her concerns regarding the company's use of microbeads	

(2 marks)

(f) **If Dipika discloses this issue through appropriate channels, either internally or externally, would any protection against dismissal be offered to Dipika under the Public Information Disclosure Act 1998 (PIDA)?**

Action	✓
No, as disclosure of the matter would be inappropriate in this situation.	
Yes, as she has reasonable grounds to believe that the environment is being damaged and disclosure was made in good faith.	
No, PIDA only protects individuals who are disclosing serious organised crimes such as money laundering.	

(2 marks)

Task 1.2 (15 marks)

The tasks are based on the following workplace scenario of Clodlands, a partnership

You are Paula, a part-qualified accounting technician employed by Radcliffe & Rutherfords, an accountancy firm.

Friends Chipo and Charlie have recently begun to trade through a new partnership, Clodlands which owns and lets several areas of land including two houses.

On reviewing Clodland's sales day books, you have found three errors:

Sales ledger control account

		£			£
01/06	Balance b/d	32,300	Bank and cash	30/06	23,500
30/06	Sales	17,800			
			Balance c/d		26,600
		50,100			50,100

- A sales invoice of £2,700 had not been posted as sales on 29 June

- A customer who owed £3,600 had been declared bankrupt on 25 June, and it is unlikely that the debt will be recovered.

- An error was made by the credit control clerk, which meant that a cash receipt for an invoice was incorrectly recorded as £1,730, when the invoice was actually for £1,370

You prepare journals to correct these errors.

(a) **What is the journal to correct the error made by the credit controller?**

		£
Debit	▼	360
Credit	▼	360

Picklist:

Trade receivable
Bank and cash
Sales day book
Sales returns book

(2 marks)

(b) **Which of the following correctly describes the type of error made by the credit control clerk?**

	✓
Error of omission	
Error of original entry	
Error of commission	
Error of principle	

(2 marks)

(c) In order to account for the irrecoverable debt, which side of the sales ledger control account will the entry be accounted for?

	✓
Debit	
Credit	

(1 mark)

(d) What is the revised carried down balance after the correction of the errors on the sales ledger control account as at 30 June?

£ [   ]

(2 marks)

(e) Which ONE of the following statements about a Limited Liability Partnership is NOT correct?

Description	✓
An LLP is a separate legal entity.	
The LLP must be registered with the Registrar of Companies.	
There is no upper limit to the number of partners a LLP can have.	
The LLP must file annual returns, accounts and an annual corporation tax return.	

(2 marks)

You have discovered that Charlie has been charging VAT on invoices, even though Clodlands is not yet registered for VAT. When questioned, he declared that he 'didn't see the problem as Clodlands paid VAT on supplier invoices anyway'. You have informed Chipo, but she does not mind either.

(f) **Complete the following statement by selecting ONE of the options below.**

The accountant should disclose this information NEXT to which of the following parties?

	✓
The Nominated Officer at Radcliffe's and Rutherfords	
HMRC	
National Crime Agency	

(2 marks)

You discover that Charlie has begun training for his AAT qualification and has signed up as a student with the AAT.

(g) **Which ONE of the following statements is correct about AAT disciplinary procedures?**

	✓
Charlie will not be exposed to disciplinary proceedings because he has not taken all of his exams yet.	
The Code of Professional Ethics is only enforceable for fully qualified members of the AAT.	
Charlie may disciplined if he fails to comply with AAT CPD requirements	

(2 marks)

(h) **Complete the following sentence by selecting the correct word from the picklist.**

The AAT has a Continuing Professional Development (CPD) cycle which comprises four steps.

These are assess, plan, [▼] and evaluate

Picklist:

action
consider
engage
mitigate

(2 marks)

Task 1.3 (15 marks)

It is Monday morning when the partner, Mr Rutherford, calls you into his office for a private meeting. He explains that he has a number of expenses relating to personal expenditure that he would like to put through the company's books of accounts. He hands you a file containing a year's worth of private bank statements and requests you to identify any expenditure relating to his expensive family holidays and post as an expense to the business travel account.

Your response is you have learnt at college that only valid business expenditure should be recorded through the business's books of account. However, his reasoning is that the holidays are there to help him relax from the stress of running a business so it is only fair this is recorded as a business expense.

The director implies that as a thank you he may able to obtain two tickets for two seats for the finals at a tennis tournament. When you return to your desk you complete an Internet search and are surprised to discover these tickets are currently selling in excess of £500 each.

(a) Outline any potential ethical issues that this work request can bring. In your answer refer to the *Code of Professional Ethics* highlighting specific threats that may apply.

(6 marks)

(b) **State your decision regarding the request from the partner and state any further action you would be required to take.**

(2 marks)

You have received the following email from one of your colleagues:

To: You@.accounts

From: Colleague@.accounts

Hi,

I am a new joiner at the partnership and will be working on the partnership end of year financial statements. I have just started my accountancy studies and have only covered sole traders. We have not covered the types of accounts and financial statements used in partnerships. This is all new to me!

Please can you help me get started?

Kind regards,

Colleague

(c) **Reply to your colleague outlining the accounts and statements used in a partnership arrangement. Your answer should be suitable for someone with no knowledge of partnerships.**

(7 marks)

Task 2.1 (25 marks)

You are Sarah-Jane Smith, a part-qualified accounting technician. You work for Winter Co, which manufactures and installs bathrooms.

You cover all aspects of bookkeeping and accounting for the business. You report to Emma Neesome, the Chief Finance Officer.

Today's date is 15 October 20X1.

Emma has asked you to do some breakeven analysis, based on the budgeted figures for the next quarter. Forecast sales are 5,000 units and sales price is £300. Cost figures are as follows:

	£
Direct materials	400,000
Direct labour	200,000
Assembly	300,000
Installation	450,000

60% of assembly costs and 80% of installation costs are variable.

Emma has told you the company's target margin of safety is 30% and its target profit is £140,000.

Download the spreadsheet file "WinterCo PA1.xlsx" from the www.bpp.com/aatspreadsheets. Save the spreadsheet file in the appropriate location and rename it in the following format: 'your initial-surname-AAT no-dd.mm.yy-Task2.1'. For example: H-Darch-123456-12.03.xx-Task2.1

A **high degree of accuracy** is required. You must **save your work as an .XLS or.XLSX file** at regular intervals to avoid losing your work.

(a) **Open the renamed file. Calculate total revenue and enter it in cell B2.**

(b) **Enter total direct materials in cell B4 and total direct labour in cell B5.**

(c) **Calculate variable assembly and packaging costs and enter them in cells B6 and B7.**

(d) **Calculate total variable costs and enter them in cell B8.**

(e) **Calculate variable costs per unit, using the budgeted sales volume of 5,000, and enter it in cell B9.**

(f) **Calculate contribution per unit, using the budgeted sales price of £300, and enter it in cell B10.**

(g) **Calculate fixed assembly and packaging costs and enter them in cells B12 and B13.**

(h) **Calculate total fixed costs and enter them in cell B14.**

(i) Calculate the breakeven point in units and enter it in cell B15, giving your answer to the nearest unit. Use conditional formatting to show this figure in green if it is less than the budgeted sales volume and red if it is more than the budgeted sales volume.

(j) Calculate the breakeven point in revenue terms and enter it in cell B16.

(k) Calculate the contribution/sales ratio and enter it in cell B17, showing it to 2 decimal places.

(l) Calculate the margin of safety in units and enter it in cell B18, giving your answer to the nearest unit.

(m) Calculate the margin of safety in % terms and enter it in cell B19, showing it to 2 decimal places. Highlight this figure with a yellow background and black border. Put an IF statement in cell C19 to show HIGHER if it is greater than the target margin of safety of 30%, LOWER if it is less than the target margin of safety.

(n) Calculate the volume of sales needed to achieve the target profit of £140,000 and enter it in cell B20, giving your answer to the nearest unit. Highlight this figure with a yellow background and black border. Put an IF statement in cell C20 to show LESS if the budgeted sales volume of 5,000 units is lower than the volume of sales needed to achieve the target profit, MORE if the budgeted sales volume is higher.

(o) Perform a spell check and ensure that the contents of all cells can be seen.

(p) Draft an email to do the following:

   • Comment on the results of your calculations.
   • Give two problems with breakeven analysis.

To:	Emma Neesome
From:	Sarah-Jane Smith
Date:	15 October 20X1
Subject:	Breakeven analysis

Task 2.2 (30 marks)

You are preparing the final accounts of a sole trader trading as Most Lotus and have been given the following draft trial balance.

Most Lotus

Open the "PA1 Most Lotus Task 2.2 QUESTION.xlsx" spreadsheet and save in an appropriate location using the following format **'your initial-surname-PA1 task 2.1'**

You should aim for a **high degree of accuracy.** You **should save your work as an .XLS or .XLSX file** at regular intervals to avoid losing your work.

Most Lotus has drafted their trial balance, however, there remains a balance on the suspense account. They have asked you to clear the suspense account, draft an extended trial balance clearly showing the adjustments and finally complete their financial statements.

The following information is also available

- The depreciation charge for the year for motor vehicles (£1,500) and fixture and fittings (£250) was correctly posted to the accumulated depreciation account, however, no expense has been posted in the statement of profit or loss.

- Coultard Co paid an invoice of £300 in respect of an invoice from Most Lotus on 31 January. This has not been reflected in the accounts receivable or the bank.

- A purchase invoice in respect of electricity charges was incorrectly posted to the electricity expense account as £850. The correct amount of £580 was posted to the purchase ledger.

Requirements

(a) **Prepare an extended trial balance to show the draft trial balance, the adjustments made to the draft trial balance and the final positions (which will be used to populate the financial statements.**

- Correct the errors and clear the suspense account on the ETB

- Insert the adjustments into the ETB, and using appropriate formula, finalise the numbers in columns

- Ensure the figures balance by using the SUM formula to total up the columns F and G.

- Label this tab 'ETB' and colour it blue.

(10 marks)

(b)   You are required to prepare the following for Most Lotus for the year ended 31 January 20X6 using the ETB you have extended:

- a statement of profit and loss; and
- a statement of financial position

Prepare your statements on separate worksheets.

Your statements should be prepared using appropriate formula and formatted in the following manner:

- All headings in bold using size 12 font
- Figures to be presented with thousand separators and no decimals
- Headings merged and centred over their respective columns
- Currency (£) symbol entered to denote currency columns
- Use top and double bottom borders on totals

Statement of profit or loss

- Name your statement of profit or loss account worksheet tab SPL and format tab in yellow
- Insert the figures of the sales revenue, cost of sales and discounts received by linking to the ETB worksheet.
- Insert the remaining expense figures (below the gross profit figure) directly into the spreadsheet.
- Use appropriate formula to calculate the gross profit, sub-total of expenses and net profit figures in the SPL.
- Apply conditional formatting to highlight any expenses in the SPL in excess of £10,000 with a light red fill. Note, this only applies to the expenses below the gross profit line.
- Using appropriate formula in cell H22, calculate the net profit as a percentage of sales revenue to two decimal places.

Statement of financial position

- Name your statement of financial position worksheet tab SOFP and format tab in green
- In rows 1-3 insert the organisation name, 'statement of financial position' and details of the period ending.

- In cells B7, C7 and D7 enter the headers 'At cost', 'Acc depn' and 'Carrying amount'. Ensure the text fits in the cells by adjusting the font to wrap the text in those three cells. Enter the information for non-current assets, splitting out the types of asset by category in rows 9 and 10.

- Complete the rest of the statement of financial position, using suitable headings and layout.

- Use formula to calculate the subtotals and totals.

- Ensure the headers for 'net current assets' and 'net assets' are in bold and block capital letters.

(17 marks)

The owner is concerned regarding the cash flow of the business and has asked you to prepare a 2-D pie chart to show the current assets of the business.

(c) You are required to prepare a 2-D pie chart to clearly show the requested current asset information.

- To the right of your statement of financial position statement prepare a 2-D pie chart to show the split of the current assets of the business.

- Title your chart Most Lotus Current Assets and ensure your chart has an appropriate legend.

Finally resave your spreadsheet as 'your initial-surname-PA1 task 2.2 finished'

(3 marks)

....

BPP PRACTICE ASSESSMENT 1
LEVEL 3 SYNOPTIC ASSESSMENT

ANSWERS

Advanced Diploma Synoptic Assessment (AVSY) BPP practice assessment 1

Task 1.1 (15 marks)

(a)

Statement	True	False
'It doesn't matter whether or not people might think my actions are unethical, it is whether or not I actually am that counts.'		✓
'As long as I comply with the principle of integrity, compliance with the other principles will be implied as a result.'		✓
'The ethical code applies to my role as a professional and my working life. My private life, on the other hand, is just that – private!'		✓
'As a professional accountant, it is more important for me to be ethical as I work in the public interest.'	✓	

(b)

	True	False
As an accountant in practice, if a member undertakes services for two clients working in the same industry, the member must always resign from one of the engagements.		✓
If a member has a family relative working in a managerial position at a company they provide services for, the member should alert their line manager.	✓	
Your close friend, Jill, has become a director at one of the clients you work for. It is recommended that an alternative manager at your firm works with Jill's business instead.		✓

Resignation would only be required if no other safeguard as available to the member. Alternative safeguards would be required and the clients made aware.

There is a familiarity threat to the member's objectivity and this should be raised with the manager internally in the first instance.

Even though work discussions may not take place, a member should be seen to be maintaining the principle of objectivity, so safeguards should be put in place to show that no breach can occur.

(c)

Action	Yes/No
Confidentiality	No
Professional competence and due care	Yes
Fairness	No

Confidentiality and fairness are Nolan Principles

(d)

Statement	True	False
Natural Beauty may have broken the law.		✓
Natural Beauty has acted unethically.	✓	

The replacement of one of the ingredients is not against the law in the country that Natural Beauty operates, however, by misleading their customers and not informing them of the substitution this can be deemed to be unethical behaviour. As Natural Beauty claims to use all natural ingredients this is not the behaviour that their customers would expect from the business.

(e)

Action	✓
Take the issue directly to the press as it is in the public interest to disclose this via the media.	
She should do nothing, the issue is not of a financial nature and therefore outside the scope of her expertise and ethical requirements.	
Discuss the findings with her immediate manager and share her concerns regarding the company's use of microbeads.	✓

Dipka should discuss her concerns with her immediate supervisor in the first instance before any further action is taken.

(f)

Action	✓
No, as disclosure of the matter would be inappropriate in this situation.	
Yes, as she has reasonable grounds to believe that the environment is being damaged and disclosure was made in good faith.	✓
No, PIDA only protects individuals who are disclosing serious organised crimes such as money laundering.	

Task 1.2 (15 marks)

(a)

		£
Debit	Trade receivable	360
Credit	Bank and cash	360

(b)

Description	✓
Error of commission	
Error of original entry	✓
Error of omission	
One-sided entry	

(c)

	✓
Debit	
Credit	✓

(d)

£	26,060

Workings

		£			£
01/06	Balance b/d	32,300	Bank and cash	30/06	23,500
30/06	Sales	17,800	Irrecoverable debt		3,600
	Sales invoice (missing)	2,700			
	Error by credit control	360	Balance c/d (balancing figure)		26,060
		53,160			53,160

(e)

Description	✓
An LLP is a separate legal entity.	
The LLP must be registered with the Registrar of Companies.	
There is no upper limit to the number of partners a LLP can have.	
The LLP must file annual returns, accounts and an annual corporation tax return.	✓

Although an LLP should file annual accounts, they are not required to file a corporation tax return as this is only for companies, not partnerships.

(f)

	✓
The Nominated Officer at Radcliffe's and Rutherfords	✓
HMRC	
National Crime Agency	

The next appropriate course of action would be to raise the matter with the designated nominated officer at the firm of accountants where you work, Only then will the matter be considered before whether it should be raised with HMRC or the NCA

(g)

	✓
Charlie will not be exposed to disciplinary proceedings because he has not taken all of his exams yet.	
The Code of Professional Ethics is only enforceable for fully qualified members of the AAT.	
Charlie may disciplined if he fails to comply with AAT CPD requirements	✓

AAT students must also comply with the *AAT Code of Professional Ethics*. Once they are registered with the AAT, they are bound by the requirements.

(h) The AAT has a Continuing Professional Development (CPD) cycle which comprises four steps.

These are assess, plan, **action** and evaluate

Task 1.3 (15 marks)

(a) When preparing financial statements only valid business expenditure is allowed to be recorded as a business expense. This is because the business is a single entity (not legal entity) and its financial affairs need to be kept separate from the owner or owners own personal dealings. Recording invalid expenses would misrepresent the results of the company and would also understate taxable profits. This can be viewed as money laundering and is a criminal offence. If the partners' own family holiday costs were recorded through the partnership this would be dishonest and a breach of the integrity principle. There is a self-interest threat the objectivity principle as I may be influenced by the promise of the tennis tickets. Due to the value of the tennis tickets this could be seen as a bribe and is a criminal offence under the Bribery Act.

(b) I must refuse to comply with the partner's request and as this can be seen as money laundering. I need to prepare an internal report to disclose this matter to the partnership Nominated officer.

A reasonable third party would view the tennis tickets as a bribe and must not be accepted.

(c)   To: Colleague@accounts

From: You@accounts

Subject: Partnership accounts

Hi,

Welcome to the partnership and thank you for contacting on this matter.

A partnership has many similarities to a sole trader as accounting principles and concepts will be the same however there are some important differences to account for two or more people sharing the business.

Here is a summary of the important differences.

Capital accounts

When an individual starts a business they will have a capital account to record the money invested in the business. This is similar to partnerships where each partner will have a separate capital account to record permanent capital invested in the partnership. An important point here is that partnership capital accounts only record long term capital investment.

Current accounts

Each partner will also have separate current account and these are used to record shorter term transactions arising from the partnership and show amounts owing to or from the partnership. Typical credit entries on a current account can be salaries, interest on capital and share in any profits made. These are amounts owed to the individual partner. A typical debit entry will be drawings where a partner extracts money from the partnership similar to a sole trader taking drawings from a business. Any drawings made by a partner will reduce the amount owed to the partner by the partnership.

Appropriation account

The appropriation account shows the total amount of profit made by the partnership with deductions for partner's salaries and interest on capital and adjustments for any interest charged on drawings. The residue amount is then available for sharing between the partners in the agreed partnership sharing ratios.

Statement of financial position

This financial statement shows the assets and liabilities of the partnership. The bottom part of the statement of financial position will show the current and capital accounts for each partner.

I hope this helps.

Please let me know if I can clarify any of the above.

Regards,

Task 2.1 (25 marks)

To:	Emma Neesome
From:	Sarah-Jane Smith
Date:	15 October 20X1
Subject:	Breakeven analysis

Hi Emma

I've carried out the breakeven calculations that you asked me to carry out. They show that the breakeven sales volume is 2,917 units and the breakeven sales revenue is £875,000. We should achieve a contribution/sales ratio of 0.24. The margin of safety in units is 2,083, in % terms 41.67%, which is greater than our target margin of 30%. We should also exceed our target profit of £140,000, as the sales volume required to achieve this profit is 4,861 units, lower than our budgeted sales volume of 5,000 units.

Two problems with breakeven analysis are:

- It assumes selling price and all related costs (variable and fixed) are constant.

- It assumes that inventory levels will remain constant, and there will be no delays or overstocks. Therefore, it assumes that sales will be the same as the production levels.

- The analysis is only possible for single products or single product mixes.

- It assumes all costs can be split into fixed and variable elements.

Best regards

Sara-Jane

[Tutorial note: more answers given for problems with break-even analysis than required, you are only asked to provide TWO problems]

Conditional formatting will require two rules in order to allow both green and red formatting dependent on the answer in the cell.

Conditional Formatting Rules Manager

Show formatting rules for:	Current Selection		

| New Rule... | Edit Rule... | Delete Rule | | |

Rule (applied in order shown)	Format	Applies to	S
Cell Value < 0	AaBbCcYyZz	=$C$20:$D$20	
Cell Value > 0	AaBbCcYyZz	=$C$20:$D$20	

The IF statements required should look like this:

15	Breakeven point in units	2,917	
16	Breakeven point in revenue	875,000	
17	Contribution/Sales ratio	0.24	
18	Margin of safety in units	2,083	
19	Margin of safety in %	41.67	LOWER
20	Target profit volume	4,861	MORE
21			
22			
23			
24			
25			

=IF(B19>0.3,"LOWER","HIGHER")

=IF(B20>5000,"LESS","MORE")

Task 2.2 (30 marks)

(a)

	Trial balance		Adjustments		Final trial balance	
	Dr	Cr	Dr	Cr	Dr	Cr
					£	£
Bank	6,930		300		7,230	
Capital		10,000				10,000
Trade payables		3,000				3,000
Trade receivables	3,080			300	2,780	
Drawings	5,000				5,000	
Fittings at cost	2,500				2,500	
Electricity	1,620			270	1,350	
Insurance	1,800				1,800	
Other expenses	40,200				40,200	
Motor vehicles at cost	15,000				15,000	
Cost of sales	162,800				162,800	
Allowance for doubtful debts		100				100
Accumulated depreciation						
Fittings		500				500
Motor vehicles		3,000				3,000
Rent	27,500				27,500	
Sales		301,100				301,100
Wages	42,000				42,000	
Closing inventory	6,000				6,000	
Depreciation expense fittings			250		250	
Depreciation expense motor vehicles			1,500		1,500	
Prepayments	2,890				2,890	
Accruals		1,100				1,100
Suspense account	1,480		270	1,750	-	-
	318,800	318,800	2,320	2,320	318,800	318,800

(b)

Less expenses			
Electricity	1,350		
Insurance	1,800		
Other expenses	40,200		
Rent	27,500		
Wages	42,000		
Depreciation expense fittings	250		
Depreciation expense motor vehicles	1,500		
Net profit			

Greater Than

Format cells that are GREATER THAN:

10000   with   Light Red Fill

OK   Cancel

	A	B	C	D	E	F	G	H	I
				Most Lotus					
				Statement of Profit or Loss					
				For the year ended 31 January 20X6					
					£		£		
	Sales revenue						301,100		
	Cost of sales						162,800		
	Gross profit						138,300		
)	Less expenses								
L	Electricity				1,350				
2	Insurance				1,800				
3	Other expenses				40,200				
4	Rent				27,500				
5	Wages				42,000				
5	Depreciation expense fittings				250				
7	Depreciation expense motor vehicles				1,500				
3							114,600		
9									
)	Net profit						23,700	7.87%	
L									
2									
3									
4									
5									
5									
7									
3									
9									
)									

ETB SOFP SPL ⊕

(c)

Non-current assets	At cost	Acc Depn	Carrying amount
Motor vehicles	15,000	3,000	12,000
Fixtures and fittings	2,500	500	2,000
	17,500	3,500	14,000
Current assets			
Bank and cash	7,230		
Accounts receivable	2,680		
Prepayment	2,890		
Inventory	6,000		
		18,800	
Less: current liabilities			
Trade payables	3,000		
Accruals	1,100		
		4,100	
NET CURRENT ASSETS			14,700
NET ASSETS			28,700
Financed by			
Capital	10,000		
Profit for the period	23,700		
Less drawings	5,000		
			28,700

Most Lotus
Statement of Financial Position
For the year ended 31 January 20X6

Most Lotus Current Assets

Bank and cash   Accounts receivable   Prepayment   Inventory

ETB   SOFP   SPL   ⊕

BPP PRACTICE ASSESSMENT 2
LEVEL 3 SYNOPTIC ASSESSMENT

**Time allowed: 2 hours and 45 minutes
(plus 15 minutes to upload your answers)**

Advanced Diploma Synoptic Assessment (AVSY)
BPP practice assessment 2

Task 1.1 (15 marks)

(a) Complete the following sentence.

A professional accountant who complies with the law, brings no disrepute on the profession and is perceived as being ethical by other people has complied with the fundamental principle of [▼] .

Picklist:

confidentiality
due care
integrity
objectivity
professional behaviour
professional competence

(2 marks)

The requirement for ethical business practices means that sustainable development and corporate social responsibility are becoming increasingly important.

(b) Which of the below is true in respect of the accountant's role in respect to the above?

Statement	✓
Sustainability and CSR are not financial matters and sit outside the remit of the professional accountant.	
Sustainability and CSR form part of the accountant's obligation to work in the public interest.	
Sustainability and CSR are only key considerations for accountants working in particular industries, such as the renewable energy industry.	

(2 marks)

Danny is a professional accountant working in practice. Whilst carrying out some work for his client, Inge, he has acted outside the limits of his professional expertise.

As a result of the work carried out by Danny, Inge has now incurred a regulatory fine.

(c) **State ONE which of the reasons below whether Inge might be able to seek compensation from Danny for this loss on each of the following grounds.**

Action	✓
Professional negligence	
Self interest	
Fraud under false representation	

(2 marks)

Sparkys Limited, a small home electricals company who you have worked with for a number of years, has unexpectedly requested your practice to help in selling a number of residential properties that they have recently acquired.

(d) **State whether customer due diligence should be carried before accepting this work.**

Statement	True	False
Due diligence procedures are not necessary as this situation relates to an existing client.		
You should report this matter urgently to the relevant authorities. There is clearly something amiss.		

(2 marks)

You are a newly qualified accounting technician working in practice. Your colleague Piers has been off work sick for the past week and your line manager asks you to go through his in-tray and deal with anything that needs urgent attention.

In Piers' in-tray you find a letter addressed to Piers from one of his clients, Martin. In this the letter Martin asks Piers to include a revenue figure in his tax return which is much lower than the actual revenue received by the client. Martin offers Piers 'the £1,000 you need to clear your gambling debt' in return for inclusion of this incorrect figure. Martin also suggests that if this is not done by the end of the month, he will inform the firm of the other ways in which Piers has helped him to present suitable figures in the past.

(e) **Complete the following sentence.**

As a result of this letter, Piers faces threats of [_____ ▼] and [_____ ▼] to his professional ethics.

Picklist:

advocacy
familiarity
intimidation
self-interest
self-review

(2 marks)

(f) **State which THREE of the following of Piers' fundamental principles are threatened by this letter.**

Action	✓
Integrity	
Objectivity	
Confidentiality	
Professional competence and due care	
Professional behaviour	

(3 marks)

(g) **Which of the following actions would it be most appropriate for you to take on discovery of this letter?**

	✓
Hide the letter back in the in-tray and pretend you never saw it; it would not do for you to get caught up in this mess	
Report the misconduct immediately to the AAT	
Discuss the situation with your immediate line manager	

(2 marks)

Task 1.2 (15 marks)

You are an Accounting Technician at Broadchurch & Co. The partner of the firm, Mr Tennant has asked you to answer some queries which have come into the office from some small clients.

Elsie has purchased a new van from Vans & Co for the business using a bank loan. She is unsure how to account for it and explains that she has 'heard of depreciation' but doesn't understand what it is and how to calculate it.

Cost of van   £13,500
Expected scrap value   £1,500

Elsie expects to use the van for 3 years before she upgrades to a bigger van

(a)   Show the double entry for the van which Elsie has purchased in the journal below, using the picklist to select the relevant accounts.

Account name		Amount £	Debit ✓	Credit ✓
	▼			
	▼			

Picklist:

Bank loan
Cash
Inventory
Non-current assets: vehicles
Trade creditor (Vans & Co)

(2 marks)

(b)   Calculate depreciation on the new van on a straight line basis.

(1 mark)

James and Suzy have been the owners of a partnership business for many years, sharing profits and losses in the ratio 3:2, with James receiving the larger share.

On 1 January 20X7, the partnership agreement was changed so that James and Suzy will share profits and losses in the ratio 2:1, with James receiving the larger share.

Goodwill was valued at £84,800 at this date. No entries for goodwill have yet been made in the partnership accounting records.

(c)   Show the entries required to introduce the goodwill into the partnership accounting records on 1 January 20X7.

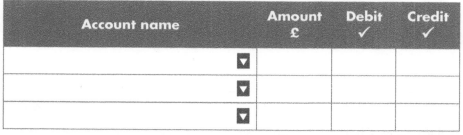

Account name		Amount £	Debit ✓	Credit ✓
	▼			
	▼			
	▼			

(3 marks)

Picklist:
Balance b/d
Balance c/d
Bank
Capital – James
Capital – Suzy
Current – James
Current – Suzy
Drawings
Goodwill

(d)   Which of the following should be included in a partnership agreement? Choose ONE.

	✓
The partnership appropriation account.	
Capital and current accounts for each partner.	
Salaries and wages to be paid to all employees.	
The rate at which interest is to be allowed on capital.	

(2 marks)

The partnership has recently disposed of a large piece of machinery, which is used to make a key item for their business.

- The machinery originally cost £35,000 on 1 January 20X6.

- The policy is to calculate depreciation on a diminishing balance basis at 25%. Scrap value is expected to be £3,000.

- The machinery was sold for £12,000 on 31 December 20X8

(e) Calculate the profit or loss on the disposal of the machinery

(4 marks)

A third client, Christie & Co are a small, but complex local business, specialising in foreign currency deals. You are unsure how to deal with this type of accounting.

(f) What is your next course of action?

	✓
Leave the work on Christie & Co for another colleague to find, after all, the client will chase if they haven't heard anything for a while	
Show a willing attitude and give it your best shot	
Request to be removed from the job	
Consult with your line manager about the task	

(2 marks)

(g) State the fundamental principle which is at risk in the Christie & Co scenario

(1 mark)

Task 1.3 (15 marks)

You are currently working on the year-end financial statements. The work involves the collection of revenue and costs from three divisions. One of your colleagues has mentioned that to speed up communication between divisions he has been using a social media site to transfer and share financial information. He has suggested that you should also do so as the present company policy of password protected data transfer is slow and inconvenient.

(a) **Referring to the AAT *Code of Professional Ethics* explain the ethical principles that are at risk here.**

(4 marks)

(b) **What actions should you take to reduce the risks to the ethical principles?**

(2 marks)

Your worst fears have been realised as the financial data your colleague uploaded onto the Internet has been deleted and lost. A back-up copy has not been made.

You have receive the following email:

To: You@accounts

From: Colleague@acounts

Subject: Missing information

Hi,

I have lost some important financial information. The information I need are amounts paid for trade purchases and sales revenue. I need these figures for the year-end statement of profit or loss.

I have been able to recover that opening payables amounted to £5,400 and closing payables were £4,800. Amounts paid from our bank account to our trade suppliers amounted to £108,000.

If it is any help the sales team have informed me that we operate on a 20% mark-up on cost and inventory values were negligible.

Please help.

Regards,

(c) **Reply to your colleague's email explaining the approach that is required and also supply the sales and purchase figures that your colleague is requesting.**

(9 marks)

Task 2.1 (25 marks)

You are Harry Sullivan, a part-qualified accounting technician. You work for Henniswoode Co, which manufactures kitchen utensils.

You cover all aspects of bookkeeping and accounting for the business. You report to Sarah Foster, the Chief Executive.

Today's date is 12 November 20X2.

Sarah has asked you to do a comparison between the actual overheads for the year 31 October 20X2 and the overheads absorbed, using the basis of labour hours. The information you need is attached.

Download the spreadsheet "PA2 Henniswoode QUESTION.xlsx" file from www.bpp.com/aatspreadsheets. Save the spreadsheet file in the appropriate location and rename it in the following format: 'your initial-surname-AAT no-dd.mm.yy-Task2.1'. For example: H-Darch-123456-12.03.xx-Task 2.1

A **high degree of accuracy** is required. You must **save your work as a .XLS or .XLSX file** at regular intervals to avoid losing your work.

(a) **Open the renamed file. In cells B3–B11, identify the basis you will use to allocate the overheads given in rows 3–11 (using the information in the tab 'information').**

(b) **Allocate the overheads in each department using the bases that you have chosen.**

(c) **In cells D12–G12 subtotal the overheads allocated to each department.**

(d) **Put an IF statement in cell H12 that will show 'Balanced' if the column totals add to the same total as the total in cell C12 and 'Check' if they do not.**

(e) **Reallocate the overheads allocated to the stores department in row 13, using the information given (see tab 'Information'). Show the overheads allocated to other departments as positive figures and the overheads allocated away from stores as a negative figure. Confirm the accuracy of what you have done by totalling in cell C13 the figures in cells D13–G13. The total should be a nil figure.**

(f) **In cells D14–F14 subtotal the overheads allocated to the two production departments and the maintenance department.**

(g) **Reallocate the overheads allocated to the maintenance department in row 15, using the information given. Show the overheads allocated to other departments as positive figures and the overheads allocated away from maintenance as a negative figure. Confirm the accuracy of what you have done** by totalling in cell C15 the figures in cells D15–F15. The total should be a nil figure.

(h)   In cells D16–E16 subtotal the overheads allocated to the two production departments.

(i)   Insert the budgeted labour hours for the two production departments in cells D17 and E17.

(j)   Calculate the overhead absorption rate for the two production departments and insert the figures in cells D18 and E18.

(k)   Colour cells D18 and E18 with a yellow background and black border.

(l)   Calculate the amount of overheads absorbed by actual production, using the information given about actual labour hours. Show this figure in cell C19.

(m)   Calculate the over or under absorption of overheads and show this figure in cell C20. If there has been an over-absorption of overheads, show this figure as a positive figure in green. If there has been an under-absorption of overheads, show this figure as a negative figure in red.

(n)   Enter the figure for absorbed overheads in cell B26 and calculate what the profit would have been using this figure in cell B27.

(o)   Enter the figure for over and under absorption of overheads in cell B28 and calculate the actual profit in cell B29.

(p)   Tidy up the calculation by showing all negative figures in brackets and all figures with comma for 000s. Ensure the worksheet tab is called 'Answer'.

(q)   Copy the whole 'Answer' worksheet to create a duplicate worksheet. Rename this 'Goal Seek'.

The directors of Henniswoode want to know what changes they can make to the depreciation charge (possibly by reviewing the useful life of the assets) in order to achieve a nil over/under absorption.

The company has also been advised that the factory rent is increasing to £95,000 for the next year.

(r)   Change the factory rent to £95,000

(s)   Using the Goal Seek function, identify what changes would be required to the total depreciation charge in order to achieve a nil balance on the under/over absorption of costs.

It is necessary to take a screenshot of the goal seek result prior to accepting the result. Paste this screenshot on the same worksheet, to the right of the result.

Save your work as a xlsx workbook prior to uploading your results.

(20 marks)

(r)   Draft an email to do the following:

- Report the actual profit and amount of overheads over and under absorbed, explaining why the over or under absorption has occurred.

- Give one advantage and one disadvantage of using absorption costing.

(5 marks)

To:	Sarah Foster
From:	Harry Sullivan
Date:	12 November 20X2
Subject:	Absorption of overheads

Task 2.2 (30 marks)

As part of your role as an accounting technician you have been requested to prepare a partnership profit appropriation account for the Awesome Partnership for the year ended 30 June 20X6.

The following information is available to you:

The partnership has three partners; Andy, Wahid and Erin and profits are shared 3:3:2 respectively

Salaries:

Andy £17,500
Wahid £15,000
Erin £10,000

Interest of 15% is paid on capital balances at the end of the year.

Capital balances as at 30 June 20X6
Andy £30,000 Credit balance
Wahid £45,000 Credit balance
Erin £35,000 Credit balance

BPP LEARNING MEDIA

Net profit for the year ended 30 June 20X6 amounted to £100,000 before any partnership distributions.

Open a spreadsheet and save in an appropriate location using the following format **'your initial-surname-PA2 Task 2.2**

You should aim for a **high degree of accuracy**. You **should save your work as an .XLS or .XLSX file** at regular intervals to avoid losing your work.

(a) **Using your saved spreadsheet you are required to prepare a profit appropriation account for the Awesome Partnership for the year ended 30 June 20X6.**

Your partnership profit appropriation account should be prepared using appropriate formula and formatted in the following manner:

* **Account heading in bold, italics using size 14 font.**
* **Heading merged and centred over respective columns.**
* **Figures to be presented with thousand separators and no decimals.**
* **Insert currency (£) symbols where relevant.**
* **Use top and double bottom borders on account totals.**
* **Name your appropriation worksheet tab AWE1 and format tab in blue.**

The partnership is considering using a spreadsheet to help with valuation and location of inventory held in the store room. The store room is split into two sections named '1' and '2'. Wahid has explained to you that the business sells many products but he would like you to prepare a pilot spreadsheet for just four products, A to D containing two 'look-up' formulae to show the current price of a product and also their location in the store room.

The following information is available:

Product	Price	Location in store room
A	£25.00	1
B	£27.80	1
C	£28.40	2
D	£30.00	2

Open a new worksheet and enter the information above.

(20 marks)

(b) **You are required to prepare a worksheet that can quickly show both price AND location of a product using appropriate look-up formulae.**

- **Your table should be set up to show the product, the unit price and the location, using the information provided (above). Put this in rows 1-5 and columns A-C.**

- **In row 7, add a box marked 'Product' in cell 7 A and B. Merge these cells together and centre the text. In cell C7, this will be a box where text can be entered to select the product.**

- **In cell F2, add your look-up formula which will reference to the selection box in cell C7 and your location information in cells A-C 1-5.**

- **Use grey infill for any non-active areas of your worksheet.**

- **Custom format in GBP currency to two decimal places.**

Finally resave your spreadsheet as '**your initial-surname-PA2 Task 2.2 finished**'

(10 marks)

....

BPP PRACTICE ASSESSMENT 2
LEVEL 3 SYNOPTIC ASSESSMENT

ANSWERS

Advanced Diploma Synoptic Assessment (AVSY)
BPP practice assessment 2

Task 1.1

(a) A professional accountant who complies with the law, brings no disrepute on the profession and is perceived as being ethical by other people has complied with the fundamental principle of ┃ professional behaviour ┃ .

(b)

	✓
Sustainability and CSR are not financial matters and sit outside the remit of the professional accountant.	
Sustainability and CSR form part of the accountant's obligation to work in the public interest.	✓
Sustainability and CSR are key considerations for accountants working in particularly industries, such as the renewable energy industry.	

(c)

Action	✓
Professional negligence	✓
Self interest	
Fraud under false representation	

(d)

Statement	True	False
Due diligence procedures are not necessary as this situation relates to an existing client.		✓
You should report this matter urgently to the relevant authorities. There is clearly something amiss.		✓

(e) As a result of this letter, Piers faces threats of ┃ self-interest ┃ and ┃ intimidation ┃ to his professional ethics.

(f)

Action	Yes/No
Integrity	✓
Objectivity	✓
Confidentiality	
Professional competence and due care	
Professional behaviour	✓

(g)

	✓
Hide the letter back in the in-tray and pretend you never saw it; it would not do for you to get caught up in this mess	
Report the misconduct immediately to the AAT	
Discuss the situation with your immediate line manager	✓

Task 1.2

(a)

Account name	Amount £	Debit ✓	Credit ✓
Non-current assets: vehicles	13,500	✓	
Bank	13,500		✓

(b) £4,000

Working

£13,500 – £1,500 = £4,000 per annum

3 years

(c)

Account name	Amount £	Debit ✓	Credit ✓
Goodwill	84,800	✓	
Capital – James*	50,880		✓
Capital – Suzy**	33,920		✓

Workings

*James £84,800/5 × 3 = £50,880

**Suzy £84,800/5 × 2 = £33,920

(d)

	✓
The partnership appropriation account.	
Capital and current accounts for each partner.	
Salaries and wages to be paid to all employees.	
The rate at which interest is to be allowed on capital.	✓

(e) £2,766 loss

Workings

As the diminishing balance basis is used, the scrap value is irrelevant. This method does not take account of any residual value, since the carrying amount under this method will never reach zero.

	£	
Cost	35,000	1 January 20X6
Depreciation	(8,750)	£35,000 × 25%
Carrying amount	26,250	31 December 20X6
Depreciation	(6,562)	£26,250 × 25%
Carrying amount	19,688	31 December 20X7

	£	
Depreciation	(4,922)	£19,688 × 25%
Carrying amount	14,766	31 December 20X8
Sale price	(12,000)	
Loss on sale	2,766	

(f)

	✓
Leave the work on Christie & Co for another colleague to find, after all, the client will chase if they haven't heard anything for a while	
Show a willing attitude and give it your best shot	
Request to be removed from the job	
Consult with your line manager about the task	✓

Consult with your line manager about your concerns about completing the work. If you are still in doubt then ask to be removed from the work. Do not attempt to complete the work if you do not feel you have the knowledge and experience to do so. It would unethical to leave the work you should contact your line manager who will be able to reassign it to someone with the relevant knowledge and experience.

(g) Professional competence and due care

....

Task 1.3

(a) The two ethical principles most at risk here are confidentiality and professional behaviour.

Organisations have a professional and legal obligation to keep data and information secure and confidential. Typically this will require strict access policies and the use of password protection. My colleague's use of social media to transfer company information is risking a breach of confidentiality and is against company policy. In respect of the data protection regulations it is likely to be illegal as well.

The second principle at risk here is professional behaviour. It were to be public knowledge that the company was using this method of transferring sensitive information this would bring disrepute to the company and the accountancy profession.

(b) I must refuse to share and exchange information in this way and only communicate information as per company policies on information and data. I should also report this matter to my supervisor as this is a serious breach of company policy and can have wider legal implications and affect respect for the accountancy profession.

(c) To: Colleague@accounts

From: You@accounts

Subject: Missing information

Hi,

Firstly I must remind you that we do have responsibility to keep proper books of accounts that would be able to supply this information.

However, when there are incomplete records we can use various techniques to reconstruct the missing information from the records we do have. Incomplete records can occur when proper records have not been kept or in unusual circumstances through fire, flood or system crashes.

Amounts that are missing can be reconstructed by the use of raw data, for example paying-in stubs, bank statements, invoices and credit notes. When opening and closing balances are known balancing figures can sometimes be inserted into workings to discover missing amounts. Other methods can include the use of percentage mark-ups and margins to calculate missing figures. This can include the reconstruction of sales revenue, cost of sales and gross profit figures.

Trade payments

The bank statement shows that £108,000 has actually been paid to trade suppliers however this has to be adjusted for the opening and closing balances to show how much should go into the statement of profit or loss. This is part of the matching or accruals concept.

£108,000 plus amounts outstanding at the end of the year = £108,000 + £4,800 = £112,800 less £5,400 that relates to the previous year = £112,800 - £5,400 = £107,400

£107,400 is the amount to be included in the statement of profit or loss for trade purchases.

Sales revenue

As we operate on a 20% plus cost basis sales revenue is £107,400 × 1.20 = £128,880.

Please keep information and data safer in future.

Regards,

Task 2.1

The following is a screenshot of an Excel spreadsheet:

			PD1	PD2	Maint	Stores	
Henniswoode Co Allocation of overheads							
Factory rent	Area	80,000	32,000	24,000	16,000	8,000	
Factory heat	Area	15,000	6,000	4,500	3,000	1,500	
Production department 1 - supervisor cost	PD1	40,000	40,000				
Production department 2 - supervisor cost	PD2	35,000		35,000			
Maintenance - supervisor cost	Maintenance	30,000			30,000		
Stores - supervisor cost	Stores	30,000				30,000	
Depreciation of equipment	NBV	20,000	10,000	7,500	2,500	-	
Canteen expenses	Employees	10,000	4,000	3,600	1,400	1,000	
Welfare costs	Employees	5,000	2,000	1,800	700	500	
Total overheads allocated		265,000	94,000	76,400	53,600	41,000	Balanced
Allocation of stores		0	20,500	16,400	4,100	(41,000)	
			114,500	92,800	57,700		
Allocation of maintenance		0	34,620	23,080	(57,700)		
Total production department overheads allocated			149,120	115,880	0		
Direct labour hours			14,912	14,485			
Overhead absorption rate			10	8			
Amount of overheads absorbed by actual production		276,414					
Over/under absorption of overheads		2,414					

Henniswoode Co Actual statement of profit or loss for the year ended 31 October 20X2	
	Actual
Revenue	2,400,000
Direct material costs	(540,000)
Direct labour costs	(620,000)
Overheads (absorbed)	(276,414)
	963,586
Over/under absorption of overheads	2,414
Profit	966,000

A closer look at some of the formulas used in this answer as follows:

Conditional formatting:

Conditional Formatting Rules Manager

Show formatting rules for: Current Selection

New Rule...   Edit Rule...   Delete Rule

Rule (applied in order shown)	Format	Applies to	
Cell Value < 0	AaBbCcYyZz	=$C$20:$D$20	
Cell Value > 0	AaBbCcYyZz	=$C$20:$D$20	

Amount of overheads absorbed by actual production:

C19   ▾   :   ✕   ✓   *fx*   =((D18*15615)+(E18*15033))

	A	B	C
.0	Canteen expenses	Employees	10,000
.1	Welfare costs	Employees	5,000
.2	Total overheads allocated		265,000
.3	Allocation of stores		0
.4			
.5	Allocation of maintenance		0
.6	Total production department overheads allocated		
.7	Direct labour hours		
.8	Overhead absorption rate		
.9	Amount of overheads absorbed by actual production		276,414
?0	Over/Under absorption of overheads		2,414
?1	**Henniswoode Co Actual statement of profit or loss for the year ended 31 October 20X2**		
??			

Over/Under absorption of overheads:

C20   ▾   :   ✕   ✓   *fx*   =SUM(C19-274000)

	A	B	C	[
.0	Canteen expenses	Employees	10,000	
.1	Welfare costs	Employees	5,000	
.2	Total overheads allocated		265,000	
.3	Allocation of stores		0	
.4				
.5	Allocation of maintenance		0	
.6	Total production department overheads allocated			
.7	Direct labour hours			
.8	Overhead absorption rate			
.9	Amount of overheads absorbed by actual production		276,414	
?0	Over/Under absorption of overheads		2,414	
?1	**Henniswoode Co Actual statement of profit or loss for the year ended 31 October 20X2**			
?2			Actual	
??			2,400,000	

IF statement for the overheads:

Maint	Stores		
16,000	8,000		
3,000	1,500		
30,000		=IF((G12+F12+E12+D12)=C12,"Balanced", "Check")	
	30,000		
2,500	-		
1,400	1,000		
700	500		
53,600	41,000	Balanced	
4,100	(41,000)		
57,700			
(57,700)			
0			

Once you have copied your Answer worksheet (right click on the tab at the bottom of the worksheet and select Move/Copy. Remember to select the correct worksheet and tick the copy box).

Goal seek formula will need to set in the cell of C20 (the under/over absorption) to the value of zero by changing the total depreciation charge in cell C9.

	A	B	C	D	E	F	G	H
20	fx =SUM(C19-274000)							
	Maintenance - supervisor cost	Maintenance	30,000			30,000		
	Stores - supervisor cost	Stores	30,000				30,000	
	Depreciation of equipment	NBV	20,000	10,000	7,500	2,500	-	
	Canteen expenses	Employees	10,000	4,000	3,600	1,400	1,000	
	Welfare costs	Employees	5,000	2,000	1,800	700	500	
	Total overheads allocated		280,000	100,000	80,900	56,600	42,500	Balan
	Allocation of stores		1,500	21,250	17,000	4,250	(41,000)	
				121,250	97,900	60,850		
	Allocation of maintenance		3,150	36,510	24,340	(57,700)		
	Total production department overheads allocated			157,760	122,240	3,150		
	Direct labour hours			14,912	14,485			
	Overhead absorption rate			11	8			
	Amount of overheads absorbed by actual production		292,062					
	Over/Under absorption of overheads		18,062					
	Henniswoode Co Actual statement of profit or loss for the year ended 31 October 20X2							
		Actual						
	Revenue	2,400,000						
	Direct material costs	(540,000)						
	Direct labour costs	(620,000)						
	Overheads (absorbed)	(292,062)						
		947,938						

Goal Seek dialog:
Set cell: C20
To value: 0
By changing cell: $C$9

Once the calculation has run, you will get a message like this. It is important that you take a screenshot of this to be pasted in your answer booklet.

	147,804	114,881	986
	14,912	14,485	
	10	8	
274,000			
0			
:tober 20X2			

Goal Seek Status

Goal Seeking with Cell C20 found a solution.

Target value: 0
Current value: 0

Step
Pause
OK
Cancel

The results will change like this:

Henniswoode Co Allocation of overheads		
Factory rent	Area	95,000
Factory heat	Area	15,000
Production department 1 - supervisor cost	PD1	40,000
Production department 2 - supervisor cost	PD2	35,000
Maintenance - supervisor cost	Maintenance	30,000
Stores - supervisor cost	Stores	30,000
Depreciation of equipment	NBV	2,686
Canteen expenses	Employees	10,000
Welfare costs	Employees	5,000
Total overheads allocated		262,686
Allocation of stores		1,500
Allocation of maintenance		986
Total production department overheads allocated		
Direct labour hours		
Overhead absorption rate		
Amount of overheads absorbed by actual production		274,000
Over/Under absorption of overheads		0

change rent to £95,000

Depreciation charge has been reduced

Word (desktop)

Henniswoode Co Allocation of overheads

			PD1	PD2	Maint	Stores	
Factory rent	Area	95,000	38,000	28,500	19,000	9,500	
Factory heat	Area	15,000	6,000	4,500	3,000	1,500	
Production department 1 - supervisor cost	PD1	40,000	40,000				
Production department 2 - supervisor cost	PD2	35,000		35,000			=IF((G12+F1
Maintenance - supervisor cost	Maintenance	30,000			30,000		
Stores - supervisor cost	Stores	30,000				30,000	
Depreciation of equipment	NBV	2,686	1,343	1,007	336	-	
Canteen expenses	Employees	10,000	4,000	3,600	1,400	1,000	
Welfare costs	Employees	5,000	2,000	1,800	700	500	
Total overheads allocated		262,686	91,343	74,407	54,436	42,500	Balanced
Allocation of stores		1,500	21,250	17,000	4,250	(41,000)	
			112,593	91,407	58,686		
Allocation of maintenance		986	35,211	23,474	(57,700)		
Total production department overheads allocated			147,804	114,881	986		
Direct labour hours			14,912	14,485			
Overhead absorption rate			10	8			
Amount of overheads absorbed by actual production		274,000					
Over/Under absorption of overheads		0					

change rent to £95,000

Depreciation charge has been reduced

Henniswoode Co Actual statement of profit or loss for the year ended 31 October 20X2

	Actual
Revenue	2,400,000
Direct material costs	(540,000)
Direct labour costs	(620,000)
Overheads (absorbed)	(274,000)
	966,000
Over/under absorption of overheads	0
Profit	966,000

Goal Seek Status

Goal Seeking with Cell C20
Found a solution.
Target value: 0
Current value: 0

OK   Cancel

Information | Question | Goal Seek | Answer | +

To:	Sarah Foster
From:	Harry Sullivan
Date:	12 November 20X2
Subject:	Absorption of overheads

Hi Sarah

The actual profit for the year was £966,000. This is calculated after taking into account an over-absorption of overheads of £2,414. This means that actual overheads were less than overheads absorbed, on the basis of total labour hours worked.

Advantages of absorption costing include:

• It allows management to ensure that the sales of their products are covering all the costs of production.

• It is more appropriate for a business using cost plus pricing (as they can ensure that there will be a profit, in theory, on the goods sold).

• Absorption costing is preferable as it is more consistent with current accounting standards and therefore favoured by financial accountants.

Disadvantage with using absorption costing include:

• The method of absorption can be arbitrary.

• It is possible to manipulate profit under absorption costing by increasing inventory levels at year end (thus reducing the cost of sales figure). This is only a short term fix though, as the cost of sales will be higher in the following year.

Best regards

Harry

[Tutorial note: more advantages and disadvantages have been given, you are only expected to provide one of each]

••

Task 2.2

(a)

	A	B	C	D	E	F	G	H
1	Interest on capital		15%					
2								
3			*Profit appropriation account*					
4			£	£			£	
5					Profit for the year		100,000	
6	Salaries							
7	Andy		17,500					
8	Wahid		15,000					
9	Erin		10,000					
10				42,500				
11	Interest on capital							
12	Andy	30,000	4,500					
13	Wahid	45,000	6,750					
14	Erin	35,000	5,250					
15				16,500				
16								
17	Balance c/d			41,000				
18				100,000			100,000	
19	Profit share				Profit for apropriation		41,000	
20	Andy	0.375	15,375					
21	Wahid	0.375	15,375					
22	Erin	0.25	10,250					
23			41,000				41,000	
24								

AWE1

(b)

	A	B	C	D	E	F	G	H
1	Product	Price	Location		Price	£27.80		
2	A	£25.00	1		Location	1		
3	B	£27.80	1					
4	C	£28.40	2					
5	D	£30.00	2					
6								
7	Product		B					
8								
9								
10								
11								

Suggested formulas

	A	B	C	D	E	F	G
1	Product	Price	Location		Price	=VLOOKUP(C7,A1:E5,2,FALSE)	
2	A	25	1		Location	=VLOOKUP(C7,A1:C5,3,FALSE)	
3	B	27.8	1				
4	C	28.4	2				
5	D	30	2				
6							
7	Product		B				
8							
9							

BPP PRACTICE ASSESSMENT 3
LEVEL 3 SYNOPTIC ASSESSMENT

**Time allowed: 2 hours and 45 minutes
(plus 15 minutes to upload your answers)**

PRACTICE ASSESSMENT 3

Advanced Diploma Synoptic Assessment (AVSY)
BPP practice assessment 3

Task 1.1 (15 marks)

Rose Well is a sole practitioner accountant who has a client, Baxter Links. She has evidence that Baxter has been selling counterfeit goods. She decides that she will discuss this with him at their next meeting

(a) **Which of the following statements is true or false about the action Rose proposes to take in this matter**

Statement	True	False
Rose may be guilty of the crime of tipping off a client		
Rose will be guilty of breaching confidentiality if she reports Baxter without discussing her suspicions with him first		
Rose should report her findings to her nominated officer prior to talking to Baxter		

(3 marks)

(b) **Complete the following statement**

The FRC aims to promote ethical [▼] and increased [▼] in the accountancy profession in the UK.

Picklist:

accounting
compliance
confidence
financial reporting
practices

(2 marks)

(c) **Are these statements true or false?**

Statement	True	False
The need to act ethically is most important for accountants employed in the public sector as they are more open to criticism if this money is perceived to be spent inappropriately.		
The *Code of Professional Ethics* sets out the required standards of professional behaviour with guidance on how these standards can be achieved.		
The *Code of Professional Ethics* adopts a principles-based approach in order to allow individuals to choose appropriate behaviour and to remove the need for professional judgements to be made.		

(3 marks)

You have recently terminated your relationship with a client after discovering a number of errors in their VAT return that they refused to correct.

(d) **You withdrew from this engagement to safeguard against which threat to your fundamental principles?**

	✓
Familiarity	
Self-interest	
Intimidation	

(2 marks)

You have now been approached by the client's new accountant who has asked you why the agreement ended.

(e) **Which of the fundamental principles does this threaten?**

	✓
Professional behaviour	
Confidentiality	
Objectivity	

(1 mark)

You have just found out that, as result of the discovery of previously withheld information, that the financial statements of a client are materially misstated. Several months ago you issued an audit report which confirmed that the statements presented a true and fair view.

(f) Which of the below statements are true?

Statement	✓
You failed to comply with the ethical principle of professional competence and due care at the time of the audit.	
You failed to comply with the ethical principle of integrity at the time of the audit.	
You complied with the ethical principles at the time of the audit.	

(2 marks)

(g) Which of the following actions should now be taken?

Action	✓
You should make a note on the audit file for next year. The report on these financial statements has already been issued and it is too late to retract it.	
You should issue a revised audit report immediately.	
You should securely destroy the new information to prevent damage to your reputation as a professional accountant.	

(2 marks)

Task 1.2 (15 marks)

You are an Accounting Technician in a small firm of accountants near Hull.

You have found a sizeable error in the information the firm sent to HMRC in respect of one of its clients. You are concerned that this may breach legislation, so you consider consulting a technical helpline set up by a local accountancy firm to determine what you should do next.

(a) **According to the ethical code, which of your fundamental principles would be under threat if you called the helpline?**

Integrity ☐

Confidentiality ☐

Objectivity ☐

(2 marks)

Another of the clients you look after has recently purchased a new forklift truck for their business. They have paid £25,000 for the forklift and have informed you that they purchased it in May 20X7.

You are preparing the financial statements for the year ended 31 December 20X7 and the policy of the business is to depreciate such assets over 5 years on a straight line basis. The scrap value of the asset is estimated to be £2,500. Costs of £250 were incurred in the delivery and set up of the forklift truck.

(b) **What is the depreciation charge for the year ended 31 December 20X7 (note policy is to charge a full year's depreciation in the year of acquisition and none in the year of disposal).**

(3 marks)

(c) **What is the carrying amount of the asset at 31 December 20X7**

£

(1 mark)

(d) Select which **ONE** of the following statements is an **ADVANTAGE** of using the FIFO method of valuation by ticking in the relevant box.

Reason	✓
Inventory is valued at a price which most closely represents the current market value.	
It complies with IAS 2 *Accounting for Inventory.*	
It is easy to calculate when there is a high volume of stock movement in and out of the business.	
Fluctuations in prices are smoothed out, making it easier to analyse the data for decision making.	

(2 marks)

(e) You have been asked to calculate the irrecoverable debt allowance for a client, Coolio Ltd. Which **ONE** of the following statements is correct?

	✓
Irrecoverable debt provision must be based on Coolio's accounting policy which takes 15% of the value held at the year-end on the trade receivable's account	
The provision should be based on specifically identified customer debts which are expected to be irrecoverable	
The provision should be adjusted to ensure the correct level of profit for Coolio at year end	

(2 marks)

(f) Select which of the following statements are true or false regarding sole traders and limited companies.

	True ✓	False ✓
Limited companies are separate legal entities from the shareholders.		
Directors can have a 'drawings' account like a sole trader.		

	True ✓	False ✓
Financial statements must always be prepared in accordance with recognised accounting standards. This is correct for both sole traders and limited companies.		
The Companies Act 2006 states that the directors of a limited company must file annual accounts.		
Only large companies may use International Financial Reporting Standards as the basis for their financial statements preparation.		

(5 marks)

Task 1.3 (15 marks)

Kasablanka Ltd has a year end of 31 December 20X8

It is just after the year-end and you are currently working on the inventory value to go into the extended trial balance. For many years Kasablanka Ltd has used a weighted average cost (WAVCO) method in the calculation of inventory values but this year one of the directors has requested you to use a 'last in first out' (LIFO) method. The reason given for this was that purchase costs increased considerably towards the end of the year so this would reflect 'economic reality' and we can change back to WAVCO next year when costs have settled down to a more normal level. Kasablanka is keen to keep their corporation tax at a minimum this financial year. The director also mentioned that he is in the process of considering the approval of your annual leave request.

(a) Identify and explain the ethical principles at risk here along with any associated threats to those principles.

(6 marks)

(b) What actions should you take in these circumstances?

(5 marks)

Bill is a new director of Kasablanka Ltd and he used to run a small vegetable stall as a sole trader. He is struggling to understand why the financial statements 'are so complex'.

(c) Explain to Bill what is the purpose of financial statements, and briefly how the results of the business are reported. Consider who is likely to use the accounts.

(4 marks)

Task 2.1 (25 marks)

You are Tegan Jovanka, a part-qualified accounting technician. You work for Miller Ltd, a company that manufactures precision equipment for workshops.

You cover all aspects of bookkeeping and accounting for the business. You report to John Stevens, the Finance Director.

Today's date is 6 December 20X3.

John Stevens has asked you to carry out an analysis of the company's overheads because he is not satisfied with the accuracy of the current absorption basis used, which is labour hours. He wants to see the results of using machine hours to absorb overheads, and using activity-based costing (ABC) to calculate absorbed overheads.

The information relating to the next accounting period that you need to carry out this analysis is attached.

Download the spreadsheet "BPP PA3 Task 2.1 Miller Ltd Question.xlsx" file from the www.bpp.com/aatspreadsheets. Save the spreadsheet file in the appropriate location and rename it in the following format: 'your initial-surname-AAT no-dd.mm.yy-Task2.1'. For example: H-Darch-123456-12.03.xx-Task2.1

A **high degree of accuracy** is required. You must **save your work as an .XLS or.XLSX file** at regular intervals to avoid losing your work.

(a) **Open the renamed file. Enter the total machine hours for each product in the period in cells C3–F3 and the total machine hours in cell G3.**

(b) **Use the total machine hours figure in your calculation of the absorption rate per machine hour. Enter this figure in B4 and show it to 2 decimal places.**

(c) **Show the total overheads absorbed per unit on a machine hour basis for each product in cells C5–F5, showing these figures to two decimal places.**

(d) **Enter the total labour hours for each product in the period in cells C7–F7 and the total labour hours in cell G7.**

(e) **Use the total labour hours figure in your calculation of the absorption rate per labour hour. Enter this figure in B8 and show it to 2 decimal places.**

(f) **Show the total overheads absorbed per unit on a labour hour basis for each product in cells C9–F9, showing these figures to two decimal places.**

(g) **Enter the number of set-ups for each product in the period in cells C11–F11 and the total number of set-ups in cell G11.**

(h)   Use the total number of set-ups in your calculation of the cost per set-up. Enter this figure in B12 and show it to 2 decimal places.

(i)   Show the total set-up costs absorbed for each product in cells C13–F13.

(j)   Enter the number of requisitions for each product in the period in cells C14–F14 and the total number of requisitions in cell G14.

(k)   Use the total number of requisitions in your calculation of the stores receipt cost per requisition. Enter this figure in B15 and show it to 2 decimal places.

(l)   Show the total stores receipt costs absorbed for each product in cells C16–F16.

(m)   Enter the number of units produced for each product in the period in cells C17–F17 and the total number of units produced in cell G17.

(n)   Use the total number of units produced in your calculation of the quality control cost per unit produced. Enter this figure in B18 and show it to 2 decimal places.

(o)   Show the total quality control costs absorbed for each product in cells C19–F19.

(p)   Enter the number of orders executed for each product in the period in cells C20–F20 and the total number of orders executed in cell G20.

(q)   Use the total number of orders executed in your calculation of the materials handling and despatch costs per order executed. Enter this figure in B21 and show it to 2 decimal places.

(r)   Show the total materials handling and despatch costs absorbed for each product in cells C22–F22.

(s)   Total the overheads absorbed on an ABC basis for each of the products and enter these totals in cells C23–F23.

(t)   Calculate the overheads absorbed per unit on an ABC basis and enter these figures in cells C24–F24, showing them to 2 decimal places.

(u)   Summarise the results, by showing the absorbed cost per unit under each of the three methods in cell range C26–F28.

(v) **Highlight the product with the highest absorbed cost per unit for each method by showing the cost with an orange background and black borders round each cell. Highlight the product with the lowest absorbed cost per unit for each method by showing the cost with a green background and black borders round each cell.**

(w) **Tidy up the calculation by showing all negative figures in brackets and all figures with comma for 000s.**

(x) **Perform a spell check and ensure that all the contents of the cells can be seen.**

(20 marks)

(y) **Draft an email on the spreadsheet to do the following:**

- **Compare the results of the different methods of absorbing overheads.**

- **Give two advantages of activity-based costing.**

(5 marks)

To:	John Stevens
From:	Tegan Jovanka
Date:	6 December 20X3
Subject:	Overhead analysis

Task 2.2 (30 marks)

You are in the process of preparing the final accounts for Velocity Partnership for the year ended 31 March 20X6.

You will need to download the spreadsheet **BPP PA3 Task2.2 Velocity Question.xls.**

You are given a trial balance for the company together with additional information.

Further information is available:

- Prepayments of £1,120 were credited to the general expenses account in the SPL, however, the other side of the entry was not entered.

- An accrual for general expenses of £520 needs to be accounted for at year end.

- Interest paid of £375 was credited from the bank and cash account, but no expense was booked in the nominal ledger.

Open the spreadsheet **BPP PA3 Task2.2 Velocity Question.xlsx** and save in an appropriate location using the following format **'your initial-surname-task 2.2'**

You should aim for a **high degree of accuracy**. You **should save your work as an .XLS or .XLSX file** at regular intervals to avoid losing your work.

Using your saved spreadsheet you are required to extend the trial balance which can be found on the tab labelled 'Information' for Velocity Partnership for the year ended 31 March 20X6.

(a)   **Your extended trial balance should be prepared using appropriate formula and needs to be presented and formatted in the following manner:**

- **Clear the suspense account and enter the adjustments required in the adjustments columns.**

- **Two new columns to be inserted for each of statement of profit or loss and statement of financial position entries.**

- **All headings to be merged and centred over appropriate columns.**

- **Insert additional rows as required to extend your trial balance.**

- **Figures to be presented with thousand separators and no decimals.**

- **Insert currency (£) symbols where relevant.**

- **Use top and double bottom borders on column totals.**

- **Name your appropriation worksheet tab ETB and format tab in red.**

(12 marks)

There are three partners in Velocity, with the following information available:

- Callisto takes a salary of £17,500, and has a 50% share of the profits

- Thebe and Leda both have a £15,000 salary and has a 25% share of the profits.

- The interest on capital is 5%

- Callisto has put £2,000 capital into the partnership. Thebe has put in £14,000 and Leda has put in £4,000.

(b) Using the profit figure calculated in the ETB you need to draw up a profit appropriation account in worksheet labelled 'Partnership' for the Velocity Partnership using the information provided.

- All headings to be merged and centred over appropriate columns. The heading 'Profit Appropriation Account' should be in bold, italics and font 14.

- Use a suitable formula to calculate the interest on capital for each of the partners, based on their capital invested in the business.

- The profit for the year will need to entered in cell G5.

- Use suitable formula to calculate the profit share of each partner.

- In cell H23, enter an IF formula which will state 'balanced' if cells H23 and C23 are equal, and 'out of balance' if they don't.

- In cell H23 also apply conditional formatting so that if the answer is 'balanced' the cell will go green with dark green font.

- Rename the tab 'Profit split' and colour it green.

(18 marks)

BPP PRACTICE ASSESSMENT 3
LEVEL 3 SYNOPTIC ASSESSMENT

ANSWERS

Advanced Diploma Synoptic Assessment (AVSY)
BPP practice assessment 3

Task 1.1

(a)

Statement	True	False
Rose may be guilty of the crime of tipping off a client	✓	
Rose will be guilty of breaching confidentiality if she reports Baxter without discussing her suspicions with him first		✓
Rose should report her findings to her Nominated Officer prior to talking to Baxter		✓

Rose may be guilty of 'tipping off' the client if she takes any action which may be deemed to prejudice an investigation – such as discussing her evidence with him in advance of notifying the NCA.

As she has specific knowledge and reasonable grounds to suspect money laundering is taking place, she will be legally allowed to breach confidentiality in this instance under the The Money Laundering, Terrorist Financing and Transfer of Funds (Information on the Payer) Regulations 2017. Rose will have a professional duty to report it.

As Rose is a sole practitioner, she will not have a Nominated Officer. Instead, she will have to consider making a report direct to the NCA.

(b) The FRC aims to promote ethical | financial reporting | and increased

| confidence | in the accountancy profession in the UK.

(c)

Statement	True	False
The need to act ethically is most important for accountants employed in the public sector as they are more open to criticism if this money is perceived to be spent inappropriately.		✓
The *Code of Professional Ethics* sets out the required standards of professional behaviour with guidance on how these standards can be achieved.	✓	
The *Code of Professional Ethics* adopts a principles-based approach in order to allow individuals to choose appropriate behaviour and to remove the need for professional judgements to be made.		✓

313

(d)

	✓
Familiarity	
Self-interest	
Intimidation	✓

(e)

	✓
Professional behaviour	
Confidentiality	✓
Objectivity	

(f)

	✓
You failed to comply with the ethical principle of professional competence and due care at the time of the audit.	
You failed to comply with the ethical principle of integrity at the time of the audit.	
You complied with the ethical principles at the time of the audit.	✓

(g)

	✓
You should make a note on the audit file for next year. The report on these financial statements has already been issued and it is too late to retract it.	
You should issue a revised audit report immediately.	✓
You should securely destroy the new information to prevent damage to your reputation as a professional accountant.	

Task 1.2

(a)

Integrity ☐

Confidentiality ☑

Objectivity ☐

(b)

£	4,550

Workings

	£
Cost	25,000
Add delivery costs	250
Less scrap value	(2,500)
Amount to be depreciated over 5 years	22,750
Charge for the year	4,550

(c)

£	20,700

Workings: £25,250 – £4,550

(d)

Reason	✓
Inventory issued is valued at a price which most closely represents the current market value.	
It complies with IAS 2 *Accounting for Inventory*.	✓
It is easy to calculate when there is a high volume of stock movement in and out of the business.	
Fluctuations in prices are smoothed out, making it easier to analyse the data for decision making.	

Option 1 is a benefit of LIFO. Option 3 and option 4 are benefits of the weighted average cost valuation method.

BPP LEARNING MEDIA

(e)

	✓
Irrecoverable debt provision must be based on Coolio's accounting policy which takes 15% of the value held at the year end on the trade receivable's account	
The provision should be based on specifically identified customer debts which are expected to be irrecoverable	✓
The provision should be adjusted to ensure the correct level of profit for Coolio at year end	

Irrecoverable debt provisions should be based on specifically identified debts which are expected to be irrecoverable at the year end. They should be based on factual evidence and the best estimation of whether they are really recoverable.

They should not be used to alter the profit required and general provisions are not allowed.

(f)

	True	False
Limited companies are separate legal entities from the shareholders.	✓	
Directors can have a 'drawings' account like a sole trader.		✓
Financial statements must always be prepared in accordance with recognised accounting standards. This is correct for both sole traders and limited companies.		✓
The Companies Act 2006 states that the directors of a limited company must file annual accounts.	✓	
Only large companies may use International Financial Reporting Standards as the basis for their financial statements preparation.		✓

Task 1.3

(a) The ethical principles at risk can include objectivity and integrity. The financial statements should be prepared without bias or any undue influence. It would be unfair to change the valuation method for one year as this would be against the accounting concept of consistency in the use of accounting policies. Intentionally changing the inventory method for this purpose would be dishonest and in breach of the integrity principle. The threats here are intimidation through the possible refusal of my annual leave request and also a self-interest threat for the director in manipulating profits to minimise tax. An added issue here is that the LIFO method is not allowed for inventory valuation under IAS 2.

(b) It can be possible to change accounting policies provided that there is a valid reason for doing so, for example a change in how an industry is regulated or if it was found that the current policies did not provide a fair reflection of the results of a business. In this case, it appears the only reason is to manipulate profits on a short-term basis, and not following guidance in the accounting standards (IAS 2, Inventories and the Conceptual Framework's principles. therefore I should refer this matter onto my immediate supervisor for authorisation to make this change in the valuation method. When I contact my supervisor I should also mention the impact the change will make on reported profits and also that LIFO is not considered an appropriate valuation method.

(c) The purpose of the financial statements is to show the financial performance of the business during the reporting period. This is reported through the statement of profit or loss. The financial statements will also show the financial status of the business through the statement of financial position. This statement shows the assets and liabilities of the business including the capital invested into the business by its owner or owners as in the case of a partnership.

The financial statements can be used by a variety of users and these can include; employees, customers, suppliers, potential investors, banks and also the tax authorities.

Task 2.1

To:	John Stevens
From:	Tegan Jovanka
Date:	6 December 20X3
Subject:	Overhead analysis

John

I have carried out the overhead analysis you requested.

Under all methods product AB absorbs the most overheads per unit, but the difference in overhead absorbed between it and the other products under ABC is much less than under the machine or labour hour methods, showing the importance of the different activities that the products generate.

For example:

AB absorbs £17.70 per unit under the ABC basis, but £48.00 per unit under the labour hour method.

Under each method a different product absorbs the least overhead per unit:

GH on a machine hours basis (£9.60 per unit)

EF on a labour hours basis (£6.00 per unit)

CD on an ABC basis (£14.57 per unit)

ABS costing is an alternative to absorption costing, and is developed for businesses which have a higher proportion of overheads.

Two advantages of using ABC are:

- It is concerned with all overhead costs
- It shows what drives overhead costs ("cost drivers")

The ABC cost drivers here are:

- Set ups required by the product in production
- Requisitions within the stores
- Quality control cost per product
- Materials handling and despatch cost per order.

As product AB incurs relatively few costs in respect of these costs, it's overheads absorped per unit under the ABC systems is only £17.70 per unit.

As you can see, the type of absorption rate can have a significant effect on the cost of a product.

Kind regards

Tegan

	B	AB	CD	EF	GH	Total
Overheads Machine hours						
Total Machine hours		700	1,500	1,600	1,200	5,000
Overhead absorption rate	4.80					
Overheads absorbed per unit		33.60	14.40	19.20	9.60	
Overheads Labour hours						
Total Labour hours		800	1,000	400	1,800	4,000
Overhead absorption rate	6.00					
Overheads absorbed per unit		48.00	12.00	6.00	18.00	
ABC						
Set-ups		4	7	6	8	25
Cost per set-up	200.00					
Set-up costs		800	1,400	1,200	1,600	
Requisitions		10	60	50	80	200
Stores receipt cost per requisition	37.50					
Stores receipt costs		375	2,250	1,875	3,000	
Number of units		100	500	400	600	1,600
Quality control cost per unit produced	3.75					
Quality control costs		375	1,875	1,500	2,250	
Orders executed		4	32	28	36	100
Materials handling and despatch cost per order executed	55.00					
Materials handling and despatch costs		220	1,760	1,540	1,980	
Total overheads absorbed		1,770	7,285	6,115	8,830	
Overheads absorbed per unit		17.70	14.57	15.29	14.72	
Summary						
Machine hours basis		33.60	14.40	19.20	9.60	
Labour hours basis		48.00	12.00	6.00	18.00	
ABC basis		17.70	14.57	15.29	14.72	

Task 2.2

(a)

Ensure that the adjustments have been correctly posted and are totalled using formula at the bottom of each column.

Ensure the split between the statement of Profit or loss and the statement of financial position has been done correctly.

Ensure the tabs have been correctly labelled and coloured.

	Ledger balances		Adjustments		Statement of profit or loss		Statement of financial position	
	£	£	£	£	£	£	£	£
Bank	4,750						4,750	
Capital		20,000						20,000
Closing inventory	2,760	2,760				2,760	2,760	
Non-current assets at cost	125,000						125,000	
Accumulated depreciation		17,500						17,500
Depreciation charge	2,500				2,500			
Long term loan		7,500						7,500
General expenses	56,260		520		56,780			
Interest paid			375		375			
Opening inventory	3,000				3,000			
Prepayments			1,120				1,120	
Accruals				520				520
Trade payables		2,320						2,320
Trade receivables	1,950						1,950	
Sales		303,405				303,405		
Purchases	155,770				155,770			
Suspense	1,495			1,495				
Profit or loss for the year					87,740			87,740
	353,485	353,485	2,015	2,015	306,165	306,165	135,580	135,580

ETB | Profit split | ⊕

(b)

Ensure correct title and examples of suitable formulas are given below

	A	B	C	D	E	F	G	H	I	J
2										
3			*Profit Appropriation Account*							
4			£	£			£			
5					Profit for the year		87,740			
6	Salaries									
7	Callisto		17,500							
8	Thebe		15,000							
9	Leda		15,000							
10				47,500						
11	Interest on capital									
12	Callisto	2,000	100							
13	Thebe	14,000	700							
14	Leda	4,000	200							
15				1,000						
16										
17	Balance c/d			39,240				=IF(C23=G23,"balanced","out of balance")		
18				87,740			87,740			
19	Profit share				Profit for appropriation		39,240			
20	Callisto	0.5	19,620							
21	Thebe	0.25	9,810							
22	Leda	0.25	9,810							
23			39,240				39,240 balanced			
24										
25										

Profit split ⊕

	A	B	C	D	E	F	G	H
	Interest on capital		0.05					
			Profit Appropriation Account					
			£	£			£	
					Profit for the year		87740	
	Salaries							
	Callisto		17500					
	Thebe		15000					
	Leda		15000					
0				=SUM(C7:C9)				
1	Interest on capital							
2	Callisto	2000	=B12*C$1					
3	Thebe	14000	=B13*C$1					
4	Leda	4000	=B14*C$1					
5				=SUM(C12:C14)				
6								
7	Balance c/d			=G5-D10-D15				
8				=D10+D15+D17			=G5	
9	Profit share				Profit for appropriat		=D17	
0	Callisto	0.5	=B20*G$19					
1	Thebe	0.25	=B21*G$19					
2	Leda	0.25	=B22*G$19					
3			=SUM(C20:C22)				=C23	=IF(C23=G23,"balanc
4								
5								

An 'IF' formula needs to be inserted (shown here in green) to check whether the calculation has balanced.

	=G5	
rofit for appropriat	=D17	
	=C23	=IF(C23=G23,"balanced","out of balance")

Appendix: Reference materials for the synoptic assessment

The information in this section is for use alongside the AAT's sample assessment and the practice assessments in this Question Bank.

This will be available to you in the assessment in pop-up windows.

Code of Professional Ethics (2017)

Code of Professional Ethics – Part A

Introduction – 100

Section 100 – Introduction and code of fundamental principles

100.1 A distinguishing mark of the accountancy profession is its acceptance of the responsibility to act in the public interest. Therefore, your responsibility as a member is not exclusively to satisfy the needs of an individual client or employer. In acting in the public interest, members shall observe and comply with the *Code* of ethical requirements set out in this *Code*.

100.2 This *Code* is in three parts. Part A establishes the code of fundamental principles of professional ethics for members and provides a conceptual framework for applying those principles. The conceptual framework provides guidance on fundamental ethical principles. Members are required to apply this conceptual framework to enable them to identify threats to compliance with the fundamental principles, to evaluate their significance and, if such threats are not clearly insignificant, to apply safeguards to eliminate them or reduce them to an acceptable level such that compliance with the fundamental principles is not compromised.

100.3 Part B and C describe how the conceptual framework applies in certain situations. They provide examples of safeguards that may be appropriate to address threats to compliance with the fundamental principles. They also describe situations where safeguards are not available to address the threats and where the activity or relationship creating the threats shall be avoided. Part B applies to Licensed members. Part C applies to members in business. Licensed members may also find Part C relevant to their particular circumstances.

100.4 In this *Code* the use of the word 'shall' imposes a requirement on the member to comply with the specific provision in which 'shall' has been used. Compliance is required unless an exception is permitted by this *Code*.

Fundamental principles

100.5   A member shall comply with the following fundamentals principles:

(i)   **Integrity**: to be straightforward and honest in all professional and business relationships.

(ii)   **Objectivity**: to not allow bias, conflict of interest or undue influence of others to override professional or business judgements.

(iii)   **Professional competence and due care**: to maintain professional knowledge and skill at the level required to ensure that a client or employer receives competent professional service based on current developments in practice, legislation and techniques. A member shall act diligently and in accordance with applicable technical and professional standards when providing professional services.

(iv)   **Confidentiality**: to act, in accordance with the law, respect the confidentiality of information acquired as a result of professional and business relationships and not disclose any such information to third parties without proper and specific authority unless there is legal or professional right or duty to disclose. Confidential information acquired as a result of professional and business relationships shall not be used for the personal advantage of the member or third parties.

(v)   **Professional behaviour**: to comply with the relevant laws and regulation and avoid any action that discredits our profession.

Each of these fundamentals principles is discussed in more detail in Sections 110–150.

Conceptual framework approach

100.6   The circumstances in which members operate may give rise to specific threats to compliance with the fundamental principles. It is impossible to define every situation that create such threats and specify the appropriate mitigating action. In addition, the nature of engagements and work assignments may differ and consequently different threats may exist, requiring the application of different safeguards. Therefore, this *Code* establishes a conceptual framework that requires a member to identify, evaluate and address threats to compliance with the fundamental principles. The conceptual framework approach assists members in complying with the ethical requirements of this *Code* and meeting their responsibility to act in the public interest. It accommodates many variations in circumstances that create threats to compliance with the fundamental principles and can deter a professional accountant from concluding that a situation is permitted if it is not specifically prohibited.

100.7 When a member identifies threats to compliance with the fundamental principles and, based on an evaluation of those threats, determines that they are not at an acceptable level, the member shall determine whether appropriate safeguards are available and can be applied to eliminate the threats or reduce them to an acceptable level. In making that determination, the member shall exercise professional judgement and take into account whether a reasonable and informed third party, weighing all the specific facts and circumstances available to the member at the time, would be likely to conclude that the threats would be eliminated or reduced to an acceptable level by the application of the safeguards, such that compliance with the fundamental principles is not compromised.

100.8 A member shall evaluate any threats to compliance with the fundamental principles when the member knows, or could reasonably be expected to know, of circumstances or relationships that may compromise compliance with the fundamental principles.

100.9 A member shall take qualitative as well as quantitative factors into account when considering the significance of a threat. When applying the conceptual framework, a member may encounter situations in which threats cannot be eliminated or reduced to an acceptable level, either because the threat is too significant or because appropriate safeguards are not available, or cannot be applied. In such situations, a member shall decline or discontinue the specific professional service involved or, when necessary, resign from the engagement (in the case of a Licensed member) or the employing organisation (in the case of a member in business).

100.10 Sections 290 and 291 (as detailed within the associated document *Code of Professional Ethics: independence provisions relating to review and assurance engagements*) contain provisions with which a member shall comply if the member identifies a breach of an independence provision of the *Code*. If a member identifies a breach of any other provisions of this *Code*, the member shall evaluate the significance of the breach and its impact on the member's ability to comply with the fundamental principles. The member shall take whatever actions that may be available, as soon as possible, to satisfactorily address the consequences of the breach. The member shall determine whether to report the breach, for example, to those who may have been affected by the breach, a member body, relevant regulator or oversight authority.

100.11 When a member encounters unusual circumstances in which the application of a specific requirement of the *Code* would result in a disproportionate outcome or an outcome that may not be in public interest, it is recommended that the member consult with AAT on the issue.

Threats and safeguards

100.12 Threats may be created by a broad range of relationships and circumstances. When a relationship or circumstance creates a threat, such a threat could compromise, or could be perceived to compromise, a member's compliance with the fundamental principles. A circumstance may create more than one threat, and a threat may affect compliance with more than one fundamental principle.

Threats fall into the following categories:

(i) self-interest threats, which may occur where a financial or other investment will inappropriately influence the member's judgement or behaviour

(ii) self-review threats, which may occur when a previous judgement needs to be re-evaluated by the member responsible for that judgement

(iii) advocacy threats, which may occur when a member promotes a position or opinion to the point that subsequent objectivity may be compromised

(iv) familiarity threats, which may occur when, because of a close or personal relationship, a member becomes too sympathetic to the interests of others

(v) intimidation threats, which may occur when a member may be deterred from acting objectively by threats, whether actual or perceived.

Parts B and C of this *Code* explain how these categories of threats may be created for Licensed members and members in business respectively. Licensed members may also find Part C relevant to their particular circumstances.

100.13 Safeguards are actions or other measures that may eliminate threats or reduce them to an acceptable level. These fall into two broad categories:

(i) safeguards created by the profession, legislation or regulation
(ii) safeguards in the work environment.

100.14 Safeguards created by the profession, legislation or regulation include, but are not restricted to:

(i) educational, training and experience requirements for entry into the profession

(ii) continuing professional development requirements

(iii) corporate governance regulations

(iv) professional standards

(v)   professional or regulatory monitoring and disciplinary procedures

(vi)   external review of the reports, returns, communications or information produced by a member and carried out by a legally empowered third party.

100.15 Parts B and C of this *Code*, respectively, discuss safeguards in the work environment for Licensed members and members in business.

100.16 Certain safeguards may increase the likelihood of identifying or deterring unethical behaviour. Such safeguards, which may be created by the accounting profession, legislation, regulation or an employing organisation, include, but are not restricted to:

(i)   effective, well publicised complaints systems operated by the employing organisation, the profession or a regulator, which enable colleagues, employers and members of the public to draw attention to unprofessional or unethical behaviour

(ii)   an explicitly stated duty to report breaches of ethical requirements.

Conflicts of interest

100.17 A member may be faced with a conflict of interest when undertaking a professional activity. A conflict of interest creates a threat to objectivity and may create threats to the other fundamental principles. Such threats may be created when:

(i)   the member undertakes a professional activity related to a particular matter for two or more parties whose interests with respect to that matter are in conflict; or

(ii)   the interest of the member with respect to a particular matter and the interests of a party for whom the member undertakes a professional activity related to that matter are in conflict.

100.18 Parts B and C of this *Code* discuss conflicts of interest for Licensed members and members in business respectively.

100.19 In evaluating compliance with the fundamental principles, a member may be required to resolve conflict in the application of fundamental principles.

100.20 When initiating either a formal or informal conflict resolution process, a member shall consider the following, either individually or together with others, as part of the resolution process:

- relevant facts
- ethical issues involved
- fundamental principles related to the matter in question
- established internal procedures
- alternative courses of action.

Having considered these factors, a member shall determine the appropriate course of action that is consistent with the fundamental principles identified. The member shall also weigh the consequences of each possible course of action. If the matter remains unresolved, the member may wish to consult with other appropriate persons within the firm or employing organisation for help in obtaining resolution.

100.21 Where a matter involves a conflict with, or within, an organisation, a member shall determine whether to consult with those charged with governance of the organisation, such as the board of directors or the audit committee.

100.22 It may be in the best interests of the member to document the substance of the issue and details of any discussions held or decisions taken concerning that issue.

100.23 If a significant conflict cannot be resolved, a member may consider obtaining professional advice from the relevant professional body or legal advisers on a confidential basis and thereby obtain guidance on ethical issues without breaching confidentiality. For example, a member may suspect that he or she has encountered a fraud and may need to discuss confidential information in order to satisfy themselves as to whether their suspicions are justified. In such circumstances, the member shall also consider the requirement under the anti-money laundering legislation to submit a report to NCA or to the firm's Money Laundering Reporting Officer (MLRO).

100.24 If, after exhausting all relevant possibilities, the ethical conflict remains unresolved, a member shall, where possible, refuse to remain associated with the matter creating the conflict. The member shall determine whether, in the circumstances, it is appropriate to withdraw from the engagement team or specific assignment, or to resign altogether from the engagement, the firm or the employing organisation.

Integrity

Section 110 – Integrity

110.1 The principle of integrity imposes an obligation on all members to be straightforward and honest in professional and business relationships. Integrity also implies fair dealing and truthfulness.

110.2 A member shall not be associated with reports, returns, communications or other information where they believe that the information:

- contains a false or misleading statement

- contains statements or information furnished recklessly

- omits or obscures information required to be included where such omission or obscurity would be misleading.

When a member becomes aware that they have been associated with such information they shall take steps to be disassociated from the information.

110.3 A member will not be considered to be in breach of paragraph 110.2 if the member provides a modified report in respect of a matter contained in paragraph 110.2.

Section 120 – Objectivity

120.1 The principle of objectivity imposes an obligation on all members not to compromise their professional or business judgement because of bias, conflict of interest or the undue influence of others.

120.2 A member may be exposed to situations that may impair objectivity. It is impractical to define and prescribed all such situations. Relationships that bias or unduly influence the professional judgement of the member shall be avoided. A member shall not perform a professional service if a circumstance or relationship biases or unduly influences their professional judgement with respect to that service.

Section 130 – Professional competence and due care

130.1 The principle of professional competence and due care imposes the following obligations on members:

- to maintain professional knowledge and skill at the level required to ensure that clients or employers receive competent professional service and

- to act diligently in accordance with applicable technical and professional standards when providing professional services.

130.2   Competent professional service requires the exercise of sound judgement in applying professional knowledge and skills in the performance of such service. Professional competence may be divided into two separate phrases:

- attainment of professional competence and
- maintenance of professional competence.

130.3   The maintenance of professional competence requires continuing awareness and understanding of relevant technical, professional and business developments. Continuing professional development (CPD) develops and maintains the capabilities that enable a member to perform competently within the professional environment. To achieve this, the Council expects all members to undertake CPD in accordance with the *AAT Policy on Continuing Professional Development*. This requires members to assess, plan, action and evaluate their learning and development needs. Licensed members should also refer to paragraph 200.3.

130.4   Diligence encompasses the responsibility to act in accordance with the requirements of an assignment, carefully thoroughly and on a timely basis.

130.5   A member shall take reasonable steps to ensure that those working under the member's authority in a professional capacity have appropriate training and supervision.

130.6   Where appropriate, a member shall make clients, employers or other users of the professional services aware of limitations inherent in the services to avoid the misinterpretation of an expression of opinion as an assertion of fact.

Section 140 – Confidentiality

In general terms, there is a legal obligation to maintain the confidentiality of information which is given or obtained in circumstances giving rise to a duty of confidentiality. There are some situations where the law allows a breach of this duty.

The following sections help to explain what this means in practice for members as well as giving guidance on the standards required of members from an ethical perspective.

140.1   The principle of confidentiality imposes an obligation on members to refrain from:

- disclosing outside the firm or employing organisation confidential information acquired as a result of professional and business relationships without proper and specific authority or unless there is a legal or professional right or duty to disclose and

- using confidential information acquired as a result of professional and business relationships to their personal advantage or the advantage of third parties.

Information about a past, present, or prospective client's or employer's affairs, or the affairs of clients of employers, acquired in a work context, is likely to be confidential if it is not a matter of public knowledge.

140.2 A member shall maintain confidentiality even in a social environment. The member shall be alert to the possibility of inadvertent disclosure, particularly in circumstances involving close or personal relations, associates and long established business relationships.

140.3 A member shall maintain confidentiality of information disclosed by a prospective client or employer.

140.4 A member shall maintain confidentiality of information within the firm or employing organisation.

140.5 A member shall take all reasonable steps to ensure that staff under their control and persons from whom advice and assistance is obtained respect the principle of confidentiality. The restriction on using confidential information also means not using it for any purpose other than that for which it was legitimately acquired.

140.6 The need to comply with the principle of confidentiality continues even after the end of relationships between a member and a client or employer. When a member changes employment or acquires a new client, the member is entitled to use prior experience. The member shall not, however, use or disclose any confidential information either acquired or received as a result of a professional or business relationship.

140.7 As a fundamental principle, confidentiality serves the public interest because it facilitates the free flow of information from the client to the member. Nevertheless, the following are circumstances where a member may be required to disclose confidential information or when such disclosure may be appropriate:

- where disclosure is permitted by law and is authorised by the client or the employer (or any other person to whom an obligation of confidence is owed) for example:

    - production of documents or other provision of evidence in the course of legal proceedings or

    - disclosure to the appropriate public authorities (for example, HMRC) of infringements of the law that come to light

- disclosure of actual or suspected money laundering or terrorist financing to the member's firm's MLRO or to NCA if the member is a sole practitioner, or

• where there is a professional duty or right to disclose, which is in the public interest, and is not prohibited by law. Examples may include:

- to comply with the quality review of an IFAC member body or other relevant professional body

- to respond to an inquiry or investigation by AAT or relevant regulatory or professional body

- to protect the member's professional interests in legal proceedings

- to comply with technical standards and ethics requirements.

This is a difficult and complex area and members are therefore specifically advised to seek professional advice before disclosing confidential information under c above.

140.8 In deciding whether to disclose confidential information, members should consider the following points:

• whether the interest of all parties, including third parties, could be harmed even though the client or employer (or other person to whom there is a duty of confidentiality) consents to the disclosure of information by the member

• whether all the relevant information is known and substantiated, to the extent that this is practicable. When the situation involves unsubstantiated facts, incomplete information or unsubstantiated conclusions, professional judgement should be used in determining the type of disclosure to be made, if any

• the type of communication or disclosure that may be made and by whom it is to be received; in particular, members should be satisfied that the parties to whom the communication is addressed are appropriate recipients.

Members who are in any doubt about their obligations in a particular situation should seek professional advice.

Section 150 – Professional behaviour

150.1 The principle of professional behaviour imposes an obligation on members to comply with relevant laws and regulations and avoid any action that may bring disrepute to the profession. This includes actions which a reasonable and informed third party, having knowledge of all relevant information, would conclude negatively affect the good reputation of the profession.

Members should note that conduct reflecting adversely on the reputation of AAT is a ground for disciplinary action under *AAT's Disciplinary Regulations*.

150.2 An example of this principle is that in marketing and promoting themselves and their work, members shall be honest and truthful. They may bring the profession into disrepute if they:

- make exaggerated claims for the services they are able to offer, the qualifications they possess, or experience they have gained

- make disparaging references or unsubstantiated comparison to the work of others.

Section 160 – Taxation

160.1 Members performing taxation services in the UK, Ireland and in other member states of the EU will be dealing with compliance and advice on direct and indirect taxes based on income, gains, losses and profits. The administrative authorities and the legal basis for direct and indirect taxes vary substantially.

160.2 Professional members working in tax must comply with the fundamental principles of behaviour outlined in the Professional Conduct in Relation to Taxation (PCRT). It is beyond the scope of this *Code* to deal with detailed ethical issues relating to taxation services encountered by members. The guidance that follows consists therefore of general principles for members which apply to both direct and indirect taxation

160.3 A member providing professional tax services has a duty to put forward the best position in favour of a client or an employer. However, the service must be carried out with professional competence, must not in any way impair integrity or objectivity and must be consistent with the law.

160.4 A member shall not hold out to a client or an employer the assurance that any tax return prepared and tax advice offered are beyond challenge. Instead the member shall ensure that the client or the employer is aware of the limitation attaching to tax advice and services so that they do not misinterpret an expression of opinion as an assertion of fact.

160.5 A member shall only undertake taxation work on the basis of full disclosure by the client or employer. The member, in dealing with the tax authorities, must act in good faith and exercise care in relation to facts or information presented on behalf of the client or employer. It will normally be assumed that facts and information on which business tax computations are based were provided by the client or employer as the taxpayer, and the latter bears ultimate responsibility for the accuracy of the facts, information and tax computations. The member shall avoid assuming responsibility for the accuracy of facts, etc. outside his or her own knowledge.

160.6 When a member submits a tax return or tax computation for a taxpayer client or employer, the member is acting as an agent. The nature and responsibilities of the member's duties should be made clear to the client or employer, in the case of the former, by a letter of engagement.

160.7 Tax advice or opinions of material consequence given to a client or an employer shall be recorded, either in the form of a letter or in a memorandum for the files.

160.8 In the case of a member in practice acting for a client, the member shall furnish copies of all tax computations to the client before submitting them to HMRC.

160.9 When a member learns of a material error or omission in a tax return of a prior year, or of a failure to file a required tax return, the member has a responsibility to advise promptly the client or employer of the error or omission and recommend that disclosure be made to HMRC. If the client or employer, after having had a reasonable time to reflect, does not correct the error, the member shall inform the client or employer in writing that it is not possible for the member to act for them in connection with that return or other related information submitted to the authorities. Funds dishonestly retained after discovery of an error or omission become criminal property and their retention amounts to money laundering by the client or employer. It is also a criminal offence in the UK for a person, including an accountant, to become concerned in an arrangement which he knows or suspects facilitates (by whatever means) the acquisition, retention, use or control of criminal property by or on behalf of another person. Other EU states have equivalent provisions. In each of these situations, the member shall comply with the duty to report the client's or employer's activities to the relevant authority, as explained in the following paragraphs.

160.10 A Licensed member whose client refuses to make disclosure of an error or omission to HMRC, after having had notice of it and a reasonable time to reflect, is obliged to report the client's refusal and the facts surrounding it to the MLRO if the member is within a firm, or to the appropriate authority (NCA in the UK) if the member is a sole practitioner. The member shall not disclose to the client or anyone else that such a report has been made if the member knows or suspects that to do so would be likely to prejudice any investigation which might be conducted following the report.

160.11 In circumstances where the employer of a member in business refuses to make disclosure of an error or omission to HMRC:

- where the employed member in business has acted in relation to the error or omission, he or she should report the employer's refusal and the surrounding facts, including the extent of the member's involvement, to the appropriate authority as soon as possible, as this may provide the member with a defence to the offence of facilitating the retention of criminal property

- where the employed member in business has not acted in relation to the error or omission, he or she is not obliged to report the matter to the authorities. However, if the member does make a report to the appropriate authority, such report will not amount to a breach of the member's duty of confidentiality.

160.12 Where a member in business is a contractor who is a 'relevant person' for the purposes of the *Money Laundering Regulations* in the UK or equivalent legislation in another EU State or other overseas jurisdictions, the member shall act in accordance with paragraph 160.10 above, as though he were a Licensed member. However, where the member in business is not a 'relevant person', he should act in accordance with paragraph 160.11 above.

160.13 All members have a responsibility to make themselves familiar with anti-money laundering and terrorist financing legislation and any guidance issued by AAT in this regard.

160.14 The tax authorities in many countries have extensive powers to obtain information. Members confronted by the exercise of these powers by the relevant authorities should seek appropriate legal advice.